C++ Games Programming

Al Stevens
Stan Trujillo

M&T BOOKS

M&T Books
A Division of MIS:Press, Inc.
A Subsidiary of Henry Holt and Company, Inc.
115 West 18th Street
New York, New York 10011

© 1995 by M&T Books

Printed in the United States of America

Library of Congress Cataloging-in-Publication Data

Stevens, Al,
    C++ games programming / Al Stevens, Stan Trujillo.
        p. cm.
    ISBN 1-55851-449-X
    1. Computer games—Programming. 2. C++ (Computer program language)
    I. Trujillo, Stan. II. Title
QA76.76.C672S74 1995
794.8/15265 20   95-30653
                                                         CIP

97 96 95 94   4 3 2 1

Editor-in-Chief: Paul Farrell   Managing Editor: Cary Sullivan
Editor: Debra Williams Cauley   Copy Editor: Betsy Hardinger
Production Editor: Anthony Washington

Dedication

To my friend and father, Art Trujillo
S. T.

To Woody
A. S.

Acknowledgments

Thanks to Ed Trujillo for introducing the authors.

We would like to thank Patrick Lujan for supplying the Sky Scrap demo, and finding bugs.

We would like to thank the following authors for letting us use and distribute their software:

Gary Maddox—Blaster Master

David Mason—Dave's Targa Animator (DTA)

John Ratcliff—DIGpack and MIDpack

Diana Gruber of Ted Gruber Software—Fastgraph Light

Paul H. Yoshimune of Handmade Software, Inc.—Image alchemy

Lutz Kretzschner of SoftTronics—Moray

Jim Conger—Midi Sequencer

Neosoft Corporation Neopaint version 3.1

Owen Thomas—Astrofire

Table of Contents

Preface

This book is the first in a series of two books about writing computer games on the PC in the C++ programming language. This book addresses games that run under MS-DOS. The second book, still under development as this book reaches the market, will be about writing game programs with the Win32 application programming interface—32-bit applications that run under Windows 3.1, Windows NT, and Windows 95.

The premise of this book is that programmers can build professional-quality games in C++ by exploiting the wealth of shareware, freeware, and public-domain graphics and modeling tools that are readily available and that support game development. You can use inexpensive tools and libraries; some of them are free, and others are shareware—available for you to try out first and then buy only when you are satisfied with the results. The CD-ROM that accompanies this book includes many of these tools. This book goes one step further by introducing and providing the source code and documentation for Theatrix, a C++ class library that encapsulates all the behavior of game programming in a simple interface. The Theatrix paradigm uses a metaphor wherein game development proceeds much like that of a theatrical production.

There can be no doubt that computer games are entrenched as a vital part of our culture. From humble beginnings, they have spawned an industry that now ranges in scope from the serious business of aircraft and spacecraft flight simulation to the whimsical trek of cute sprites through mazes of obstacles and rewards. Astronauts learn to handle orbiting spacecraft by using flight simulator software. At the same time, ordinary people stand in line to pop in their tokens and use the latest simulators at the local mall's arcade. They fly through space, drive the Grand Prix, or engage in street battles with ominous cybernetic opponents. New home computer games such as Myst sell out as soon as they arrive at the stores. Games such as Under A Killing Moon have the appearance of movies, with real actors who seem to interact with the game player. TV series and movies are being produced with computer games as their central themes.

People have always played games. It is in our nature to create imaginary environments and situations in which we play roles and fulfill our inner wishes. An infant concentrates on toy objects, centering its play activities on the toys themselves. As the child matures, objects take increasingly smaller roles in playtime and give way to imagination. The objects become artifacts in a larger imaginary world that the child creates in its mind, often with the collaboration of other children. And thus the child invents role playing.

The games and roles that we play as children prepare us for adulthood. Our ability as adults to relate to one another on civilized levels stems from the social skills and lessons we learn as children when we play together. In a nonhostile environment, we as children learned about appropriate and inappropriate behavior—what works and what does not. And we did that by creating circumstances and situation within which we could act out various roles, trying out different behavior. Our reactions to one another conditioned us to associate different behavior with approval and disapproval at the peer level. The disapproval was nonjudgmental and was soon forgotten by the disapproving party, but the object of that disapproval (and of approval, too) learned valuable lessons from the experience.

Gradually the fantasy worlds of the child assume lesser importance as adult responsibilities require us to deal routinely and effectively with the world. The success that we achieve in the world is often a measure of the quality of our childhood and the degree to which we as children enjoyed meaningful play.

But the child in us never dies. Despite the challenges and obstacles of survival and adult responsibilities, we continue to enjoy playful activities throughout our adult lives. Over the years the games change, and so do the shape, function, and cost of the artifacts of our play. As we invent increasingly convenient ways to provide our basic needs, we must likewise invent new ways to occupy the leisure time that results. Adult games and their artifacts are more complex, challenging, and expensive than those of children. Golf clubs. Sport and recreational vehicles. Stereos. Vacations. Club memberships. Computers.

Computers, indeed. The computer has changed or influenced virtually every aspect of the human experience in the half-century that usable computers have been around. Computer games are an example of that phenomenon.

No one knows for sure who played the first game on a computer or what that game was, but from at least the mid-1950s, and perhaps earlier, people have been using the computational features and storage of computers to simulate worlds, universes, and the rules of game play. For many years, access to computers was limited to those who worked with them. However, due to the size and operating costs of those early computers, personal and recreational use was mostly discouraged, and game technology did not advance much. The personal computer revolution changed all that.

There have probably been more different game programs developed and distributed for personal computers than programs of any other kind, and that circumstance continues today. But most such programs fade quietly into obscurity: Perhaps a game fails to interest users; maybe the author does not adequately market, distribute, and support the game; in many cases, the game's implementation is simply amateurish, unreliable, or inefficient. This book does not tell you how to design the concept for a successful game or how to bring it to market, but it does provide the tools with which you can build games that exhibit the professional touch—animation, photo-realistic scenes and characters, integrated sound effects and music, and fast displays. Lights, camera, action.

The evolution of PC game technology and the complexity of PC game software have kept pace with the advancing technology of personal computer display, storage, and processing speed. Until recently, however, the evolution of game development did not track advances in programming technology.

Object-oriented programming languages and graphical user interface operating systems were not among the options of serious game developers. As effective as those tools are for developing commercial software and hosting its operation, those environments were traditionally far too demanding of the computer's resources to support games of any consequence. Most games were written in C, assembly language, or a combination of the two, and they "took over the machine," which means that all the computer's resources had to be dedicated to the game while it was executing.

All that has changed. Contemporary mainstream desktop computers possess sufficient internal memory, removable mass storage, and processing speed to support not only the operating systems of today but also applications with heavy resource demands—and those applications include games. The work represented by the contents of this book and its accompanying CD-ROM reflects this revolution and its consequences.

From Al Stevens:

In the summer of 1994, Stan brought his Theatrix C++ class library to me for my opinion. I've never been a game programmer, but the level of abstraction in the class design was so impressive that I decided to give it a try and write my first computer game. In a couple of days and with only about 500 lines of C++ code, I built an arcade-style game with background scenery and sprites that move around the screen like the characters in an animated cartoon. Most of the work was the artistic part—designing the scenery and the sprites with a paint package. That one facet of the project is what fascinated me. By using good tools and a well-designed class library, you can concentrate most of your effort on the important stuff—the artwork.

After realizing that virtually all the game-building tools we were using are shareware or free software, Stan and I decided to enhance and improve the library and develop example games that people could use in the development of their own games. The project was compelling. I found myself engrossed in subjects that I had long ignored: 3-D modeling, ray tracing, image palettes, animation, sound generation, MIDI music files.

Eventually, we had to decide what to do with the project. As far as I was concerned, there was no problem finding a medium with which to distribute our work. I'm already a book author, and game programming books are popular now. Fortunately for me (and for you, too, I think), Stan agreed, and this book is the result.

From Stan Trujillo:

For as long as I've been playing video games, I've been fascinated by them. As soon as I saw a game, I'd want to play it, and as soon as I played it, I'd want to figure out how to win. Beating a game wasn't enough, though, because after winning, I'd want to win all over again, but this time with style. All the while, during each stage of involvement, one question plagued me:

> *How did they do that?*

This question bothered me for years, and the answer (which I was slow to realize) was: *with tools that you don't have.*

Behind each game, I pictured teams of eggheaded computer scientists who were so smart that each of them was in a perpetual state of creative bliss. I though that each one of these geniuses was capable of sitting down at any computer and writing a complete game from scratch without any special tools and without once needing to consult a manual.

This fantasy could not be farther from the truth. Every game that you've ever seen was written by normal people on normal computers. What do they have that you don't have? Tools. Not just generic tools such as compilers and editors, but game-specific tools such as game engines, sprite designers, palette utilities, and sound clip editors.

When I finally figure this out, I decided to write a C++ class library that was designed specifically for the development of games. I planned to use it to develop my own games, and perhaps I still will, but in the meanwhile, I showed it to Al. Much to my amazement, he suggested that we co-author a book on the subject. There was no question about it (but I tried to act as if it was a tough decision anyway). We spend a few months enhancing the library, writing demos, and collecting great shareware and freeware utilities. It was a lot of fun, and I couldn't be more pleased with the outcome.

Introduction

"Play it, Sam,"
Ingrid Bergman

Welcome to the world of PC game software development with the C++ programming language. You are about to embark on a rewarding and enjoyable journey, one from which you may not want to return. Whether you go beyond this book to build the next great, wildly successful, player-addicting game remains to be seen, but one thing is sure--if you venture any further than this chapter, your life will be changed. Among the pursuits of craftsmen, none gives greater satisfaction than the creation of something that delights its audience. And nothing on a computer is more delightful than a well-crafted game. Follow this road and you will be hooked, we promise you.

This chapter introduces these subjects:

◇ The Theatrix C++ class library

◇ Objectives of a game library

◇ You, the game programmer

◇ What to expect from this book

1

Theatrix

This book is about writing C++ programs that implement computer games to run under MS-DOS. We provide and describe tools for game construction and give explanations of how and when to use them. The underlying technology in this approach is Theatrix, a C++ class library and toolkit that encapsulates the functionality of computer games. A survey of the existing books on game development reveals that most of them teach game programming at the lowest, most primitive levels. Programmers learn about the details of hardware and low-level application programming interfaces (APIs) that address the video, sound, mouse, and keyboard. Then they write programs at those levels, usually in C or assembly language. With Theatrix, programmers concentrate on the high-level components and logic of the game itself, leaving the details to the library's hidden C++ implementation. This approach brings game development into the modern software development environment of the present. By using the C++ class mechanism and proven tools, the game development process becomes structured and object-oriented and provides the fastest way available to get a graphical computer game up and running.

In addition to being a class library, Theatrix includes a suite of game-construction tools collected from the many shareware, freeware, and public domain programs that are widely available. The class library and game-building tools are included on the accompanying CD-ROM.[1] We provide many examples of complete games that we developed by using only these tools. The CD-ROM contains the C++ source code for all the games. In fact, this book contains more demo games than any other game programming book available today. The demos represent the kinds of games that you can build, from the simplest to some complex examples. The CD-ROM contains all the artwork in each of its forms throughout the game development cycle. Everything you need to build the artwork is there: the fonts, conversion programs, graphics construction programs, 3-D modelers, and sample image files for scenery and sprites. All sound and music clips are there in each of their forms, too.

---

[1]There is one exception. The POV-Ray ray-tracing program is not on the CD-ROM, but it is easily obtained by download from the CompuServe Information Service. An agreement between the tool's creators and another book publishing firm restricts us from distributing POV-Ray. We do, however, describe how we used the program, include examples of the image source code and image files, and explain how you can get a copy of the program. Chapter 11 has details.

This book is more about the technology of game construction than it is about game design. We discuss some of the components of game design, but no book can cover all the possible ideas. A computer game is an expression of someone's ideas. A jazz musician cannot tell someone else how to improvise a riff. A painter cannot explain how to conceive a great picture. A writer cannot just tell someone how to effectively describe in deathless prose a particular scene. Those artists can teach only their craft, which consists of the tools and techniques that underpin their art. It is through the practiced application of that craft that the student's inner ideas find their own expression and art is formed. Any artist will tell you that you do not find true artistic freedom in your own expressions until you master the medium. Ultimately the quality of art is a collaboration of the artist's skill with a medium and his or her ability to have unique ideas and the freedom to express them. The ideas behind your games are, therefore, necessarily yours, although we encourage you to use our examples to stimulate your imagination. The freedom to express your ideas becomes yours when you master the tools and techniques. This book gives you the tools, explains the techniques, and teaches you how to use them.

Many people use and enjoy computer games. As long as there are computers, there will be an active market for new games. By now we must realize that it is not possible to saturate the game market. Why not? Simply this: First, many games cease to be interesting to the player once the player has conquered the game. Second, every new game whets the player's appetite. There are some exceptions to the first property. Flight simulators, card games, and 3-D maze games, for example, can offer infinite varieties of game scenarios, so their novelty does not wear off so quickly. There is no exception to the second property. Every new game makes the chronic player hunger for more. That's where you come in. An eager market awaits your games.

Objectives

A computer game's construction involves all the components of a theatrical production. Later you learn to carry that metaphor forward through the use of Theatrix, the C++ class hierarchy that implements it. This discussion concentrates on the objectives of the Theatrix class library and its suite of game-construction tools.

Details: What to Know, What to Hide

In the old days, a computer game builder had to know and do it all. You needed an intimate understanding of the computer's video, keyboard, mouse, joystick, and sound-generation hardware—an imposing scope of knowledge, to be sure, but not nearly as daunting then as it is today. The typical computer game of yore was written to run on a particular suite of hardware; the programmer had to master only one small set of configurations. Not only do the PCs of today have various and incompatible hardware options, but also their architectures are arcane and esoteric.

It is our position that programmers do not need an intimate understanding of details of SVGA/XVGA memory and register architecture in order to display images and text on a screen. Entire volumes have been written on video architecture, and you can read them if you wish, but you do not need to.

You do not need to know how to poll the mouse to see where its cursor is or whether a click has occurred. The mouse architecture and interface are standard now, and its interface involves a moderately complicated API. There is an accepted reference work on using the mouse, but you do not need to understand those details.

The same thing is true of the keyboard. There are many ways to read the keyboard on a PC. You can intercept the keyboard interrupt vector and read the keyboard input port. You can use calls into BIOS to poll and read keystrokes. You can call the higher-level (and less efficient) MS-DOS console input functions. You can use the standard C++ *istream cin* object, which encapsulates the MS-DOS console input functions. Each of these techniques represents a higher level of abstraction.

In the same vein, your understanding of image page swapping, animation, sprite Z-ordering, and screen scrolling need not extend beyond knowing how to make them work at the highest possible level of abstraction.

Levels of Abstraction

How much you must understand about low-level details of implementation describes the *level of abstraction* at which you operate. You may view level of abstraction as an imaginary line somewhere between the hardware at the lowest level and the application problem being solved (in this case, the game being developed) at the highest level. As the level of abstraction falls, it exposes more details of implementation. Furthermore, the lower that line gets, the more complex the details become. As the programmer, you must understand everything from the highest level down to your particular, personal lowest level of abstraction. It follows that the higher that line, the fewer details you have to deal with and the more details you can forget about.

People who understand details of implementation have built detailed functionality into libraries for others to use. By using those libraries, we raise our level of abstraction. The higher our personal level of abstraction, the fewer details we need to be concerned about. It is, therefore, advantageous to use those libraries.

Consequently, an objective of Theatrix is to raise the game programmer's level of abstraction as far as possible above the details of implementation.

Because no single programming metaphor suits every possible programming need, a concomitant objective permits the programmer to use interfaces that exist at several levels of abstraction.

Encapsulation

Theatrix encapsulates the details and interface of a game-construction metaphor. Its objective is to provide an interface that hides the details of video page management, video effects, animation, sound and music generation, keyboard and mouse event processing, and message dispatching. The implementation uses driver libraries for video displays, the keyboard, the mouse, and the sound card. The interface hides the details of those libraries so that programmers can ignore them.

The Theatrix Metaphor

A metaphor is like a parable. It tells a story that uses an analogy to make a point. The analogy associates something that we already understand with the lesson that we are about to learn. The familiar helps to explain the unfamiliar. One of Theatrix's objectives is to provide an intuitive metaphor through its class design. By associating game construction with more familiar human activities, Theatrix helps programmers understand and remember what the components are, how they relate to one another, and when it is appropriate to use each one in the development of a particular game.

The Theatrix game-construction metaphor equates the components of a game with the participants in a theatrical production. There are directors and players. The directors manage scenery and direct the actions of the players. The players control their own movements and originate their own voices and sound effects. There are conductors that generate music. This metaphor is modeled in a class hierarchy. A game program derives game-specific classes from the Theatrix classes and instantiates objects of those game-specific classes. The objects register for and receive cues from each other and from Theatrix—keystrokes, mouse events, timer events, and game-defined messages.

Performance

For a game to be taken seriously by the game-playing public, it must perform well. Sluggish games will be rejected. It follows that a class library that encapsulates game components must likewise perform well. We used performance as the major criterion for the selection of our tools, and we kept performance in the forefront throughout the development of the Theatrix library.

A Comprehensive Toolkit

We wanted the Theatrix toolkit to be complete, comprehensive, and obtainable. A game developer needs good tools for building graphics, sound effects, music, and video. There are expensive commercial packages that support those activities, and if you like them and can afford them, then by all means use them. But we did not want to limit the use of Theatrix to people who could afford high-end tools. So we went in search of and found quite acceptable tools that support all our requirements yet are within the budgets of most independent developers. Many of these tools are free.

You can use the tools on the CD-ROM to test and experiment with the example games, and you can use them to begin development of your own games. We selected tools that are available and supported. In some cases, the tools are free for you to use as is. Others are shareware, and, if you expect to continue to use them, you should pay the nominal registration fees to their authors. Still others are freely distributed for you to develop with, but you must pay a nominal license to use them in game products that you distribute.

Extensibility

We designed Theatrix to be extensible. If you want to incorporate other features into the library, you can derive from the existing classes. If you prefer to use different libraries for graphics, sound, and so on, you will find those functions isolated in the class system and you can build or derive new classes to replace the classes that use the supported libraries.

Who Are You?

Building a killer computer game involves many skills and much imagination. The best games employ the talents of conceptual designers who create the game's premise and objectives, creative writers to write the scenarios and design the levels, graphics artists to design the scenery and sprites, musicians to compose and record the score, sound technicians to create effective sound effects, and computer programmers to write the code that brings together all of the above.

You may have these skills, but you are definitely a programmer, and this book assumes that you have a working knowledge of the C++ programming language. We do not spend time explaining object-oriented programming, C++ class design, or C++ language constructs. If you are not familiar with C, you should read *Al Stevens Teaches C*, by one of the authors of this book. (It should be obvious which author.) If you do not know C++, we suggest that you read *Teach Yourself C++, 4th Edition*, also by Al Stevens. We assume that you understand how to compile and link programs and what an object library is. You are expected to understand the implications of source code header files and C/C++ macros. Beyond that, all you need is a desire to understand and build computer games.

It is a lucky coincidence that building a computer game requires the skills of a programmer. Programmers are the most inveterate of game players. We enjoy challenges, puzzles, and complex constructions. The very nature of programming involves building and solving the mysteries of the most intricate of mazes, the computer program. We are qualified game builders because we are inherent game players.

There are two possible reasons that you might be reading this book. Either you are fascinated with computer games—love them, fixate on them, can't live without them—and have a white-hot burning desire to build games of your very own; or you are just a programmer who sees all the money that the game builders are making, and you want a piece of that action. If you fit into the first category, you are the perfect candidate to read this book. If the second category describes you better, then you are in for a happy awakening. In addition to being rewarding, game development is pure fun. This subject matter is compelling. Unless you are a completely boring person, which we doubt very much, you will get into it, and we mean really into it.

What Do You Need?

To run the example games on the CD-ROM, all you need is a PC with a VGA that supports the mode-X video mode (320 x 240 resolution with 256 colors). To compile the source code and build your own games with Theatrix, you need a DOS C++ compiler that supports ANSI runtime type information (RTTI) additions. We developed this software with Borland C++ 4.5. You cannot go wrong with that package.

Your Rights and Some Restrictions

The Theatrix source code is copyrighted by the authors. You may use it to your heart's content to build games, and you may distribute those games in any manner that you like. We hope you build cool games (that we can play, too), and we hope that you make a million bucks doing it. We encourage you to give copies of the Theatrix source code to anyone, but you may not sell it unless you are selling a copy of this book along with it, which, we presume, you acquired through legitimate channels. Under no circumstances may you publish any part of the source code and represent it as your own work.

The tools on the CD-ROM come from many vendors and have different copyright and licensing restrictions. View the *readme* files for each tool to see what your rights and responsibilities are.

The songs in the MIDI files are copyrighted. You are encouraged to play them for your own entertainment, but please do not use them in programs that you intend to publish commercially.

The example games are just that, examples. With a little practice you can defeat any of them in short order. You may use them as launching pads for your own game programs. The sprites and backgrounds are not particularly exotic or original, so we do not mind if you use them. Your games, however, should be unique and unlike any others. You should build your own sprites. The POV-Ray source files (those that have the extensions **.POV** and **.INC**) are hereby released to the public domain.

Getting Help

If you have questions about the Theatrix software, you can E-mail us on CompuServe or the Internet. Al Stevens can be reached at astevens@ddj.com or on CompuServe as 71101,1262, and Stan Trujillo is on CompuServe as 75233,1506.

For help with a particular tool from another vendor, see the documentation file with that tool. Most of them can and will help you with technical support if you have registered their product. Some of them maintain a presence on CompuServe or the Internet and offer to answer questions that way.

The Organization of This Book

This book describes the theories of game construction and provides tutorials, examples, and reference material on the use of Theatrix and its tools. You will not find much hardware detail about how sound is generated or how video circuitry makes the phosphor pixels glow. The purpose of class libraries such as Theatrix is to hide those details from those who do not need to know them. The treatment of those subjects is, therefore, brief and superficial.

Chapter 2 is about game theory. It uses the history and evolution of computer games to explain the components of games and the various kinds of games that run on computers.

Chapter 3 provides brief descriptions of the technologies that games use. Its purpose is to provide a common ground for later discussions and to ensure that you understand enough of the PC's architecture to build games that fit within its operating limits.

Chapter 4 discusses the technical aspects of game-building strategies. This is where you learn to assemble the game components that are outside the program code. You learn to create scenery using techniques that depend on whether you want photographic realism or an arcade appearance. You learn to design and build animated sequences for the action in your game. This chapter describes how to build sound effects and the game's musical score.

Chapter 5 is an introduction to Theatrix, the C++ class library with which you integrate the game's components into a running program. This chapter gives an overview of the class hierarchy and explains the theatrical production metaphor.

Chapter 6 is the Theatrix user's guide. It contains operating instructions for the utility programs.

Chapter 7 is the Theatrix reference manual, which documents the public interfaces of the C++ classes in the Theatrix class library.

Chapter 8 is the Theatrix technical specifications, which describe the operation of the software and the formats for the various data library files that game programs use.

Chapter 9 describes the Theatrix development environment. The approach taken here organizes the games into projects with makefiles that build every game component automatically. The chapter includes a discussion on using a small network to coordinate the efforts of a game-development team and to share resources.

Chapter 10 explains each of the example game programs that are included on the CD-ROM. This chapter is where you learn to use Theatrix, because it teaches, by example, each of the features that the library supports. The discussion addresses the operation of the games and the code and data files that implement them.

Chapter 11 describes each of the tools in the Theatrix toolkit, explaining when and how you use each one of them in the development of a game.

Appendix A explains what is on the CD-ROM, how you install the programs, data files, and source code on your PC, how to run the games, and how you can modify and recompile the software.

Appendix B lists the C++ header files for the Theatrix class library.

Game Theory

"Final kiss at seven."
Guy Tibbets

This chapter is your introduction to computer games in general. We discuss some of the early computer games to provide a historical perspective on how they started and to illustrate how the evolution of games reflects advances in computing power. Then we address the factors that go into the design and development of a contemporary computer game.

You will read about these subjects:

◇ Early computer games

◇ Different kinds of games

◇ The components of a computer game

◇ The issues of violence and programming standards

Early Computer Games

In the early 1960s, one of the authors of this book played his first computer game. The computer was an IBM 1410, and it belonged to the U.S. government. I (Stevens) was a civilian programmer, and an Air Force sergeant named Guy Tibbets was the operator. The IBM 1410 was a character-based machine with 100,000 characters of memory and a Selectric-ball typewriter console device. The game was Tibbets's idea. We would fill memory with the NOP instruction (which consumed an instruction fetch and execute cycle but did nothing), press the **Reset** button to position the instruction pointer at address zero, and then press the **Start** and **Stop** buttons in rapid succession. The console displayed the instruction pointer address where the stop occurred. Our game was to see who could stop the computer faster, as measured by the lower stop address. I could never beat Tibbets. It was a simple and mindless exercise, but it passed the time on the night shift when we ran out of jokes to tell.

The point of this story is twofold. First, given the opportunity, most computer users will use a computer to have fun—when the General isn't around. Second, the manner in which a computer can entertain us is usually a function of its processing power. That 1410, which filled a room, was actually slow enough that a human being could move a hand from one button to another in less time than it took the computer to execute 100,000 NOP instructions. Thus the limitations of the 1410 computer permitted the game that Tibbets[1] contrived.

Chess

Computer games predate that early experience with a 1410. In 1959, an MIT mathematics professor named John McCarthy wrote a chess-playing program on the school's IBM 704 computer. Chess programs are common today—you can buy small microprocessor-based chess machines at Radio Shack for a song—but at the time the program was a monumental achievement. It gave credibility to a new discipline called *artificial intelligence*, one that was

---

[1]Tibbets loved mind puzzles of any kind. He devised anagrams by scrambling the letters of your name with an insulting comment. He'd give you the anagram and smirk while you tried to figure out what it meant. Mine was the quote at the top of this chapter, which unscrambles to "Al Stevens is a fink." Tibbets also built a fully functioning merry-go-round from scratch out of junk parts for the neighborhood children. I often wonder what became of him.

generally regarded among the knowledgeable as showing little promise. Computer game construction continued for several years at MIT's Artificial Intelligence (AI) Laboratory, where students had relatively unrestricted and unmonitored access to government-funded computers.

Spacewar

In 1961, Steve Russell, one of McCarthy's students, was given access to the school's DEC PDP-1, which had an oscilloscope display device that you could control from a program—an early video terminal. Russell set about to create the first video game, an outer-space confrontation between two players. Each player controlled the movements and weaponry of a rocket ship by pressing switches on the computer's front panel console. The point of the game was to destroy the opponent's ship by firing a torpedo while at the same time avoiding the opponent's torpedoes.

The game survived for years, with improvements added by the programmers at the AI lab. One of those improvements was the invention of the first computer joystick, created from scrap parts by the programmers because computer console switches were difficult to use to fly spacecraft and fire torpedoes.

Life

The game of Life was invented by British mathematician John Conway and was published in *Scientific American* in 1970. Life simulates a universe of neighboring cells. Each cell, identified by its x/y address in a coordinate system, may have one of two possible states. The cell is either populated or unpopulated and is surrounded by eight neighboring cells. The game consists of a sequence of generations. Each generation examines each cell to see (1) whether it is populated and (2) how many populated neighbors it has. A neighbor is one of the eight adjacent cells in the 3 x 3 array of nine in which the target cell is the center cell. If an unpopulated cell has a certain number of populated neighbors, the cell becomes populated in the next generation. Conversely, if a populated cell has too few or too many neighbors, its population expires in the next generation. A cell is born if there are enough neighbors to spawn it and dies if there are either too few neighbors to support it or too many neighbors with which it must share resources. Some implementations of Life use screen character positions to represent cells, and the universe of cells is limited to the number of screen character positions. Others use dense graphical screens on which to display the simulation.

The game of Life simulates the evolution of generations. To play the game, you create the universe by specifying which cells are initially populated. Then you run the evolution and observe how each generation modifies the pattern of populated cells. The universe often takes on interesting symmetrical patterns as the generations pass. Some patterns result in a totally expired universe after a few generations. Other patterns result in a stable universe. Still other patterns endlessly repeat a cycle of births and deaths. A culture of Life players blossomed in the 1970s, and its members often published and shared interesting starting patterns.

As with Spacewar, Life was given its own life at the MIT AI lab in the early 1970s. For a time, Life dominated the concentration and lives of researchers and students, who programmed Life to run on the lab's PDP-6 and spent most of their time experimenting with Life patterns.

The executable and source code for a DOS text-mode version of Life is included on the CD-ROM that accompanies this book. See Michael Abrash's *The Zen of Code Optimization* (listed in the Bibliography) for a discussion of Life as a study in how to optimize computer simulations.

Adventure

Adventure was developed in the early 1970s at the Stanford AI Laboratory by Will Crowther and Donald Woods. Adventure uses keyboard input and console output to establish a dialogue with the human player. Adventure simulates a world of caves, dragons, dwarfs, and so on. The game tells the player where the player is located and what the surroundings hold. For example, when you first begin to play, you see this message on the console:

```
Somewhere nearby is Colossal Cave, where others have found fortunes in
treasure and gold, though it is rumored that some who enter are never seen
again. Magic is said to work in the cave. I will be your eyes and hands.
Direct me with commands of 1 or 2 words. (Should you get stuck, type "help"
for some general hints. For information on how to end your adventure, etc.,
type "info".)


You are standing at the end of a road before a small brick building. Around
you is a forest. A small stream flows out of the building and down a gully.
    >
```

From the prompt you type terse commands and directions. Following each command, the program tells you where you are. For example, at the first prompt you can type **enter** or **go in** and the next message appears:

```
You're inside building.


There are some keys on the ground here.
There is a shiny brass lamp nearby.
There is tasty food here.
There is a bottle of water here.
>
```

Subsequent commands retrieve items and navigate you through the world of Adventure. It is a compelling and addictive game, particularly until you have mastered it and retrieved all the treasures in Colossal Cave.

Adventure is typical of the first generation of action games, using text displays and the player's keyboard commands. Joysticks were not widely available then, the mouse had not been invented, and computer graphics were too slow and too low in resolution to display the kind of images that Crowther and Woods described with words. If Adventure were being developed today, it would be very different than it was twenty-five years ago.

The CD-ROM with this book includes the executables and source code of Adventure as ported to C to run on a PC. The original program was written in FORTRAN and displayed all its messages in uppercase, another example of how the limits of computers influenced their games.

Contemporary Games

Early computer games had a certain charm and appeal that contemporary games lack. Because of the limitations of the hardware, early games used text mode or very primitive graphics. As a consequence, a principal ingredient in games was the player's imagination. The experience is akin to that of reading a book; the reader's mind provides the visual and audible details based on the writer's descriptions. Another analogy compares radio drama (for those of you who remember it) to that of movies and television. The radio listener supplied the scenery, the action, and faces for the actors. The medium provided only voices, sound effects, and background music to tell its story.

With vast improvements in display, controller, and sound technology, game development has advanced far beyond the simple interfaces from the early days, and the current crop of games reflects those improvements. Typical of modern entertainment, today's games emphasize action represented by the visual and audible, leaving very little of those elements to the player's imagination. As a result, players concentrate more on honing motor skills or using deductive reasoning to unearth the clues and beat the game than they do on visualizing the scenery and characters.

Contemporary games come in many varieties; four common types are simulators, real-time 3-D mazes, static photo-realistic displays, and arcade-style animated sprite games.

Simulators

Not long after IBM introduced the PC in 1981, Microsoft began selling Flight Simulator, a program that it acquired from a company called SubLogic. Flight Simulator was a milestone program for two reasons. First, it was a realistic simulation of the cockpit of a small airplane in which the player-pilot could execute takeoffs, landings, and flight maneuvers. Second, the program became the benchmark for compatibility when the PC clone market was born. If a would-be PC-compatible computer could run Flight Simulator, chances were good that it would run anything that a true blue PC could run.

The first Flight Simulator was truly impressive. It ran in a 4.77-MHz 8088 machine with no hard disk and 512K of internal memory. The Color Graphics Adapter display had a monochrome graphics resolution of 640 by 200 pixels. By today's standards, the original PC was tiny and underpowered. Yet Flight Simulator managed to display a full instrument panel with moving needles and changing digits; a pilot's view through the windshield that rendered the outside world in real time; a computer model of the terrain, a few buildings, and an airport in Chicago; and engine sounds through the PC's tiny speaker.

Flight Simulator has kept pace with advances in hardware. The latest version (5.0) uses a photo-realistic instrument panel, fractal scenery, and enhanced visuals of some scenery that maps digitized aerial photography over the terrain renderings. It also requires a fast processor and many megabtyes of hard disk space.

There are many other flight simulators for the PC. Most of them emphasize air combat missions, although a few, such as Chuck Yeager's Advanced Flight Trainer 2, teach the elements of flight rather than combat. Others include simulators of bombers, fighters, helicopters, ultralights, gliders, biplanes, and even the space shuttle. An air traffic control simulator allows Flight Simulator pilots on networks to fly in controlled airspace. One player is the air traffic controller; the others are the pilots.

Simulators are now available for race cars, submarines, tanks, and every imaginable kind of spacecraft, including the *Starship Enterprise*. They all have one thing in common. They render their scenery in real time. The program maintains a computer model of the world in which the simulated object moves. That model describes the terrain and features such as buildings, bodies of water, towers, statues, trees, pylons, and so on. As the simulated object moves through this world, the program uses the model to render each frame of the player's view as the view changes.

This book is not about writing simulators, although you could use the Theatrix class library to implement one. Two books in the Bibliography address flight simulator technology and construction in detail. They are *Flights of Fantasy* and *Taking Flight*.

3-D Mazes: Doom

In the early 1990's, Apogee Software introduced a shareware game called Wolfenstein. In the game, the player is a hero of sorts who wanders through a 3-D maze of corridors and doors and does battle with Nazi types who appear at random from inside doorways and around corners and who shoot at the hero. The game and its display techniques launched a new generation of games culminating with Doom, the most successful shareware game ever produced. Doom was developed by the programmers who wrote Wolfenstein after they split off from Apogee. Doom originated as a DOS shareware game.

Wolfenstein, Doom, Blake Stone, Descent, and other 3-D maze games use a display software technology called *ray casting*, which is a way to rapidly compute successive frames of complex scenery in real time. The Theatrix library does not encapsulate the functions of ray casting, and this book is not about developing 3-D maze games. Two books in the Bibliography specifically address game development with ray casting. They are *Tricks of the Game Programming Gurus* and *Gardens of Imagination*.

Static Displays: Myst

Myst is completely different from Doom. Although the two games represent different game development strategies, they are also the two most successful of contemporary computer games. Myst was originally a Macintosh game that was later ported to Windows. The Windows version is by far the more popular. A sequel to the original game is now under development, and it promises to be a runaway best seller.

Myst plays out its scenario beginning on an island where the player moves about and gathers information. From that information the player learns to travel to and return from other islands where the player gathers more clues. Gradually the clues combine to reveal the purpose and eventual completion of the game. At first, players do not know the purpose—or even the premise—of the game. The magic of Myst is in the way the mystery unravels itself as players move around in the beautiful and mystical worlds that the game provides.

The scenery in Myst consists mostly of static displays. The player moves about by clicking the mouse on points on the screen. The program changes the player's view accordingly. These views are rendered in advance by a technique known as *ray tracing*, which provides photo-realistic images of scenes represented in a computer model.

Myst frequently uses small inserts of video clips superimposed over the static displays. Some of the video clips are actual video images created with a video camera. Others are constructed from animated sequences of scenes rendered in advance with ray tracing and compiled into video files that the computer can play back.

Sound effects and music are an integral part of Myst. Many of the clues depend on sound effects. The music provides no clues or information, but greatly enhances the visual effects of the game by adding to the mood.

The Theatrix library supports the development of games such as Myst. The toolkit includes 3-D modeling and ray tracing tools, and the library supports static displays, selective mouse control, coordinated sound effects, video clips, and music.

Sprites and Backgrounds

Games such as Putt-Putt and Leisure Suit Larry may be at opposite ends of the family values spectrum, but they use similar animation techniques. A static background provides the scenery, and small animated characters, called *sprites*, move around the scene and provide the action. The player controls the game with the keyboard and mouse. When the scene changes, the game displays a new background.

Some games use scrolling backgrounds. As the sprites move around, the background scrolls to keep the sprites in view. This technique allows the game to seem to cover more territory without changing scenes. Arcade games such as Super Mario Brothers use scrolling backgrounds.

Theatrix supports animated sprites and both static and scrolling backgrounds.

Your Game

All the discussions until now have been about games that other people have developed. Now it's time to consider your game, and that's what we'll concentrate on from this point forward. This chapter addresses the theory behind the components of a PC game and the options you have when you build one. Chapter 3 is about the technology, and Chapter 4 is about the strategies that you apply in building your game.

After you have decided to write the next killer game and sweep the market, you have to build it. To do that, you start with the game's purpose (other than to make you a pile of money, of course). What is its point? What are the objectives? What is expected of the player? What does the game itself provide?

Develop a theme. Will your players kill or be killed? Or will they explore, collecting treasures and gathering clues? Must they manipulate a vehicle? How about weapons? Will there be one player at a time or more? Will the game support multiple players at a single PC session, or is a network involved?

Develop a scenario. Sketch out the scenes and the game's progress. Identify items that appear in each of the scenes and their consequence to the player.

Who are the players going to be? Small children? Teenagers? Adults? Senior citizens? Does the game make assumptions about the players' cultural or ethnic backgrounds?

Will music play a role? Sound effects? Video clips?

How will the player control the game? With the keyboard? With the mouse? With a joystick?

Will the scenery and characters be realistic? Surrealistic? Have an outer-space look? Be pastoral? Have an arcade look?

All these decisions help you select the technique for presenting the game and the tools that you need. The example games in this book have all the scenery and use all the features just mentioned—music, sound effects, video clips, mouse, joystick. You won't find all the elements in every game, but everything just discussed exists in one or more of the example games.

Scenery

Designing scenery is a major part of game design, but it's something that doesn't call on your programming skills at all. Whether you use a paint program to construct a scene or render a 3-D model into a ray-traced, photo-realistic image, the result is a screen full of colored pixels that the program copies into video memory. When you use a class library such as Theatrix, all you do in the program is provide the name of the file. All the real work is done in the construction of the scene.

There might be parts of the scenery screen that are significant to the program. If a mouse click has meaning on a particular feature, you must record the pixel coordinates of the click boundaries. You will need to eventually plug these values into the program. If the scene includes a door that opens and closes, you need to record the coordinates that define the door's rectangle. If sprites move about in the scene, you need to map a path of screen coordinates that represent the movement.

Characters

The characters in a game—the sprites—are like the actors in a play. They move about among the scenery, speak lines, and make things happen. Through animation, sprites provide the action in the game.

Not all sprites represent living creatures. A door that opens and closes can be a sprite. So can a table that slides across the floor. Anything that moves against the static background scenery is a sprite.

Animation of a sprite involves rendering in advance all the frames necessary to represent motion. A walking sprite needs frames to display the character in each of the configurations of steps. If the character moves toward and away from the player's view of the scene, there must be frames of different sizes to suggest perspective. Sometimes you render these frames in advance. Other times you have one set of frames for each motion and compute and render the size at runtime.

Video Clips

Not all moving things in a game are implemented as sprites. Sometimes you use video clips. These clips can be animated sequences built from 3-D models or individually painted frames. They can also be real video sequences captured onto disk from a video input card connected to a video camera or VCR. There are standard formats for these video files, and Theatrix supports their display.

Myst uses many video clips. The scenes where the characters speak from behind books in the library are video clips. The porthole view of flying into the island of another world in a spaceship is a video sequence made by many renderings of a 3-D model of that flight.

Sound and Music

Sound effects and music add an extra dimension to a game. The PC has a programmable speaker, but its small bandwidth limits its use for effective sound generation. However, most game players have add-on sound boards in their PCs. These boards are capable of producing high-quality sound effects and synthesized or sampled music. By using these sound boards, even games that do not depend on sound to communicate with the player are more fun to play. If the game slams a door or fires a shotgun, the sound adds to the effect. Music, as played from MIDI files, adds mood and texture to a scene.

Menus

If there is more than one place for a player to start when playing a game or if the player can make choices at strategic points in the game, a menu is a good way to present the choices and get the selection. A *menu* shows a list of the possible selections and provides a way for the player to make a choice. Every computer user is accustomed to menus. Game programmers have the freedom to use any menu technique they like. Unlike other development environments, Theatrix does not impose a standard for menus on the game programmer. (See "What About Standards" later in this chapter.) For that reason, there is no menu class in the library. You should design a menu to reflect the atmosphere that your game presents and use the Theatrix paradigm to display the menu and retrieve the player's choices. The menu should be simple and easy to use. Some of the example games on the included CD-ROM use menus, and you can use these examples as a guide.

Options

A game's options can be as simple as allowing the player to specify a skill level or as complex as letting the player modify the game itself. Most action games allow you to join in as a rookie or trainee and then raise your skill level as you become more experienced. This approach allows players to get into and enjoy the game well before they are proficient with it. If you do not provide such an option in a difficult action game, then either your game is not so difficult after all—it is too easy, in fact—or players will give up in frustration before they have discovered all that the game has to offer. This concept does not apply so much to passive games of discovery such as Myst, where players can take their time. It is more important in games—such as Doom—that require the player to apply refined motor skills and fast reflexes to survive.

As with menus, the way that you display options and get their values should look as if it belongs to the game. The example programs on the included CD-ROM show you ways to do this.

Saving Games in Progress

If a game is complex and takes a while to complete, you should provide the ability to save and restore the game's status. There's not much that a library can add to what Standard C++ already provides for reading and writing disk files, but you should understand the concept.

Saving a game's progress consists of recording a number of status indicators and values into a disk file that the game can read during the initialization of a subsequent session. You should identify each of these items when you design the game's scenario to facilitate designing the save and restore software logic. The current status of a game consists of the progress that the player has made and the options under which the game is running. If the game has successive levels, the current level is one item of progress. If there are foes that have been vanquished, that fact should be recorded for each one. If items have been moved or bodies are strewn about, the location and identity of each one is saved. Any persistent data value that influences how the computer plays the game or that affects the player's location, skill, or progress should be saved.

When the player shuts down without having won or lost, the game program should ask whether the player wants to save the game. If so, the game program writes the status data into a disk file.

When the game begins at another time, the player must have the option to restore a previous game, in which case the game loads the status data into memory and proceeds from the last point of departure.

Suppose more than one person plays the game at different times but on the same computer. The game program needs to tell them apart. There are two ways to do this. One way is to name each saved game data file. When saving the game, the player specifies the saved game's name. That name is used later to retrieve the game. Another way is to provide a sign-on log. When a player starts the game, the program displays a list of players and allows a player to select from the list or to sign on as a new player to be added to the list.

Multiple Players

There are two ways to support multiple players in a game. One way is to let both players have their own controllers and use the same computer. Such games usually use a joystick, because sharing a keyboard or mouse can be awkward. The other way is to connect two or more computers in a network. The computers all run the game in a multiple-player environment, and they communicate by exchanging packets across the network.

The network can be as simple as two computers connected with a serial cable or by modem across telephone lines. Although many multiple-player games run on local and wide area networks, the demands of a game are small. The programs exchange small packets about such things as where the sprites are and who is shooting in what direction.

Keeping Score

If a game has scores or levels of achievement, then the game should offer the player an opportunity to record the results. A typical game displays a list of the highest scores and scoremakers, adding the latest score to the list if it ranks among the highest. This list gives new players an objective to aim for.

Simulators often maintain and record levels of player achievement. A pilot or driver can accumulate hours of experience and advanced ratings by successfully executing prescribed maneuvers, such as cross-country trips, instrument approaches, bombing raids, dogfights, and so on.

A game that records the progress of several players can use the same disk file to record the players' individual scores.

The Question of Sex and Violence

When people gather to discuss the issue of sex and violence in entertainment media, you have to watch for outside agendas. It seems that the only people whose opinions can be trusted are those who have no personal stake in the outcome, and no one seems to fit that description. Politicians posture for votes. The entertainment industry holds forth for profits. Parents worry about wrong influences on their children. Civil libertarians guard our rights to free speech and expression. It seems that everyone has a stake in sex and violence.

Leisure Suit Larry depicts a couple of cute sprites having sex—under the covers, to be sure, but there is no question about what they are doing. The game may have more sexually oriented action than that one scene, but we never got much further with it.

Doom is violent. It depicts death and carnage, complete with screams, blood, and bodies scattered all over the landscape. The player does most of the killing, selecting weapons from a deadly and varied arsenal.

Most flight simulators involve bombing or shooting down the enemy, who, it must be presumed, are human beings.

Myst has no active violence, but it tells the story of long-ago acts when beings did harm to one another. In one scene, a skeleton is seen hanging from a gallows, a remnant of earlier, unseen atrocities.

Descent takes a different approach to its violence. The player shoots down unmanned drones that are themselves programmed to mindlessly shoot down the player. The player never actually kills anything that is alive.

Some arcade games depict neo-gladiators tearing off one another's arms, legs, and heads. These games have come under public scrutiny, and a cry has gone up for some form of industry self-regulation and a ratings system.

Despite what you hear during political campaigns and on talk shows, no empirical evidence exists to support the position that children receive negative influences from seeing improper behavior in entertainment media. That is only emotional opinion. The absence of such evidence does not mean that the opinions are without merit, however, only that they are unproven by scientific means.

You must decide how you feel about this issue, because you have the opportunity to add to and influence this culture in one way or another. One thing is clear: There is a strong market for games that allow the player to fire weapons and vanquish the enemy. You may draw whatever conclusions you wish about a society that desires and seeks out such a release. If you think that you know what's right and acceptable, then you have found the answer for yourself, and that's what matters.

Until there are government regulations to control what people can publish in a computer game (which is inevitable, we fear), everyone has to exercise good taste and judgment. The market should guide us. If programmers make the right decisions and the games are good ones and are properly marketed, people will use and praise them. If, on the other hand, someone puts out an obvious piece of trash where evil nuns slaughter little fuzzy puppies (we hope we haven't given anyone an idea here) or something equally stupid and gratuitous, that work will be rejected and the programmer can move on to other pursuits.

What about Standards?

Every aspect of programming involves standards. There are standards for writing code, for documentation, and most particularly for the user interface.

When DOS reigned, applications prided themselves on their proprietary user interfaces. If you copied the menu and data entry screens of another application, the chances were good that you would find yourself the object of a *look-and-feel* lawsuit.[2] Now that Windows prevails, applications pride themselves on their common user interface, and they all look and feel alike. Go figure.

Should all games look and feel alike? We don't think so, not even if they are Windows games. Each of the example games on the included CD-ROM has its own unique interface. Some have menus, and others have options screens. Their screens are designed to consistently maintain the aura that the game supports. Some of the games use the mouse, others use the keyboard, and still others use both. They do not necessarily use those things in exactly the same ways.

The charm of games such as Doom and Myst is that their user interfaces reflect the underlying theme of the games and are unique. Their menus and options screens sustain the overall theme of the particular game. Command structures are designed to facilitate effective play based on how the game works rather than on a rigid definition of a standard way to do things.

Imagine playing Myst if you had to pop down menus and use dialog boxes to rotate the tower in the Library and view constellations in the Planetarium.

Imagine Doom with radio buttons to set the level of play and command buttons to fire a weapon.

It's a game, folks. It's supposed to be fun. It's for after hours. Leave the stuffy and constraining standards to those who wear ties and socks and who write and use commercial applications with databases, reports, and scheduled processing cycles. That description may fit you during your day gig, but when you are off the clock, you can forget the standards and have some fun.

---

[2]In a famous litigation, Lotus sued Borland because Quattro Pro's DOS user interface resembled that of Lotus 1-2-3 for DOS. It has been reported that during that period, Philippe Kahn, then Borland's CEO, greeted Mitch Kapur, CEO of Lotus, in a restaurant by saying, "Good morning, Mitch. How do you look and feel today?"

PC Game Technology

"Go play with the town you have built of blocks..."
Stephen Vincent Benet

This chapter deals with the hardware and software technologies that underpin a computer game. We discuss hardware architecture, multimedia techniques, and software issues. We also address the creative aspects that apply to generating the multimedia components of a computer game.

You will learn about the following subjects:

- ◇ Events and messages
- ◇ Video
- ◇ Graphics
- ◇ Sound
- ◇ Music
- ◇ Game controllers

Why Learn about Hardware?

Programmers who build conventional computer applications can usually concentrate on the problem and ignore the hardware. The operating system insulates the programmers from such details. Lucky them. Game programmers, on the other hand, have always had hardware to contend with. To a large extent, Theatrix hides those details, and it is possible to write a game program without knowing very much about hardware. It always helps, however, to understand how things work. In the case of subjects such as the video palette, you need to generally understand the hardware's operations so that you can recognize their consequences and deal with them.

This chapter provides only an overview of hardware architectural issues so that you understand them well enough to write effective games. Entire books have been written about PC video architecture, programming the mouse, MIDI music cards, and so on. Although you do not need to understand all the technical complexities of these devices to develop a Theatrix game, you might find them interesting. In that case, refer to the Bibliography for a list of books on these subjects.

Event-Driven, Message-Based Programming

Theatrix implements an event-driven, message-based programming model. The model vaguely resembles the way that Windows programs are written, although the Theatrix message system is not nearly as complex as the one that Windows programmers have to learn.

A Theatrix game program instantiates its game objects, registers for event messages, and then turns everything over to Theatrix. The system then watches for events to occur, intercepts them when they do, and dispatches event messages to the registered functions.

Events are things that happen outside of and asynchronous to the game program. Clock ticks, keystrokes, mouse movements, mouse clicks, joystick motion, joystick button presses, and receptions of network packets are all events.

Messages are function calls that the system makes to registered functions of the game program. Messages report events to the game program. The game program gets only those messages for which it has registered. A message registration specifies the function for Theatrix to call when the event occurs.

Game programs may specify internal application-dependent messages, too. One function registers for the message. Some other function in the game sends the message. Theatrix takes care of dispatching the message to the registered function. In this case, the event is whatever the sending and receiving functions agree that it is. Using messages loosens the functional coupling between program components.

Game Controllers

The player controls the game with input from controlling devices. In arcade games, unique devices designed for the particular game are installed on the arcade machine. PCs, being general-purpose computers able to play many different games, have common keyboard and mouse devices that were designed for typing, menu selection, and other such mundane computing tasks. Games must use those devices as controllers. There is one standard device in the PC architecture that is a concession to game players—one that seems to be used for little else—and that device is the joystick. Theatrix also permits a game to be controlled remotely through a serial port.

Keyboard

The keyboard has been used for virtually every kind of game control. Many champion Doom players prefer the keyboard to the joystick for moving through the maze and firing weapons. Flight simulators always include keyboard commands to control pitch, roll, and yaw in case the pilot's computer does not have a joystick. Real-life airplane pilots are often surprised when PC simulator pilots become proficient at flying a simulator by using the keyboard instead of more intuitive and realistic flight controls.

Action games often require the coordinated use of different sets of keys at the same time. You might be changing direction with an arrow key to avoid being shot while at the same time firing a weapon. BIOS and DOS keyboard input functions cannot report such keypress combinations. Sensing them requires a low-level device handler that intercepts the keyboard hardware interrupt vector and reads the keyboard data port.

Unlike a typical video terminal, the PC keyboard device is not an ASCII input device. Pressing a key interrupts the running program. An interrupt service routine executes and reads the keyboard data port, which delivers a keystroke *scan code*. Each key on the keyboard has a unique scan code; the code is unlike the key's corresponding ASCII value. The BIOS function that services the keyboard interrupt translates those keystroke combinations into the ASCII value that your C++ program reads when it extracts from the *cin* object.

The event-driven, message-based programming model used by Theatrix permits elements of the game to register functions with keyboard events. When a registered key is pressed, the system calls the game program's function. There are two ways to register. You can register for a regular ASCII keypress such as the one you get from a BIOS function call, or you can register for an asynchronous keypress, which calls your function as soon as the registered key is pressed irrespective of other key presses at the same time.

Mouse

The mouse is an asynchronous pointing device. When enabled, the mouse driver displays a cursor on the screen. The cursor points to a screen position related to the smallest unit of resolution in the current video mode. For example, if the program uses Mode X, the mouse's cursor points to positions from 0 to 319 in the X axis and 0 to 239 in the Y axis.

The cursor's screen position is coincidental to the mouse's location on your desktop. You can pick up the mouse and move it, and the cursor does not move. You need to roll the mouse on a flat surface to move the cursor on the screen.

A program can turn the mouse cursor display on and off, specify the graphics configuration of the mouse cursor, set and read the current mouse cursor coordinates, and read the setting of the mouse buttons. Mouse cursor movements occur independently of the running program. When the user moves the mouse, the mouse driver moves the cursor. The driver saves what was displayed under the mouse cursor so that it can restore the screen before moving the cursor to another position.

A game program needs to be aware of the mouse cursor. The program should turn the mouse cursor display off during writes to the screen in graphics modes. Otherwise the program's write could erase all or part of the mouse cursor. Also, the mouse driver's cursor-save video buffer would not be current if the application program wrote to the current mouse cursor position. Ignoring the mouse during typical animation sequences leaves mouse trails all over the screen. Fortunately, you do not have to worry about these details. Theatrix takes care of mouse displays for the game program by turning the cursor display off and on at strategic times when writing to video memory.

A Theatrix game program can register for mouse events in several ways. It can specify functions to be called when the mouse moves and when the player clicks a mouse button. The functions receive as parameters the current mouse position at the time of the event. By using these registered functions, a program can use the mouse to select menu items, press game buttons, drag game parts around the screen, and so on.

The game program can provide a table of screen regions with associated mouse cursor shapes. This table tells Theatrix how to change the cursor's appearance depending on where the mouse cursor is positioned. You might use arrow cursors to indicate that a click in that region changes direction, a finger cursor to indicate that a button can be pressed, and an open hand cursor to indicate that an object can be picked up.

The table can also include game-dependent functions for Theatrix to call if the user clicks the mouse while the cursor is in the associated region. These table entries allow the game to take actions that depend on where the mouse was when the user clicked. For example, you might open a door, pick up an object, move closer to a scene, or turn to the right or left based on what item in the display you are touching with the mouse when you click the button.

Joystick

The standard PC joystick is a poor relation to the high-resolution joystick devices found in high-end CAD workstations of 10-plus years ago. The PC joystick is a crude, low-resolution, mostly inaccurate device that is used in games mainly for direction and motion control.

Flight simulators use the joystick for attitude control because its function resembles that of the control stick in older aircraft and modern jet fighters. The name *joystick* comes from aviation. It is what World War I and barnstorming pilots called the control lever in their craft. Some PC joystick devices resemble the control wheel in modern airplanes and are intended for more realistic flight simulation, although professional pilots often complain that PC joysticks are not sensitive enough to simulate true flight conditions.

How well a program works with the joystick depends on how well the programmer understands the vagaries of the device. The shareware version of Doom uses the joystick to move the player through the maze. Either those programmers did not understand the joystick or they did not care much for it as a controlling device. They built in a wide dead spot at the center of the stick's travel, apparently overcompensating for the flutter behavior that some joysticks display. By the time you get the stick outside the dead spot, the programmed degree of motion is too fast and you overshoot where you intended to point. Perhaps that is why serious Doom players (if there could be such a thing) prefer the keyboard. Other 3-D maze programs make better use of the joystick.

A program can sense four things from the joystick's input: the distance from position zero at the left to a maximum rightmost value on the X axis, the distance from zero at the top to a maximum bottommost value on the Y axis, whether button 1 is pressed, and whether button 2 is pressed. The X/Y readings range from a possible zero/zero at the upper left to device-dependent maximum values at the lower right. Unlike with the mouse, these coordinates are unrelated to the screen resolution and do not change when the video mode changes.

Because of the inherent mechanical and electrical instability of the joystick design, its readings and sensitivity vary from device to device. Processor speed is one of the variables.

The crude A/D converter logic in the standard joystick uses a simple RC circuit that discharges two capacitors, one for each axis, at rates that get slower the farther away from upper left the stick gets. The stick's position adjusts two potentiometers, one for each axis. The potentiometers supply a variable resistance that controls the rate of discharge of the capacitors. The circuit is normally charged. The discharge begins when the program writes any value to the joystick port. The write operation closes a switch and grounds the positive side of the capacitor, which is connected to an inverter gate that the program reads as a bit in the joystick port. When the capacitor is fully discharged, the inverter gate output flips from logic 0 to 1. By timing the two discharges, the program can roughly determine the joystick's distance from its upper left position.

There are several problems with the joystick operation. First, the stick position value computed by the program is a function of processor speed and, curiously, the operating system. Presumably, the faster the CPU, the higher value it counts, but the same hardware running under plain DOS gives different readings than it does when running in a Windows DOS box. Table 3.1 shows the ranges reported by the same joystick on different 486 computers and under different operating systems. The table illustrates that you can't make any assumptions about the joystick based on the system you are using.

Table 3.1 Joystick range comparison

CPU Speed/OS	Low X/Y Value	High X/Y Value	Center X/Y Value
66 MHz/DOS	87	216	130
40 MHz/DOS	3	105	43
33 MHz/DOS	6	224	90
66 MHz/Win DOS Box	45	110	67
40 MHz/Win DOS Box	12	216	94
33 MHz/Win DOS Box	6	110	45

The second problem is that the joystick's position values are influenced by the imprecise electrical and mechanical characteristics of the particular joystick and controller. The upper left resistances, lower right resistances, and the center resistances depend on potentiometer tolerances; the discharge rate depends on the capacitor tolerances; the ranges and center position values depend on mechanical stops built into the joystick.

The third problem is that the center and outer positions are electrically unstable, delivering values that flutter several increments even when the stick is motionless.

We can conclude, therefore, that PC joysticks are imprecise and that the software needs to know about and compensate for that.

Many games calibrate the joystick by having the user move the stick to the center, the upper left corner, and the lower right corner and press a button at each position. This action permits the software to adjust itself closely to the characteristics of the player's particular joystick.

Other programs use a rough self-calibration routine that assumes that the joystick is centered when the game begins. Its starting position is stored as the probable center position, double its X and Y values are stored as approximate lower right positions, and zero/zero is stored as an approximate upper left position. These values work when you are using the joystick to indicate rough directional controls. They work well for flight simulator operations, where the distance from center determines the roll and pitch rate. Anything more precise than that needs better calibration and probably needs better hardware.

Theatrix calibrates the joystick and sends button and position messages to the game program. Theatrix converts the joystick's values to 0/0 at the center. A forward stick position is reported as a positive Y value, rear as negative Y, left as negative X, and right as positive X. Components of the game program register for joystick button clicks and mouse movements, and Theatrix sends messages to the registered game functions to report these events. The program can ask for the extreme values of the X and Y axes, which depend on the device and operating system, and can adjust itself accordingly.

Serial Port

Theatrix allows components of a game to register for serial port input messages. Each message is a byte value transmitted from a remote device connected to the PC's serial port. By using this feature, a game can be written that runs in two-player mode with the players sitting at different computers.

Theatrix does not attempt to encapsulate support for multiple serial ports at one time. You could implement that feature in your game by instantiating multiple objects of the serial port class and coordinating the input and output yourself, bypassing the message system.

The Theatrix serial port server assumes a direct connection of the serial port. One of the Theatrix utility programs is a modem shell that permits the players to make the connection through modems before launching the game executions.

Video

A computer program displays words and pictures on the screen by writing data values into video memory. The video controller translates those data values into pixels that light up dots of phosphor on the face of the cathode ray tube. That translation is a function of the video memory contents, the current video mode, and, in the case of a graphics video mode, the video palette.

The standard PC video configuration is the Video Graphics Array (VGA). Early PCs had video controllers with less memory and lower resolution, and the VGA can emulate those older devices. But the VGA is the mainstream display device today, and most game programmers target the VGA as a minimum configuration. Theatrix programs run on VGA-equipped PCs.

Video Memory

Video memory is addressable RAM in conventional memory space (which is the first megabyte of memory) above the 640KB boundary. VGA graphics video modes require a minimum of 256KB, and Super VGA (SVGA) modes can have as many as 4MB, so not all the memory is addressable at the same time. The program selects banks of memory to address by using the controller's status and data registers.

Interpreting controller registers and writing data into video memory is not usually the concern of the conventional application programmer. The operating system takes care of doing that. Similarly, the application programmer is not usually concerned with translating text or graphics renditions into bit streams that the video controller can translate. These functions are handled by lower-level drivers. The DOS game programmer, however, does not have the convenience of an operating system that understands game displays. The DOS game programmer has to do it all. Theatrix encapsulates most of that so that you do not have to worry about it.

Video Modes

The VGA supports a number of *modes*, which determine how the controller interprets the contents of video memory. When you turn your computer on, it starts out in a text mode. The data values in video memory are ASCII characters and display attribute bytes in a 24 x 80 array. The controller displays those characters with those attributes on the screen. Each attribute byte determines the colors and intensity of its associated character byte.

The graphics modes define the screen *resolution* and the number of supported colors. The VGA supports several graphics modes, and the SVGA supports even more. At its lower levels of abstraction, Theatrix permits you to use most of these graphics video modes. At higher levels of abstraction, which free the programmer from these details, Theatrix uses the XVGA mode, which has a 320 x 240 pixel resolution and 256 colors. The XVGA was nicknamed *Mode X* by Michael Abrash in *Dr. Dobb's Journal*. For a complete discussion of Mode X and the other graphics video modes, read Abrash's book, *Zen of Graphics Programming*, listed in the Bibliography.

Video Page Buffers

A VGA controller has at least 256KB and maybe more. Depending on the currently selected video mode, not all of that memory is used to hold the data being displayed. Under Mode X there are three page buffers of video memory, each one able to hold an entire screen full of data. At any one time only one of those pages is the *visible* page, which contains the display data that the user sees. The other pages are hidden in the background. Programs can rapidly set one of the two background pages to be the visible page, putting the previous visible page in the background. The switch is instantaneous, so programs typically write updates to a background page and switch the page to the visible status when the page is updated and ready to be seen. This technique avoids the annoying flicker that the user might see if the program were to update the screen directly in the visible page. Theatrix encapsulates management of the video page buffers for scene changes and sprite animation.

Bitmapped Graphics Files

A bitmapped graphics file records the pixel values for a picture in a raster graphics representation. Each dot on the screen is a picture element, nicknamed *pixel*. In Mode X there are 320 dots horizontally and 240 dots vertically. Each dot is represented by an eight-bit byte, and the value, from 0 to 255, represents the pixel's color taken from the picture's palette. The file has header information that identifies the picture's resolution, number of colors, color selection palette, and so on.

Table 3.2 lists the most common bitmapped graphics file formats.

Table 3.2 Bitmapped graphics file formats

BMP	Microsoft Windows Bitmap Format
GIF	CompuServe Graphics Interchange Format
PCX	ZSoft PC Paintbrush Format
TGA	AT&T Targa Format
TIFF	Aldus Tagged Image File Format

Theatrix uses the .PCX format during a game's execution, but your construction tools might produce files in any of several formats. The toolkit includes a conversion utility that translates between the various formats.

We chose the .PCX format for several reasons. First, virtually every raster graphics tool for the PC supports the .PCX format. Second, the .PCX format supports eight bits of color per pixel, consistent with Theatrix's 256-color objectives. Third, .PCX is a comparatively simple format, lacking the complexity and overhead of the more complex formats. Finally, .PCX's run-length-encoded (RLE) compression format is not protected by software patents, and programmers are free to use the .PCX format in any manner.

For a complete discussion of bitmapped graphics file formats, read *Bitmapped Graphics Programming in C++*, listed in the Bibliography.

The Palette

Mode X can display 256 different colors at any one time. Those 256 colors represent a subset of the 256KB colors available on the VGA. Each display consists of two parts: the display data array and a *palette* of colors from which to choose. The display data array consists of eight bits for each pixel position on the screen. The eight-bit value is offset into the palette, which contains 256 entries (one for each color that is available). Any given image can have a palette made up of any 256-color subset of the 256KB possible colors.

Image construction utility programs, such as paint programs and ray tracers, determine the palette for the image being constructed. You can easily wind up with several components of a game that have different and incompatible palettes. The VGA can work with only one palette at a time. If you superimpose a sprite on a background and if the palettes of the sprite and the background are incompatible, the sprite's colors will be wrong. If you use a system-generated mouse cursor and if the cursor's palette conflicts with the current image, the cursor's color will not be what you expect. It is even possible for frames of a video clip to have different palettes.

Ray tracers, which are discussed in more detail in Chapter 4, cause the biggest problem. They generate images from subtle combinations of colors to achieve their photo-realistic effects of lighting, shading, reflection, refraction, and diffusion. Two renderings of the same 3-D model with a slight change of camera angles will surely result in two different palettes. This is no problem if you are simply changing scenes. The VGA adjusts to new palette information instantly. But if you are using a common sprite or cursor on the two scenes, the palettes of those images will conflict with at least one of the palettes of the scenery.

With all these palette collisions to worry about, you might well wonder how you can get it all coordinated. The Theatrix toolkit includes utility programs that process sets of images and normalize all the palettes so that the pictures display the way you want them to. Chapter 4 discusses the strategy of palette correction, and Chapter 6 describes the Theatrix tools for doing that.

Graphics

An old cliché says that a picture is worth a thousand words. True enough, and unless you are writing one of those text-mode adventure games, you will involve pictures in your game. Chapter 4 discusses the strategies for building pictures to depict static scenery and animated characters. Here we are concerned about designing them and getting our ideas closer to an implementation. To do that we need to understand the strengths and limitations of the VGA's ability to display pictures from a technical as well as an artistic viewpoint.

The background scenery is a 320 by 240, 256-color picture displayed from a .PCX file. It can come from nearly anywhere. Chapter 4 discusses these strategies in more detail, but you can build the picture with a paint program from a 3-D model. You can use a ray tracer to build a photo-realistic picture.

You can even use a photograph, print, or painting that you scan into a .PCX file with a flatbed color scanner. Keep in mind, though, that paintings and photographs are artistic creations and are subject to the laws protecting intellectual property. If you are going to use the work of others, be sure that you have the right to do so.

Be careful, also, about what you yourself photograph. You might hold the copyright to pictures that you take, but if the picture includes people, make sure that you have their permission to use their images in your published work. Remember that people not in the public view have certain rights with respect to privacy, and you must observe those rights or bear the consequences. The same caution should be shown with the pictures of the property of others, particularly where business icons or logos are involved. If you are going to use these things in your game, make sure that a lawyer has blessed the practice. Neither of the authors of this book is a lawyer, and the advice we give here should not be interpreted as authoritative legal opinion. When in doubt, get professional legal advice.

Theatrix does not care about the source of the background file or the complexity or realism of what it depicts. The library's performance is not affected by those parameters. Once you have a .PCX file of the correct resolution, it's all the same to Theatrix. The file sizes vary, depending on the density of the material and the .PCX file's compression algorithm, but the software to display the files and, for the most part, the overhead required to fetch and write them to video memory is about the same. And it is fast. Theatrix can flip scenes instantaneously.

The characters in a Theatrix game are displayed from libraries of graphics inserts built with 256 colors but at lower resolutions. The height and width of the sprites are determined by the resolution of the inserts when compared to the 320 x 240 pixel resolution of Mode X. You build or render in advance all the views of the sprite to support the animation frames of its action.

The VGA supports higher resolutions than Mode X does, and the resulting realism can be better, but performance degrades somewhat. It takes longer to fetch and display a 640 x 480 picture and longer still for one with a resolution of 800 x 600. If you make rapid scene changes, you can see the difference at the higher resolutions on slower machines with slower video cards. It also takes much more disk space to record those pictures.

Bear in mind that you are building a game. It's supposed to look like a game. It's not necessarily supposed to look like a movie, although some contemporary interactive multimedia games are getting close to that kind of realism.

Choose an artistic genre in which to display scenery. Be consistent in that choice. A cartoon-like character wandering around a photo-realistic moonscape looks more like a cheap TV commercial than it does a game. Likewise, a shiny, ray-traced robot trekking through a Grandma Moses-like scene is unconvincing. We can believe in cartoon characters in cartoon worlds, and we can believe in photo-realistic characters in a photo-realistic world, but it takes creative energy to effectively mix the two.

Also be consistent in the appearance of different scenes in the same game. If you jump about from one style to another just because you happen to have the pictures and it is convenient to use them, your players will be, if not turned off, then at least confused about the story you are trying to depict.

Some games, such as flight simulators and 3-D maze games, render their scenery in real time at runtime. They have to because the scene being viewed is a function of where the player has positioned the viewport, and the game permits a view from virtually anywhere in the three-dimensional universe. It would be impossible to compute every possible position and viewing angle and then render in advance every scene as viewed from every position.

Flight simulators typically use static graphics with animated inserts to represent the instrument panel. Then they render the outside scenery in real time by computing the view of each frame from a 3-D model of the scenery and features. They employ all the computer graphics tricks to provide solid geometric shapes with surface generation and hidden line removal. The technique is effective and impressive, but it limits the amount of texture and shading that the scenery can have. The incidence of buildings is sparse because the program can compute only so many features during the brief time it has to render each frame.

Three-dimensional maze games use techniques called *ray casting* and *texture mapping* to compute every frame of an indoor scene. They map the frames of animated characters over this scenery by choosing from a fixed number of views and sizing the view in real time to represent the distance of the character from the player's view. The result is a dazzling display of rather fuzzy scenes that suggest, rather than accurately depict, the walls and doors of the maze as they slide by. Players do not mind, because the action is so fast that the passing scenery would be a blur anyway. If you hold still long enough to regard the scenery, something ugly will kill you.

Sound

Sound effects dramatically enhance a game's operation. The Shootout example on the accompanying CD-ROM illustrates this principle. The game works as well without the sound effects, but it is much more fun when you can hear them. Doors open and close, guns fire shots, bodies thump when they hit the ground, the sheriff's gun clicks instead of fires when it is empty, and the citizens applaud when you win the game.

What Is Sound?

Sound occurs when something disturbs the air. The movement of the air vibrates our eardrums, which send signals to our brains. If a tree falls in the forest and no one is there to hear it, the air still gets moved around whether or not anyone or anything is there with ears to interpret it.

Sound can be viewed as a waveform. Push the air one way and the waveform rises. Pull the air the other way and the waveform drops. Increase the frequency and the pitch rises. Increase the amplitude and the volume rises. Mix two different signals and you combine sounds.

Anything sensitive enough to move with the air vibrates in a pattern that resembles the waveform. If you turn it around and cause the air to vibrate in the same pattern by duplicating the waveform mechanically or electrically, you can reproduce the sound.

Recording Sound

Edison recorded and played back sound mechanically. He simulated an eardrum with a diaphragm at the base of an amplifying horn. At the center of the diaphragm he positioned a needle. Edison spoke the words of "Mary Had a Little Lamb" into the horn. His voice moved the air, which vibrated the horn, which vibrated the diaphragm, which vibrated the needle, which etched a groovy pattern across a wax cylinder that Edison rotated with a crank as he spoke. Thus the waveform of Edison's voice was recorded. Then he tracked the needle back through the etched pattern's groove to vibrate the needle, which vibrated the diaphragm. The horn amplified the vibrations, and Edison's recorded poem was reproduced—played back.

You can demonstrate this principle for yourself in the kitchen. Get a tin can and a sewing needle. Remove the lid from one end of the can. Dump out the string beans. Punch a tiny hole in the other end and wedge the blunt end of the needle into the hole. Connect a piece of tableware to the can with tape to act as a tone arm. Now get out an old phonograph record that you don't particularly treasure, maybe something by Barry Manilow. Put the record on a salad spinner and get it turning. Lower the needle into the track and listen to the sound being amplified by the tin can. Throw away the Barry Manilow record. Eat the string beans.

Records and audio tapes are *analog* devices[1]. They store their information as analog signals that represent, as accurately as possible, the waveform of the original sound. The recording equipment starts with air moving a microphone's sensitive diaphragm the same way that Edison did. But from that point the process is quite different. Instead of mechanically transferring the vibrations to an etched track, the electronics convert the vibrations into an analog, amplitude-modulated electrical signal and store the signal as charged particles of emulsion on magnetic tape. If a vinyl record is to be made (rare today because of the popularity of compact disks), the master pressing is made in fundamentally the same way that Edison made his first recording except that an electrical signal played back from the master tape vibrates the etching needle.

Digital Recording

The recordings just described are analog recordings. Computers reproduce sound as *digital* recordings. They store sound signals as binary strings. Except for synthesized sound, which uses algorithms to approximate sound waveforms, computer sound originates as real sound that is recorded digitally. If Edison had owned a PC with a Sound Blaster, he would have recorded "Mary Had a Little Lamb" onto a hard disk file as a digital bit stream.

---

[1] An exception is the digital audio tape (DAT) preferred by most sound engineers today.

Sampling

The digital bit stream that records sound in a computer is a *sample* of the original analog sound signal waveform. The computer samples the amplitude of the waveform at fixed intervals. The interval frequency is called the *sampling rate*. At each of these intervals, the computer stores a binary value that represents the amplitude (the height on the waveform) as a signed integer. The higher the sampling rate, the more accurately the digital bit stream represents the original audio sound.

Another variable in a bit stream sample is its *resolution*, which is the number of bits available for each sample. The more bits you use, the wider the dynamic range of the signal when it is played back. Eight to 16 bits are typical. Professional recording equipment uses 16 bits of resolution. Sixteen-bit sound cards are not unusual on PCs now, but eight-bit cards are far more common.

The combination of signal length, sampling rate, and resolution determines how much storage space is needed to record the signal. This value is an important concern. The game program needs to store the sound clips in a disk file to distribute with the game, and it needs to load them into RAM to play them back.

Most game sound effects play back well with a sampling rate of 5,000 to 11,000 and with eight bits of resolution. One thing is certain: You must play back a sound clip with the same sampling rate and resolution with which it was recorded. Otherwise the sound is garbled and its duration is wrong.

VOC Files

Theatrix uses the standard Sound Blaster .VOC file format for sound effects. This format is readily adaptable to the different sound card drivers that Theatrix supports. The VOC file format assumes an eight-bit sampling resolution and a variable sampling rate specified by header information in the data stream.

The format is convenient because it is a standard and because there are utility programs that convert between .VOC files and the formats of other kinds of sound files. Theatrix organizes the .VOC files into disk file libraries of sounds. Each character in a game can have its own library. If different sprites use different sound effects and voices, you can maintain their sound clips independently.

Music

Every game programming book that we have read either ignores the subject of music or addresses only the technical issues of how to play back a MIDI file. The authors defer the creation of their music to contributors to their book, make no effort to explain the process, and suggest that you do the same. Yet many programmers are musicians, too, and can understand the creative side of the musical aspects of game construction. We discuss some of that here, assuming that you have some understanding of musical theory or, at least, an appreciation of the implications of music in any kind of entertainment medium.

How important is music to a game? Many arcade games do not use music. The creators of Myst considered leaving music out of their production. Fortunately, they reconsidered and applied the additional effort to include background music in each scene. As you move from place to place in the five Myst islands, mood music dramatically enhances the visual effect at every change of scenery. The game would not be nearly as effective without background music.

Adding background music requires several steps. First, you identify where in the game the music occurs and what kind of music you want at each scene. Next, you compose or acquire the music. Then you translate the music into a format the computer can read and play back. Finally, you integrate the musical score into the game.

Setting the Mood

Background music sets a mood. Imagine the Lone Ranger without the *William Tell Overture*. Ta da dum. Ta da dum, ta da dum dum dum. The two go together. Rick's without Sam playing "As Time Goes By" wouldn't be Rick's. When, in *Psycho*, the corpse of Mrs. Bates spins around in the chair to face the audience, the effect would not be nearly as scary without the pulsating, piercing, screaming music.

As in the movies, each scene in a game has a theme, and music can dramatically reinforce that theme. If the player is deep in the bowels of a dark cave, the cave music could have an ominous, dank feeling. Eerie, scary music could accompany a trip through a haunted house. A child's game might use a happy tune that the child recognizes, such as "Here We Go 'Round the Mulberry Bush."

We learn through experience to associate different kinds of music with certain moods, and thus our mood changes when we hear the music. A funeral dirge elicits sadness. The Charleston is a happy dance. The blues make us feel sorry for ourselves. Old-time rock and roll is uplifting. Heavy metal is mind-numbing. A march evokes rousing feelings of patriotism. Some music is scary. Some music is romantic.

Some music is foreboding. Music prepares the player for coming events by foreshadowing a mood. You look at a closed door. Without music, the door is nothing more than that—a door. Add a low, sustained diminished chord played on an organ, and you know that something bad will happen if you open that door. The mood created by the music compels you to either run away or open the door and accept the worst.

Watch contemporary TV commercials to see how music sets a mood. Sad music plays quietly. A woman speaks. "I didn't realize that Sam's funeral would set us back six thousand dollars." The message: Don't be sad. Buy our life insurance. A contemporary blues singer sings, "Your true voice," bending her notes around in a way to suggest a caring, soulful mother. The message: We care for you deeply. Come back to our long distance service.

Try not to use music inappropriately. An urban scene of cars, noise, and street people does not fit with excerpts from the *Grand Canyon Suite*. Ragtime would be out of place in a funeral parlor. The *1812 Overture* would not work with a scene of fluffy clouds, flowers, songbirds, and butterflies. A polka would not particularly enhance a scene set in the House of Parliament. Watch movies, particularly older ones, to see how music is used to enhance scenes.

MIDI

Even though music is sustained sound, game programs do not usually use .VOC sound files for music clips. The storage requirements would be too restrictive. Music clips are usually longer than sound effects, and they require a higher sampling rate to prevent the distortion that people don't notice with voice and sound effects. Fortunately, you have an alternative, something called the musical instrument digital interface (MIDI).

Several years ago, the electronic music industry did something that the computer industry is rarely able to do: It established standard protocols and formats for data streams of packets that represent musical sounds. All the industry members uniformly adopted and implemented the MIDI standard in their products. The effort was collaborative, cooperative, and friendly, and was undertaken without rivalries or market pressures. The computer industry could learn a lot from the music industry.

The MIDI protocol was designed to allow various electronic synthesizers to be connected in a standard way. A *synthesizer* is a device that produces musical sounds electronically. Electric pianos, organs, drum machines, and so on are synthesizers. The synthesizer produces the sound of each note electronically either with an algorithmic synthesis of the desired instrument sound or by playing the note from a library of samples.

A sample is a recording of one note made with a musical instrument. The note is digitized and stored in a sample library. Sample libraries usually have several versions of each note for each instrument, reflecting various attacks, dynamics, and so on.

The MIDI protocol specifies digital packets that tell synthesizers what notes to play, how long to sustain them, and other variables such as the level of attack to apply when the note is first sounded, the pressure to apply while the note sustains, and so on.

A stream of MIDI packets tells one or more synthesizers how to play a song. A MIDI stream is the electronic equivalent of a player piano roll but with much more potential.

You can create MIDI packet streams in real time by playing music on a synthesizer (typically a keyboard). The synthesizer translates the notes you play into MIDI packets and transmits a stream of packets through the synthesizer's MIDI output port.

Synthesizers and sequencers (discussed soon) read MIDI streams into their MIDI input ports and play the notes from the stream. MIDI synthesizers can be connected in series so that you have several synthesizers interpreting and playing from the same stream.

Each MIDI note packet specifies one of 16 channels. Each of the synthesizers in the series typically processes the packets addressed to only one of the channels[2].

---

[2]It is not uncommon, though, for a MIDI instrument to incorporate more than one instrument device. Electric pianos often come equipped with integrated drum machines and sometimes with a complete set of 128 instrument patches.

A *sequencer* is a device that can read files of MIDI data and transmit the packets to the instruments. A sequencer can also record MIDI files by reading the notes being played on a MIDI synthesizer. You can record the notes from each synthesizer independently, adding each new channel to the channels already laid down. In this way one person can independently record all the instruments of an entire orchestral arrangement.[3] Each of the 16 channels in a sequencer is assigned a unique instrument voice selected from a standard table of 128 instruments. The sound assigned to an instrument is called its *patch*.

With a sequencer you can make corrections and modifications to the notes in a MIDI file. This permits a sequencer programmer to touch up a performance after it has been originally laid down. You can also change the patches that have been assigned to selected instruments and change the instrument voices assigned to selected channels.

Contemporary PC sound cards have all the hardware necessary to support sequencing. They have MIDI input and output ports, and they can produce the sounds of all 128 of the standard patches. This means that you need only a PC, a good sound card, speakers, a MIDI keyboard, and a sequencer program to record and play back MIDI files. Furthermore, all that the game player needs is a PC with a sound card and speakers to play your game and hear the background music.

Composing Music

Several of the example games on the included CD-ROM have original songs composed for this project or adapted from other original compositions from the author's portfolio. Three of them were composed extemporaneously at the keyboard by using a sequencer program to capture the MIDI data. You can listen to them in the Town demonstration game on the CD-ROM.

Two of the extemporaneous songs have no structure and are meant to imply a mood. When you get close to the church door in the game, you hear what sounds like a funeral processional played on a church organ. This song consists of random chords played in slow succession with an occasional but

---

[3]A joke among musicians tells about the studio musician who showed up at work for a recording session. To his surprise, a full, 40-piece orchestra was already there getting ready for the session. He looked at them all and said, "I hope you people realize that you're putting three sequencer operators out of work."

mostly unintentional harmonic resolution. We dubbed another track with a constantly repeated chime to suggest the church bell ringing mournfully in the background.

The second formless song plays at the front of the brick house. It uses a Hammond organ voice and is meant to suggest something ominous. The song consists mainly of a progression of minor and diminished chords, although anyone could get the same effect with a random pattern of chords of three and four unrelated notes each.

The third extemporaneous song is a ragtime improvisation on a common eight-bar chord progression (A7-D7-G7-C) repeated twice. This song plays during the video clip sequence of the Town game and is the background music for the street scene in the Shootout game. One of the benefits of MIDI is that musicians can produce music beyond their own technical abilities. By using a sequencer program, you can record the stride style of the ragtime piece in two passes at a slower tempo. One pass provides the octave-chord pattern of the left hand, which you can play with two hands in the first pass. Then you can overdub the right hand patterns in the second pass. This technique is how intricate player piano rolls of long ago were often made.

Even if you do not play the piano, you can transcribe music manually into a sequencer program by reading the score and using the manual note entry features of the program. Most of the songs that you download from on-line services were built that way. The result is usually a mechanical effect with no emotion or human interpretation built into the performance.

Acquiring Music

Not every programmer possesses the musical ear or skills to build an effective musical score for a game program. Likewise, not every skilled musician knows how to get the best effect from a MIDI system. Sometimes you have to look elsewhere for what you need. Locating someone who can get the job done might not be as difficult as you think.

To start with, you can probably find professional MIDI composers and scorers in your home town. Look in the Yellow Pages for recording studios and audio technicians. Call around. You will find someone who has the skill and equipment to build effective MIDI files. Be prepared to pay dearly for this service, particularly if you want original compositions.

Amateur musicians are plentiful, too, and you might be able to find someone who is willing to help you in exchange for a royalty arrangement or perhaps even for the exposure of an acknowledgment in your credits.

Be careful about downloading and using MIDI files from on-line services and the Internet. There are plenty of such files, but the issues about who owns the intellectual rights to the compositions, the arrangements, and the files themselves are rarely clear. The CompuServe Information Service recently removed many of the MIDI files from its libraries and suspended accepting any more uploads of MIDI files because of complaints that distribution of the files might violate copyright law.

Public domain songs are usually a safe way to go if you cannot compose original music yourself or if you cannot afford the services of a composer. Most classical compositions, hymns, and old traditional folk songs are in the public domain.

Use extreme caution with respect to public domain material. Make sure that you know the status of anything you use. You wouldn't want to wind up in court. Make no assumptions about anything, and do your research. Not everything that is old is necessarily in the public domain. For example, in the early 1950s the copyright was about to expire on Debussy's "Claire de Lune." To retain the copyright for an additional period, the beneficiaries of Debussy's estate had lyrics added to the melody. The result was an abomination called "Moonlight Love." The popular crooner Perry Como, in an uncharacteristic lapse of taste, recorded the song.

Once again, we are not lawyers. Ask one if you are not sure.

Recording Music

If you know how to use a MIDI keyboard, you can use a sequencer program to enter musical tracks into your computer and create a MIDI file. Once everything is connected and the program is running, you can begin to construct your song one channel at a time. You choose a channel and assign an instrument to the channel from the standard instrument table. By convention, channel 10 is assigned to the drum sounds, and specific drum sounds—cymbals, snares, bass drums, wood blocks, and so on—are assigned to the notes of the scale.

Some sequencer programs allow you to select from a collection of musical styles. The sequencer adds drum machine patterns to the song in keeping with the style—bossa nova, swing, rock, and so on—that you have chosen.

While you record a new channel, the sequencer plays back the existing channels so that you can stay synchronized with the song.

Most sequencers allow you to *quantize* a channel after you have entered the notes. It is impossible for human beings to accurately play precise sixteenth, eighth, quarter, half, and whole notes, no matter how well they read music. The sequencer captures exactly what you play, and the musical score, if you were to print it out, would be unreadable due to the many thirty-second and sixty-fourth notes that represented what you really played. The quantizer normalizes those notes to the resolution that you specify.

A sequencer can *transpose* a song, which changes the key signature in which the song is played. Perhaps you can play only in the keys of C, F, and G,—not uncommon among amateur pianists—but the song sounds better or better conveys the mood in a different key. You can transpose the song into any key at all after you have it programmed.[4]

Adding the Musical Score to the Game

A Theatrix game program plays music by using the MIDPAK library, as described in Chapter 4. The library includes a utility that puts MIDI files into a collection that Theatrix treats as a score. The game program instantiates an object whose purpose is to play selected songs from the score on demand. That object's class encapsulates the interface to the MIDPAK library.

32 Bits and Protected Mode

Theatrix, as published in this book, is not a 32-bit protected mode library. If you plan to build huge game programs with enormous collections of media clips, you might need the 32-bit flat memory model provided by DOS extenders.

---

[4]Many professional lounge pianists would love to have that feature built into their pianos to support the amateur singers who hang around the bar hoping for a moment in the spotlight.

One of the reasons that we did not start with a 32-bit model was that Fastgraph, the graphics library that we used, does not have a 32-bit version released as shareware. It does, however, support 32-bit development in its commercial version.

To convert Theatrix to a protected mode library, you must modify several things. First, you must look at all usages of the *int* data type to see whether they need to be changed to *short int* to preserve their 16-bit type size. Second, you should eliminate the uses of extended memory in the *Media* class for storing sound and graphics clips. Third, the few places where the library attaches interrupt vectors must be examined and converted to the conventions of whichever DOS extender is to be used.

For the time being, Theatrix works only with the Borland C++ compiler because that compiler implements the RTTI extensions to standard C++. Therefore, you probably want to use Borland's Power Pack as a DOS extender to convert to 32-bit code.

If this project is well received, we will publish a second edition that implements the DOS version of Theatrix as a 32-bit, protected mode library.

These issues are, of course, irrelevant to the Win32 version now under development.

Game-Building Strategies

"Show me a good loser and I'll show you a loser."
Common paraphrase of a Knute Rockne quotation

This chapter shows you how to build the components of a game by using the tools in the Theatrix toolset. You learn about the application of those tools in the construction of your game. We will describe the procedures and identify the tools that we use for each step of the design process. The tools are described in Chapters 6 and 11 and in the documentation files that accompany them. In this chapter you will learn about these subjects:

- ◇ Scenery
- ◇ Animation
- ◇ Video clips
- ◇ Palette correction
- ◇ Sound effects
- ◇ Music

Scenery

Scenery is the background of a scene in a game. You build scenery by building a bitmapped graphics file. There are three strategies: You can scan in a scene from an existing picture, manually design the scenery by using a paint program, or render the scenery by ray-tracing a 3-D model of the scene. We discuss each of these strategies in this chapter.

Scanning

We've never seen a game in which the background scenery was scanned in from a photograph or a print of a painting, but there is no reason why you could not do it. Imagine a game that uses photos of Mount Rushmore, the Grand Canyon, or the Eiffel Tower as its background.

Suppose that you have a print of an old painting or a photograph of an appropriate scene. Perhaps you went to the city or country on a vacation, took some photos, and had them enlarged.

First review the discussions in Chapter 3 about intellectual property rights. Then proceed.

To use these pictures as Theatrix scenery, you need a flatbed color scanner and software to scan the pictures and translate them into .PCX files of 320 x 240 pixels with 256 colors. The translation is simple enough with the tools in the Theatrix toolkit. Alchemy and NeoPaint are discussed later in this chapter and in Chapter 11, and both of these packages can translate bitmapped file formats.

> Color flatbed scanners are expensive (about $1000 at this time). They are also as difficult to install properly as any other nonstandard PC extension (IRQs, DMA, ports, and so on). But when you need one, there is no substitute. If you will be scanning rarely, you might be able to find a local business that offers the service. Be aware, though, that once you scan your first color photo, you will be hooked. Greeting cards and invitations take on a new dimension when they include color snaps of the kids. Of course, then you need a color printer...

As an alternative to scanning, you can use the services of companies that develop your film as diskette images to display on your computer. The local photo shop should be able to refer you to the right companies. If you can get that picture display in a Windows application, for example, you can use the Clipboard to import it into Windows Paint or another image program to convert it to 256-color .PCX format.

Painting with NeoPaint

The easiest way to build a background scene is to paint one using a paint program. The Theatrix toolkit includes NeoPaint, a full-featured shareware DOS paint program.

If you like NeoPaint and intend to use it, you must register the product. Text files on the CD-ROM along with the program files explain how to register.

Figure 4.1, the scenery for the Shootout game, was created with NeoPaint. (You can see a full-color rendering of this scene in the color insert pages at the middle of the book.)

Figure 4.1 Shootout background scenery

Shootout's scenery has an arcade look, which is consistent with the game that it supports. With the exception of the mountains on the horizon and the cloud in the sky—which we drew manually with the pen tool—the picture was built from standard NeoPaint primitive shapes and patterns. The buildings, windows, and doors are rectangles. The sidewalk and street are simple lines. The bricks and shingles and the textured chimney pipe on the jail are standard NeoPaint fill patterns. The lettering is from the standard NeoPaint fonts. We used the Fill tool to color the sky, mountains, sidewalk, street, and scoreboard.

It took no longer than five minutes with NeoPaint to draw this scene. Once it was drawn, we zoomed in on various points of the picture and moved the cursor to record the coordinates of critical locations. For example, the characters in the game appear in windows, from behind buildings, and from behind doors. The game program must know specifically where to clip the images as they come into view. It must also know where the sidewalk is for the bodies to fall and where to superimpose the open door images. The digit positions where the score is displayed are also important.

3-D Modeling with MORAY

The third option for creating scenery results in photo-realistic scenery but with a computer-rendered look. The scenes don't always look like actual photographs (although they could), but they have realistic features based on textures, shadows, reflections, refraction, diffusion, and so on.

First you build a 3-D model of the scene, and then you render ray-traced images of the scene taken from various views. We'll discuss the first step, creating the model, first.

A 3-D model is a computer representation of planes and objects organized to resemble something real. You build the model with a 3-D modeling tool. The Theatrix toolkit includes MORAY, a DOS shareware 3-D modeler that produces files in the POV-Ray source code format. POV-Ray, the tool used in the second step of this procedure, is discussed later in this chapter.

If you like MORAY and intend to use it, you must register the product. The author updates MORAY frequently. As this book goes to press, there is a new beta with many new features. We encourage you to download and register the new version when it is available. The MORAY documentation on the CD-ROM explains how to register, get support, and get new versions.

MORAY resembles a typical CAD system in that it allows you to build a wire-frame 3-D model by manipulating views from three coordinates and displaying an isometric view. MORAY is not as intuitive a program as NeoPaint because MORAY assumes that you have a basic understanding of

3-D models and the capabilities of POV-Ray. But with practice, a designer can do impressive work with MORAY.

Figure 4.2 shows the MORAY screen with a model of a Jeep that we built from standard shapes.

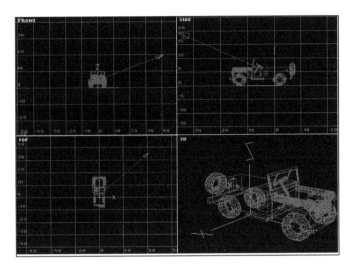

Figure 4.2 MORAY 3-D model of a Jeep

The Jeep model is complex, but it is only one element in a scene. The Town example game on the CD-ROM has scenery that includes several buildings, and each building is a separate model created from common component models. For example, we built one house frame, one door, one window, one dormer, and so on, and then built several house models from those MORAY components. Figure 4.3 shows one of the house models loaded into MORAY's design screen.

To complete the scene, we built a town model with the three houses, a church, two streets, some trees, and two copies of the Jeep. Figure 4.4 shows the town model loaded into MORAY's design screen.

You add textures and lighting to a model from within MORAY, but it does not render the picture itself. For that, it launches POV-Ray. You can make sample renderings as you go along, and you should do that at a low resolution. Rendering is a time-consuming operation. Eventually, however, you want to render the actual scenes for the game.

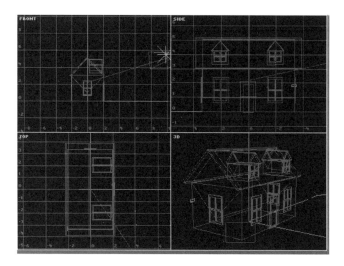

Figure 4.3 MORAY 3-D model of a house

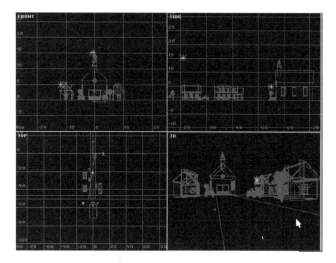

Figure 4.4 MORAY 3-D model of a town

Ray Tracing with POV-Ray

The second step in producing scenery from a 3-D model is to render the various scenes from the POV-Ray source code that MORAY produces. MORAY exports its model to POV-Ray source code. POV-Ray is a ray tracer. It reads files of ASCII source code and translates the statements in the source code into an image.

POV-Ray is a freely available program that anyone can download from CompuServe and the Internet. There are no fees for its use, and you are free to render images and distribute those images without obligation.

POV-Ray source code statements specify shapes, textures, planes, lighting, camera position, and so on, and POV-Ray uses those data to compute every pixel of the rendered image. POV-Ray writes rendered images to files in the .TGA bitmapped graphics format.

The POV-Ray source code includes the camera positions and lighting that you established with MORAY; those values, as written by MORAY, define only one scene. Even though the game will have several scenes, only one POV-Ray source code file is needed. Each scene's source code file differs only with respect to its camera position. Every thing else is the same.

First you decide how many background scenes the game uses from this model. The Town game, for example, uses 11 different scenes built from the same model. To build those scenes, we used MORAY to determine the ideal camera locations, directions, and apertures for each scene. This procedure involved loading the model into POV-Ray and moving the camera until the scene looked right in the isometric view. Then we wrote down the camera position for each scene. Next, we used a text editor to create alternative camera positions in the source code file, but we commented out all the settings except one. Listing 4.1 shows part of the *camera* statement in the TOWN.POV file. This example assumes that only three scenes are used instead of the actual 11, but it illustrates the point.

Listing 4.1 TOWN.POV, camera statement

```
camera {  //  Camera Camera01
    location  < 0.000, -10.000, 1.600>  // TOWN01
//  location  < 0.000, -24.500, 1.600>  // TOWN02
//  location  < 0.000, -24.500, 1.600>  // TOWN03
    direction <0.0,     0.0,  1.0>       // All scenes use these values
    sky       <0.0,     0.0,  1.0>       // "        "    "     "      "
    up        <0.0,     0.0,  1.0>       // "        "    "     "      "
    right     <1.3333,  0.0,  0.0>       // "        "    "     "      "
    look_at   <  0.000, -55.000, 1.600>  // TOWN01
//  look_at   <  0.000, -55.000, 1.600>  // TOWN02
//  look_at   <-10.000, -24.500, 1.600>  // TOWN03
}
```

The *camera* statement declares the camera parameters for the scene. The *location* statement specifies coordinates in the model where the camera is positioned. The *look_at* statement specifies the point in the model where the camera is focused. These are the statements you will change for each rendering. In this example, all the statements except for TOWN01 are commented out. After TOWN01 was rendered, we commented out its statements, uncommented the statements for TOWN02, and rendered the scene for TOWN02. We repeated this procedure until all 11 scenes for the Town game were rendered into .TGA bitmapped graphics files.

POV-Ray source code looks a lot like C++ source code, so programmers are comfortable with it. Some programmers and modelers work directly with the source code rather than use MORAY. Most people, however, prefer to work in a visual medium rather than use the abstract expression of source code.

An advantage of this approach is that you do not need to be concerned with perspective when you design scenery the way you would if you hand-painted every scene. If you build a set that has objects whose relative sizes are consistent with one another, then the ray-tracer will properly render the scene with correct perspective. All you have to do is position the camera.

Converting Bitmapped Graphics Files with Alchemy

POV-Ray's output is in the .TGA bitmapped graphics format. To use the pictures as scenery in a Theatrix game, you have to convert them to .PCX format. For that purpose we use a shareware program named Alchemy.

If you like Alchemy and intend to use it, you must register the product. Text files included on the CD-ROM along with the program files explain how to register.

Alchemy reads bitmapped graphics files and translates them to other bitmapped graphics file images. We use it to build eight-bit .PCX files from the .TGA files that POV-Ray produces.

Figure 4.5 shows TOWN01.PCX as POV-Ray rendered the scene and as Alchemy converted the .TGA file into the .PCX format.

Figure 4.5 TOWN01.PCX, a rendered scene

Before the .PCX files for the game's scenery can be integrated into the game, you must normalize the palettes for all the graphical elements. That procedure is described in this chapter in the section titled *Palette Correction*.

Sprites

Sprites are the characters in your game. As with scenery, you build sprites in one of three ways depending on the look you want. You can use NeoPaint to build sprites, you can use MORAY to build a 3-D model and POV-Ray to render sprite images, or you can make photographs of actual models, all of which create .PCX files with sprite images.

Before these .PCX images can be integrated into the game program, you must normalize their palettes with the other graphical elements in the game. This procedure is described in this chapter in the section titled "Palette Correction."

Painting Sprites

Figure 4.6 is the skating figure from the Skater game as built with NeoPaint.

Figure 4.6 A skating sprite

Sprites such as the skater have an arcade, cartoon look. In the enlarged figure, you can see all the jags and increments. With more work, we could have made this sprite look better. By using different color tones, you can suggest form, shading, and texture. This sprite is small, though, and its movement is fast. Much of the detailed work would be lost in the motion.

3-D Modeled Sprites

When the sprite in Figure 4.6 is displayed in its actual size and moving on the screen, the effect is more realistic, although not as realistic as ray-traced sprites (see Figure 4.7).

The sprites in Figure 4.7 were built from MORAY 3-D models and rendered with POV-Ray. The only difference between the sprites in Figure 4.6 and those in Figure 4.7 is the technique used to create the .PCX files.

Figure 4.7 Ray-traced sprites

Using Real Models

For this approach, you need more equipment: a good camera with lenses and filters, a tripod, and good color-corrected lighting. You also need a studio environment where you can photograph the model in various poses against a solid background with minimal ambient light interference.

You make a snapshot of every pose of the sprite in its animated role. (See the "Animation" section.) Then, as with photographed scenery, you translate those photographs into .PCX files with a scanner or by using a diskette medium developing service.

What can you use for models? Toys are good. You may use anything that isn't copyrighted. This could be a problem. A game featuring Ken and Barbie is bound to get the attention of a lawyer or two at the Mattel Corporation. Almost every toy is protected by copyright law, and yet toys provide the best source for game models.

You might be able to alter a toy in such a way that it no longer resembles the original. For example, costumes and makeup could help you turn GI Joe into a drag Dracula. For vehicle sprites, you could build and drastically customize plastic models that you buy at the hobby shop, perhaps using components from several models to create a hybrid. There should be no problem using models of military aircraft and commercial automobiles, but models of the *StarShip Enterprise* or Han Solo's space junker are off limits—unless you get written permission from the copyright holders, of course (fat chance).

The best approach is to create something original. If you can sculpt or sew creatively, you can make models of anything you like. A pleasant afternoon spent watching *The Nightmare before Christmas* on your VCR will give you ideas of what can be done with original models.

Whatever you use for a model, it must be able to maintain a rigid pose long enough for you to photograph it. To support animated sequences, it should permit small changes in its appendages. You might have to suspend it from a wire or mount it on a black shaft to get the pose you want. Figure 4.8 is a photographed sprite.

Figure 4.8 A photographed sprite

Animation

Animation is where the action is. To add action to a game, you make a sprite move around the screen and do interesting things. Whether the sprite is a spaceship or a cowboy, a street fighter or an ice skater, the underlying principle is the same: Animation is the product of showing a sequence of frames, with each frame representing the next increment of motion in the sequence. The motion is an illusion. Nothing really moves. Every picture that we see is a still frame. But when the frames are shown in rapid succession, our brains are tricked into thinking that we are seeing motion.

Motion: One Frame at a Time

Figure 4.9 shows five successive frames that, when shown in rapid succession, make the sheriff in the Shootout game seem to be walking. The sequence of five frames repeats until the game program wants the sheriff to do something other than walk to the right, at which point the program changes to a different sequence of frames. Each repetition of the five frames reverses the order in which the frames are shown so that the complete walk sequence is an eight-frame sequence as follows: 1-2-3-4-5-4-3-2. Then the sequence repeats itself.

Figure 4.9 The sheriff's animated frames

Prove it to yourself. Make several copies of Figure 4.9 on a copier. Cut the images into uniform rectangles, stack them up in the sequence we just described, and staple them together at one of the edges. Now you have one of those flip comic books from the 1950s. Flip through the pages and watch the sheriff take a walk.

We drew the five pictures of the sheriff with NeoPaint. We started by drawing the first picture. Then, to build the second frame, we copied the first and modified it so that the swinging left arm was closer to the body and the two legs came closer together. In the third frame, we made the arm and legs straight down. The legs of frames four and five are duplicates of those in frames two and one, except that we changed the line that defines which leg is closer to the front of the scene.

There are several other sequences in the game. One sequence has the sheriff walking in the opposite direction. To build that sequence, we used NeoPaint to reverse the frame images of frames five through one. Because the sheriff carries only one gun, we erased the gun and holster from each of the frames in the right-walking sequence, and we put a badge on the left side of his chest.

Other sequences depict the sheriff drawing and shooting in four directions, reloading his gun, and getting shot from both directions.

Each sprite has its own frames and its own update frequency. The sheriff gets updated every two clock ticks, or approximately nine times per second, so it takes about one second for the sheriff to start out with his left foot forward and take two steps ending with his left foot forward.

Plotting the Two-Dimensional Coordinates

The screen is a two-dimensional plane with an X coordinate and a Y coordinate. The coordinate ranges are the same as the resolution of the video mode. Mode X games have X coordinates of 0 to 319 horizontally and Y coordinates of 0 to 239 vertically.

As a game program displays the frames of an animated sprite, the program must also provide the screen coordinates where the frame is to be displayed. The Theatrix coordinate system uses 0/0 as the upper left coordinate and 319/239 as the lower right coordinate. Sprite frame positions on the screen are assigned according to where the upper left corner of the sprite image is positioned, *even though that point might be transparent*. (See "The Transparent Regions of a Sprite" later in this chapter.) Therefore, if the sprite moves around the screen, the game program computes the path and provides the correct coordinates for the upper left corner of each frame.

A Theatrix game may be computing frames and frame positions for many sprites for each full-screen display, so the action on the screen can be complex and the demands on the CPU can be considerable.

Smooth Animation

The sheriff in Figure 4.9 walks along the street shown in Figure 4.1. The scenery remains static and the sheriff walks. Animating a sprite consists of telling the video system where in the two-dimensional coordinate system to paint each frame. The sheriff moves from left to right during this sequence. To make the walk believable, we plot each position in the first five frames of the eight-frame sequence so that the toe of the sheriff's left boot is always in the same X/Y coordinate on the screen. For frames six, seven, and eight and frame one of the next sequence, the toe of the right boot is held in the same X/Y coordinate. This procedure gives the sheriff's walk a smooth, natural appearance.[1]

Z-Order

When a game has more than one sprite and the sprites' paths cross, the game must display the intersecting sprites so that the one closer to the player passes in front of the one closer to the background. This relationship between sprite positions is called their *Z-order*, because it reflects each sprite's location in the Z axis of a pseudo three-dimensional coordinate system. However, instead of being a scalar as in a true three-dimensional graphical system, the Z axis is represented by the positional relationship of the game's components. The background is at the lowest (most distant from the player) position in the Z-order, and the sprites are at various Z-order positions toward the front.

There are no integer Z values analogous to X and Y values. Instead, Theatrix maintains a list of sprites. The Z-order of a sprite depends on its position in the list relative to the other sprites. A sprite's initial position in the list depends on the order in which the game program instantiates the sprite object. The last sprite object instantiated has the nearest Z-order. Figure 4.10 is a screen shot of the Skater game, which uses Z-ordering to control sprite placement.

---

[1]In *Tricks of the Game-Programming Gurus* (see the Bibliography), Andrè LaMothe calls this technique "animotion."

Figure 4.10 Z-order

The skater in Figure 4.10 skates a figure eight around the two stationary sprites. At first the skater is foremost in the Z-order because he is in front of the other two sprites. When he makes his first turn to go between the other two, his Z-order changes to put him in front of the rearward sprite and behind the forward sprite. When he goes behind the rearward sprite, his Z-order changes to put him behind both of the other sprites.

A Theatrix game program tells Theatrix to change a sprite's Z-order in one of three ways: by putting the sprite at the rearmost Z-order, at the forwardmost Z-order, or behind the Z-order of a specified other sprite. Theatrix takes care of the rest.

Perspective

Because Theatrix is not a true 3-D graphical system, you have to manage certain aspects of the 3-D effect yourself. For example, as the skater moves around the figure eight in Figure 4.10, the program computes the coordinates where the skater displays. To suggest a third dimension, the game moves the skater up the Y axis when the skater is skating away from the player and down the Y axis when the skater is skating toward the player.

As objects get farther into the distance they appear to get smaller. That illusion is due to *perspective*. Observe that the rearmost stationary sprite is smaller than the forward one, which is smaller than the skater. When the skater is between the two sprites, then, it should be bigger than the one at the rear but smaller than the one at the front.

There are algorithms to shrink and expand graphical images to support perspective in real time, but we do not need to use them for the kinds of games that we build with Theatrix. Because animation is a function of selecting the correct frame, proper perspective is a matter of painting or rendering enough frames to display the sprite at whatever Z-order locations the game allows it to occupy. If you are rendering or photographing sprites, you must position the real or virtual camera far enough away to capture each frame. If you are painting the sprites with NeoPaint, you should paint the first set of frames in their largest configuration. Then, using the Scale command you can make smaller and smaller copies of the frames for the more distant Z-order images. Scaling pictures down sometimes loses critical pixels from the details, so you should keep an eye on the results and touch them up when necessary. Figure 4.11 shows the skater at its farthest location away from the player.

Figure 4.11 Sprite perspective

The Transparent Regions of a Sprite

Sprite images are 256-color rectangular .PCX files of a size appropriate to the sprite's role and position on the screen. No matter which technique you use to build sprites, you must deal with the issue of transparency the same way. Every sprite image has regions that must be transparent to let the background show through. For example, all the space around the outer edges of the sprite and to the borders of its image rectangle must be transparent. If the sprite has holes, you have to let the background show through them, too.

Transparent regions are marked by color zero—that is, each pixel in a transparent region must have a palette offset value equal to zero. It does not matter which actual color is assigned to color zero in the palette—color zero is the transparent color when Theatrix displays the sprite. Color zero is usually solid black.

Black backgrounds are easy to make when you use NeoPaint or POV-Ray to build sprite images. With NeoPaint, you start out with a white background because it's easier to see what you're painting that way. When you are finished, you use the Fill tool to replace the white background with black. You can still have black elements in the sprite's image by assigning black to a nonzero palette offset.

When rendering POV-Ray sprites, don't provide any background objects such as the sky, walls, and floors. The background will be rendered all black.

Creating transparent regions from photographed and scanned sprites is more difficult but still possible. Even though you use a solid black background in the photo session, chances are that some stray ambient light source will create subtle textures that are not completely black. To do some touchup, load the .PCX files into NeoPaint and use the Eraser tool to change rough areas to all black. Then zoom in and touch up the remaining pixels.

Sometimes there are points of solid black in the image that you do not want to be transparent. They show up as dots of background bleeding through when you run the game. This can happen with rendered and photographed sprites. You have better control over colors when you manually paint the sprite, but it can still happen if you make a mistake. To correct for these unintended holes, load the offending frame into NeoPaint and manually change the holes from color zero to another color in the palette that is black.

How Animation Works in Theatrix

Theatrix manages the animation of a large number of sprites against a common background. Follow along with Figure 4.12 as we explain how it works.

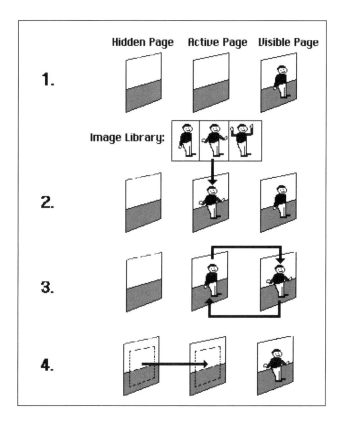

Figure 4.12 Animation

When a scene in the game begins, Theatrix saves the scene's background scenery image in one of two hidden page buffers and designates that buffer as the permanently *hidden* page. Remember from Chapter 3 that Mode X has one visible page and two hidden pages. The permanently hidden page buffer retains the scenery image unmodified for the duration of the scene. Theatrix copies the same scene into the *visible* page and the other hidden page—

which it designates the *active* page—and makes sure that they are different physical page buffers. So, to begin, all three pages have the same image, that of the background scenery, and one is the hidden page, one is the active page, and one is the visible page.

As the animation proceeds, the visible page contains what the player is looking at, the active page is where Theatrix makes its updates, and the hidden page remains constant with only the scenery in it. Step 1 in Figure 4.12 reflects that condition.

The scene consists of scenery and a list of sprites. Each sprite is an object instantiated for the scene. Each sprite registers for a refresh rate based on the 18.2/second ticks of the clock. The scene is actually refreshed once every tick, but the sprites get an opportunity to specify how often Theatrix asks them to update their frame image and position.

On each tick of the clock, Theatrix tests each visible sprite in the order that it appears in the scene's Z-order list. If the sprite's refresh rate has gone by, Theatrix calls the sprite to have it specify its frame image and screen coordinates. The sprite determines from its circumstances in the game whether there are to be any changes in its frame image and position and posts these changes to itself.

Now let's look at step 2 of Figure 4.12. Immediately following the image and position posting for each sprite, Theatrix copies the sprite's posted image from a resident sprite image library to the active page at the sprite's posted position. The active page is not visible during this process. At the end of the loop, the active page contains the screen images for all visible sprites superimposed on the scenery. This full-screen image represents what is to be viewed for the next frame in the total animation of the scene.

In step 3 of Figure 4.12, Theatrix swaps the active page with the visible page, and the player is now looking at the current frame for the game.

In step 4 of Figure 4.12, to prepare for the next frame, Theatrix iterates through the sprites again and erases their previous images from the active page by copying the positions they previously occupied from the static hidden page into the active page.

This four-step procedure permits each sprite to independently specify its next frame and its position based on whatever intelligence you, the programmer, build into the sprite's class. Usually, a sprite will maintain a mode data item that tells it what its current circumstances are. Other parts of the program—other sprites, perhaps—can cause the sprite to modify its mode variable. This variable, which you build into the sprite's class, is the sprite's insight into what it should do next. When Theatrix calls upon the sprite to update its image and position, the sprite uses its mode variable to determine what to do.

Several sprites in a scene can be modifying their images and positions independently of one another, and you can have completely random sprite movements throughout the game. They can watch one another and react accordingly. For example, when the sheriff in the Shootout game gets within shooting range of an outlaw, that outlaw takes a shot at the sheriff.

Mouse Cursors

Theatrix supports a small set of mouse cursors. The usual default arrow points up and left. Theatrix adds hands that point up, down, right, and left and block arrows that point toward the four corners of the screen. Figure 4.13 shows the Theatrix mouse cursors.

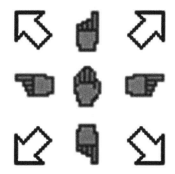

Figure 4.13 Theatrix mouse cursors

A game program that uses these cursors can specify any of these standard shapes, or it can use custom cursor shapes that you build with NeoPaint. A cursor is a color graphical picture similar to a sprite except that cursors are always 16 x 16 pixels. When used in a game, a cursor must also specify a *hot spot*, which is the relative pixel position of the cursor's pointer.

To use a custom cursor, you first build it with NeoPaint. Create a new file with 256 colors and a custom resolution of 16 x 16. That's a tiny picture, and you will have to build your cursor by zooming in and setting each pixel's color individually. Set the transparent parts of the cursor to solid black.

After the cursor's .PCX file is finished, you must translate its color representation into a C++ source code file that your game makefile compiles and links. The Theatrix toolkit includes a utility program named GMICE that reads one or more cursor .PCX files and generates a file of source code that you compile and link with your program. The GMICE program includes a table of hot spots that it selects from based on the first two characters of the .PCX file's name. You will need to modify this table to use the program for mouse cursors other than the standard ones.

Before the .PCX images for custom mouse cursors can be integrated into the game program, you must normalize their palettes with the other graphical elements in the game. Furthermore, if you use the standard cursors in a game with graphical elements that do not use the default palette, you must rebuild the standard cursors, normalize those palettes, and treat them just like custom cursors. That procedure is described in this chapter in the section titled "Palette Correction."

The Town game on the included CD-ROM uses the GMICE program to build source code files from mouse cursor .PCX files that have been palette-normalized.

Video Clips

Video clips are movie shorts. If you have a video capture board, such as the Creative Labs Video Blaster, you can hook up to your computer a CamCorder, a VCR, or any other standard video source to your computer and generate a video file. You can also create one from graphical tools such as NeoPaint; use the same animation techniques that you use to animate sprites and process the resulting frames through one of your tools.

The difference between video and animation is that your game program itself manages frame image and position during sprite animation, reacting to the conditions of the game. The motion of a video clip, on the other hand is predetermined; the clip plays in the background, and it plays an unchanging sequence of frames.

Theatrix allows you to display a video file in the standard FLC format. FLC is a format originally defined by Autodesk Animator Pro. An FLC file consists of header information and frames. The frames are optimized so that the pixels are compressed and each frame contains only the pixel information that is different from the frame that precedes the current frame. This approach allows the minimum storage for the animation sequence and the minimum processing time to refresh the screen. Each frame has its own palette information, too.

To add video to your game, you must first build or acquire an FLC file. Now for the usual caveat. We're sure you're tired of hearing this, but, as with everything else in a creative production, be reminded of your responsibility to observe the rights of others and the consequences of ripping off someone else's intellectual property.

Building Video Clips with DTA

Among the Theatrix Tools is a shareware program called *Dave's .TGA Animation Program* (DTA). For complete documentation on DTA, the Bibliography lists *Morphing on Your PC*, by the program's author, David K. Mason. The text file with the software on our CD-ROM should get you going.

We used one video clip in an example game. The Town game on the CD-ROM superimposes over a scene a video clip as seen through an open door. The video clip shows a player piano playing and a cat wagging its tail. There are 13 frames in the clip, and the program repeats the clip as long as you stay on the scene. We built the frames for the clip with NeoPaint and built the FLC file with DTA.

Building the frames for a video clip uses essentially the same procedures as building animated sprites, and either approach would have worked except that Town is a Myst-like game that moves from static scene to static scene. Its scenes are not derived from the parts of Theatrix that support animation.

Before the .PCX images for video clips can be built into an FLC file, you must normalize their palettes with the other graphical elements in the game as described later in this chapter. This is true even if you are using an existing FLC file. DTA has procedures for extracting and applying a common palette, and you can use the extracted palette to normalize the rest of the game's graphics. As an alternative, you can use DTA to extract the individual frames to .PCX files, use these frames in the normalization procedure, and rebuild the FLC file from the normalized .PCX frame files.

Playing Video Clips with Fastgraph

Theatrix encapsulates the operation of playing and stopping a video clip. The game program tells Theatrix to begin displaying a particular video clip file, provides the coordinates for the upper left corner of the clip, and specifies whether the clip is to be played once only or repeated until the game tells Theatrix to stop playing the clip. Theatrix plays the clip over the top of whatever scene is currently being displayed.

Palette Correction

Before the .PCX files for a game's scenery, background, sprites, video clips, and cursors can be integrated into the game, you must normalize the palettes for all the graphical elements.

We discussed the problem in Chapter 3. Every graphical element in a video game can have a different palette. When you mix more than one element in the same display and the elements use different palettes, only the ones that are consistent with the active palette display properly. The others have strange colors. In our games, the flesh tones are always green if we forget to normalize the palettes.

Chapter 6 describes the Theatrix utility tools in detail. This discussion explains the process of palette correction.

Given that you have some number of graphical entities with different palettes, you first have to derive a common palette from all of them. That procedure involves three steps.

First, extract palette files from all the graphical elements. Palette files contain the palette information taken from a .PCX file.

Second, use all these extracted palette files to compute a common palette file. This procedure finds all the colors in all the palettes and tries to squeeze them into one. For example, if seven .PCX files have the color green in seven different color slots in their respective palettes, the common palette chooses one slot for green. The object is to get each of the colors in use in all the palette files assigned to only one slot. The hope is that, altogether, the images don't use more than 256 different colors. When they do, the utility program finds the closest possible match for the excess colors.

Finally, use the common palette file to modify all the original .PCX files so that they use the common one in place of their originals. This modification changes the palette offset value for each of the .PCX file's pixels so that it points to the correct color in the new palette.

When this procedure is complete, all the raw .PCX files in your game operate with the same palette.

Sound Effects

Sound effects begin as .VOC files that you install into .SFX libraries. Chapter 6 explains the procedure for building the libraries.

Again, be careful about using someone's copyrighted sound effect. You can download many quotes from movies and TV shows, but don't use them in your games. Find someone who can imitate Bogie if you want his voice.

CD-ROMs are available with sound effects that you are permitted to use. Most computer supply stores have a rack of CD-ROMs where you are likely to find such material.

Recording Sound Effects

The best choice is to make your own noises and voices. You'll need a Sound Blaster or another sound card that supports recording. For voices you need a decent microphone. Radio Shack has several that work well.

You can also go out into the wilderness and record the birds and bees and make .VOC files by patching your tape player into the line input jacks on the Sound Blaster.

Beyond that, all you need is your imagination. The Myst guys tell about how they made clock chimes by banging two wrenches together, adding echo effects, and changing the playback rate of the sound. They got water gurgling sound effects by flushing the company commode.

Your sound card comes with a recording utility program. As an alternative, you can use the Blaster Master shareware program from the included CD-

ROM. It is particularly convenient if you are going to convert from other sound file formats or make special effects enhancements to your sounds.

Blaster Master supports a number of sound effects enhancements. You can speed up or slow down the playback, add reverberation, and reverse the playback, just for starters. There are many other things you can do with a sound effects waveform.

Playback with CT-VOICE or DIGPAK

Theatrix uses one of two sound drivers to play back sound effects. Sound Blasters comes with a driver named CT-VOICE.DRV. If the player of your game has that configuration and has properly set the SOUND and BLASTER environment variables, Theatrix plays the sounds back correctly.

Theatrix also uses DIGPAK, a commercial sound driver system that supports many other sound cards. Chapter 11 describes DIGPAK in more detail. You can use DIGPAK in your own games, and you can distribute the driver with your games free without licensing concerns, but if you are going to sell your games and distribute DIGPAK with them, you must pay a one-time nominal license fee ($500) to the author.

DIGPAK comes with a setup program that the user runs to generate the correct copy of the sound driver. The sound driver is named SOUNDRV.COM, and Theatrix loads and uses it if it is there.

Music

Theatrix plays MIDI music files only if the player has the commercial MIDPAK music driver. Chapter 11 describes MIDPAK in more detail. You can use MIDPAK in your own games, and you can distribute the driver with your games free without licensing concerns, but if you are going to sell your games and distribute MIDPAK with them, you must pay a one-time nominal license fee ($500) to the author.

The same setup program that builds the DIGPAK driver also builds the MIDPAK drivers. There are three files, and all of them must be available to the Theatrix game program at startup time. The files are named MIDPAK.AD, MIDPAK.ADV, and MIDPAK.COM.

Recording Music with MT

Chapter 3 discussed the creative side of making MIDI files. The included CD-ROM contains a shareware sequencer program, named MT, that runs on a PC with a music card that implements the Roland MPU-401 protocols. The Sound Blaster 16 is one such card.

You can use the MT sequencer to lay down as many as 16 tracks and produce multichannel MIDI songs, selecting from all 128 instruments in the standard MIDI instrument list.

Playing Back Music with MIDPAK

Theatrix does not have its own MIDI library format for songs. MIDPAK uses a format with the .XMI extension. MIDPAK comes with a utility, named MIDIFORM, that you use to build an .XMI file from a set of MIDI files.

The game program instantiates an object of the MusicHand class. A game typically has only one .XMI file, which is treated as the musical score for the whole game. The score contains individual songs that can be played whenever the game needs music. A game can start a song, stop a song, and test to see whether a song is still playing. The music plays in the background asynchronously and does not affect the rest of the program.

Theatrix, A C++ Class Library

"Generally speaking, the American theater is the aspirin of the middle classes."
Wolcott Gibbs

This chapter describes Theatrix, a C++ class library from which you build PC game applications. You will learn about:

- ⬥ The Theatrix metaphor
- ⬥ Class hierarchies
- ⬥ Hands
- ⬥ Cues
- ⬥ Directors

The Theatrix Metaphor

Theatrix uses a theatrical production metaphor to provide an easy and intuitive way for us to think about our task of building games. The paradigm also provides terminology that we can use to communicate.

Games written with Theatrix use a theatrical production as a model. In a play, the director coordinates a cast of actors, stagehands, and technicians to present a performance. Each member of the crew has specific tasks to perform for the play to be a success. Some members, such as actors, are visible to the audience, whereas others, such as stagehands, are not.

Timing is important in a play. The director cues members of the crew when it is time for a member to perform a task. Sometimes, a cast or crew member takes cues from the actions of others instead of directly from the director.

This concept has stood the test of centuries and works well for plays. What about games though? Is it possible to describe a game using these ideas? Sure it is. All the games and demos in this book are written using the theater model. Remember, however, that the metaphor is only a model and not a strict set of rules. The metaphor makes it easier to think about a game; use it to an extent that you find comfortable.

Theatrix Class Hierarchies

Theatrix consists of two class hierarchies: one that encapsulates your game and another that encapsulates all the graphical, musical, and vocal components of your game.

The Theatrix Class

Figure 5.1 shows the class hierarchy within which you encapsulate the components of a game.

Figure 5.1 Encapsulating the game

The *Theatrix* class in Figure 5.1 encapsulates the controls needed to run a game. The class manages events and message queues, and it initializes and shuts down system components such as timers, sound and music generators, the joystick, the mouse, and so on.

The Game Application bubble in Figure 5.1 represents your game program. It is a class named by you and derived from the *Theatrix* class. It contains data members that are objects and references to objects of classes derived from the Theatrix class library (discussed next) that you need to run your game. It can also contain anything else specific to the game itself. We will show you soon what this class looks like in a real program.

The Theatrix Class Library

Figure 5.2 is the Theatrix class library. To build a game, you derive specialized classes from these classes, and, in some cases, you instantiate objects of these classes. These classes implement the Theatrix metaphor.

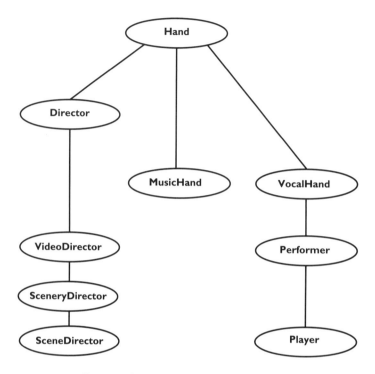

Figure 5.2 The Theatrix class hierarchy

The five levels in Figure 5.2 represent the five levels of abstraction at which you can design your game. The highest level of abstraction is shown at the bottom of the hierarchy, and the lowest is shown at the top.

Most of the classes in Figure 5.2 are designed to be base classes. You build your games by deriving from them. The *MusicHand* class, however, is designed to have an object of the class instantiated. Any game that plays music does so through one instance of the *MusicHand* class.

As you work at lower levels of abstraction, you must understand and use—and in some cases, provide—more of the details of implementation. The higher levels of abstraction encapsulate those details. When you work at higher levels you can ignore the details of the lower levels.

The example games on the included CD-ROM work at different levels of abstraction. Table 5.1 lists the games and shows where they fit on the chart.

Table 5.1 Levels of abstraction of example games

Example Game	Level of Abstraction
Textmode	1
Planet	3
Theatris	3
Marble Fighter	3
SkyScrap	3
TicTacToe	4
Mouse	4
Town	4
Skater	5
Shootout	5

A game can use the details from several levels of abstraction. For example, the Shootout game, implemented at level 5, uses level 4's *SceneryDirector* to implement introductory screens and level 2's *MusicHand* class to play music selections from a musical score.

The Hand Class

You do not usually directly derive anything from the *Hand* class, although it is possible. This class hosts and manages the events and messages that game program components use to communicate between themselves and the system. Usually your program derives classes from the classes that derive from *Hand*.

The *Hand* class allows its derived objects to request *cues*, which are messages that the system sends to *Hand* objects. Messages are usually associated with system events such as keystrokes, but they may also be messages posted by game components to be received by *Hand* objects that register for the messages.

The CUELIST Table

A derived *Hand* class requests cues for its objects by defining a CUELIST table, which specifies the cues to be received and the class's member functions to receive them.

The class declaration includes a DECLARE_CUELIST statement that declares the existence of a CUELIST table for the class:

```
class MyHand : public Hand  {
    // ...
    DECLARE_CUELIST
};
```

Then the class definition includes the CUELIST table:

```
CUELIST(MyHand)
    KEYSTROKE('a',on_key_a)
    TIMER(1,on_timer)
ENDLIST
```

The CUELIST statement specifies that a table of cues follows. The ENDLIST statement terminates the table. The CUELIST statement's parameter identifies the class for which the cues in the list are being registered, which means that the CUELIST statement must be within the scope of the class declaration. A CUELIST declaration generates a memory-resident table, so you should put it in the .CPP source code file of your program rather than in the header file that declares the class.

The CUELIST table just shown includes a KEYSTROKE entry that registers objects of the class to receive a keystroke cue. It also includes a TIMER entry that registers for a cue based on the system clock.

The *on_key_a* and *on_timer* parameters to the KEYSTROKE and TIMER statements are member functions that are called *callback* functions because the table entries pass to the system the addresses of functions to be called. Whenever the user presses the *a* key, for example, the system calls the registered class's *on_key_a* member function, once for each instantiated object of the class. The *on_key_a* function defines the object's behavior when the *a* key is pressed. The callback function might be defined like this:

```
void MyHand::on_key_a()
{
    print_string("the 'a' key has been pressed!");
}
```

There are nine types of cues. Table 5.2 lists the cues and gives examples of their entries in the CUELIST table.

Table 5.2 CUELIST events

Event	CUELIST Entry
Keystroke	KEYSTROKE('a',on_key_a)
Hotkey pressed	HOTKEY(SCAN_CTRL, on_ctrlkey)
Clock tick	TIMER(1, on_timer)
Message posted	MESSAGE(on_message)
Mouse click	MOUSECLICK(LEFTMOUSEBUTTON, on_mousebutton)
Mouse movement	MOUSEMOVE(on_mousemove)
Joystick moved	JOYSTICKMOVE(on_joystickmove)
Joystick button	JOYSTICKBUTTON(on_joystickbutton)
Network packet	NETPACK('X', on_netpack)

Callback Function Signatures

The callback function for each cue type has its own function signature depending on what the system passes as arguments. The class and callback identifiers are up to you, but callbacks should have return types of *void* and, if you are expecting to use the arguments, parameter lists that match the signatures. The discussions that follow identify the signatures for the callback functions.

Callback Functions

A callback function must be a member function of a *Hand* class or of a class derived from *Hand*. When the system calls a *Hand* callback function, it passes data arguments depending on which cue is being sent. Table 5.3 lists the cues and the prototypes for their associated callback functions.

Table 5.3 Callback function prototypes

Event	Callback Prototype	Arguments
Keystroke	void cb(int key)	ASCII keystroke
Hotkey pressed	void cb(int scancode)	Keyboard scan code
Clock tick	void cb()	
Message posted	void cb(int p1, long p2)	App-dependent values
Mouse click	void cb(int x,int y,int b)	Coordinates, Button
Mouse movement	void cb(int x,int y,int b)	Coordinates, Button
Joystick moved	void cb(int x, int y)	Coordinates off center
Joystick button	void cb(int x, int y)	Coordinates off center
Network packet	void cb(int pkt)	Packet byte value

These prototypes indicate what the system passes when it calls the callback functions. You can use a callback function without the parameters if the function does not need them. The CUELIST table uses C++ casts to build its table, so there are no compile-time checks for parameter numbers and types. For example, a keystroke callback function does not need the keystroke value if it is registered for only one cue, so it can be declared without any parameters. Be careful to specify only those parameters that the system actually sends. The casting mechanism effectively bypasses C++'s static type-checking mechanism for function parameters, and you could get into trouble by expecting something quite different than what the caller passes.[1]

KEYSTROKE

A keystroke cue is sent whenever the key associated with the cue is pressed. Keystrokes are useful, but they have a limitation. Keystrokes use the BIOS keyboard mechanism, which means that only one keystroke can be detected at a time, even if the user is pressing two keys.

---

[1]Purists might be offended by this apparent override of the type-safety built into the C++ language. Perhaps they are right, but this mechanism has been used in such class libraries as the Microsoft Foundation Classes for years.

The keystroke cue callback function has this signature:

```
void ClassName::callbackname(int k);
```

The parameter's argument is the key that was pressed. If this callback is registerd to be cued for only one key, then the parameter's argument will always have that one value. If, however, you use one callback to handle multiple keys, you will have to test the value of 'k'.

HOTKEY

Hotkey cues bypass BIOS and read the keyboard directly, so multiple keys can be detected at the same time. Hotkeys are great for intense arcade action, but it is difficult to write a menu using hotkeys because they often report multiple cues even if the user pressed the key once. Hotkey cues specify keyboard scan codes rather than ASCII key values. The header file named **scancode.h** provides global symbols for keyboard scan codes and for ASCII key values for keys such as the Esc key that do not have character constant literal expressions in C++.

The hotkey cue callback function has this signature:

```
void ClassName::callbackname(int k);
```

Like keystrokes, hotkey callbacks take a single, integer parameter, which is the keyboard scan code currently detected as being pressed.

TIMER

Timer cues are a vital part of any arcade game. The first argument in the TIMER entry specifies the number of cues sent each second. Because the system's hardware timer runs at 18.2 ticks per second, the argument's value is approximate.

The system sends timer cues at a regular rate, regardless of the processor's speed. Games use timer cues to float objects across the screen or to maintain a constant speed for bullets, rockets, and so on. The timer cue also paces the frame refresh rate of animated sequences.

The timer cue callback function has this signature:

```
void ClassName::callbackname();
```

Timer callbacks take no parameters.

MESSAGE

Message cues are different from the other types of cues. They are sent by a component of the game rather than in response to an event. Messages allow the *Hand* objects in your game to communicate. When a *Hand* object posts a message, other *Hand* objects that have registered for the message are cued. Messages may have data values associated with them.

The message cue callback function has this signature:

```
void ClassName::callbackname(int msg,long data);
```

Message callbacks have two parameters. The first is the message that was posted. The second parameter is the optional data value that can be sent along with the message.

MOUSECLICK

Mouse click cues are sent whenever either button on the mouse is pressed. The mouse click cue callback function has this signature:

```
void ClassName::callbackname(int x,int y,int b);
```

Mouse click callbacks are sent three integer parameters. The first two parameters are the X/Y location of the mouse on the screen at the time of the click. The third parameter is set to either LEFTMOUSEBUTTON or RIGHTMOUSEBUTTON, depending on which button was pressed.

MOUSEMOVE

Mouse movement cues are sent whenever the player moves the mouse. The mouse movement cue callback function has this signature:

```
void ClassName::callbackname(int x,int y,int b);
```

Mouse movement callbacks are sent three integer parameters. The first two parameters are the X/Y location of the mouse on the screen at the time of the click. The third parameter is set to zero if no button is being held down or is set to LEFTMOUSEBUTTON or RIGHTMOUSEBUTTON if a button is being held down. Programs can use the button parameter to implement mouse drag operations.

JOYSTICKMOVE

Joystick movement cues are sent whenever the joystick is positioned away from the center position. The joystick movement cue callback function has this signature:

```
void ClassName::callbackname(int x,int y);
```

Joystick movement callbacks are sent two integer parameters indicating the distance from the center position. A negative x value indicates left of center; positive x indicates right of center; negative y indicates below center, and positive y indicates above center.

JOYSTICKBUTTON

Joystick button cues are sent when a joystick button is pressed. The joystick button cue callback function has this signature:

```
void ClassName::callbackname(int x,int y);
```

Joystick button callbacks are sent the same two integer parameters that joystick movement callbacks receive.

NETPACK

Network packet cues are sent when Theatrix reads a packet from the serial port. Network packets are present only in games that use serial port communications. The network packet cue callback function has this signature:

```
void ClassName::callbackname(int p);
```

The single parameter is simply the value that was sent across the serial cable.

Requesting and Stopping Cues During the Game

A *Hand* requests cues either with the CUELIST table or by calling member functions that make the requests at runtime during the course of the game. The CUELIST table establishes an initial list of registered cues when the game begins.

If your game has a *Hand* that requests and stops cues during the course of the game, you can use *Hand* member functions that perform those operations. Table 5.4 lists the *Hand* member functions that request and stop cue callbacks during the game's execution.

Table 5.4 Cue request and stop functions

void request_keystroke_cue(int key,callback);

void stop_keystroke_cue(int key,callback);

void request_hotkey_cue(int scancode,callback);

void stop_hotkey_cue(int scancode,callback);

void request_timer_cue(int rate,callback);

void stop_timer_cue(int rate,callback);

void request_message_cue(int msg,callback);

void stop_message_cue(int msg,callback);

void post_message(int msg,long data);

void request_mouseclick_cue(int b,callback);

void stop_mouseclick_cue(int b,callback);

void request_mousemove_cue(callback);

void stop_mousemove_cue(callback);

void request_joystickbutton_cue(int b,callback);

void stop_joystickbutton_cue(int b,callback);

void request_joystickmove_cue(callback);

void stop_joystickmove_cue(callback);

void request_netpack_cue(int,callback);

void stop_netpack_cue(int,callback);

Level 1: Directors and Hands

Level 1 in Figure 5.2 is the lowest level of abstraction for a Theatrix game program. Game-dependent classes at this level derive from the *Director* and *Hand* classes. Nothing at this level supports graphics, sound effects, or music. Level 1 will launch a game program and manage events and cues.

The Director Class

The *Director* class implements objects that control the running of the game. A game may declare many *Director* objects, usually of classes derived from *Director*, but only one *Director* object is in control of the game at any given time.

Stopping the Director

A game cannot go on forever, so there must be a way to stop it. A *Hand* object calls *stop_director* to terminate the *Director* object that directs its activities. If the *Hand* is itself a *Director*, it terminates itself by calling the *stop_director* function.

When the terminated *Director* object is the only *Director* in a game, *stop_director* terminates the game. You learn later how games with multiple directors pass control among one another.

Level 2: MusicHand and VocalHand

Abstraction level 2 derives classes from *Hand*. *VocalHand* provides sound support, and *MusicHand* supports playing selections from a musical score. Contemporary games do not often use text mode displays with music sound effects, so we do not include demo games at this level. If you have such requirements, then, by all means, derive from *VocalHand* and work at the second level of abstraction. We have chosen not to do that. Two demos— Town and TicTacToe—derive classes from *VocalHand* and use objects of those classes to play sound clips.

The MusicHand Class

Theatrix provides support for music in games with the *MusicHand* class. *MusicHand* reads .XMI files, which are files that can store multiple MIDI files. The interface is simple. *MusicHand* takes the name of an .XMI file as a parameter to the constructor:

```
musichandptr=new MusicHand("tunes.xmi");
```

The file represents the game's musical score. When the time comes to play a selection from the score, a call to the *MusicHand* object can be made:

```
musichandptr->play_music_clip(clip);
```

The *clip* argument in the *play_music_clip* function call is an integer that is relative to one. It must be greater than zero and less than or equal to the number of clips in the .XMI library that was specified as an argument to the *MusicHand* constructor. If a previous selection is playing, this function stops that one and starts the new one.

To ask the *MusicHand* object whether it is still playing a selection from the score, call the *music_clip_is_playing* member function:

```
while (musichandptr->music_clip_is_playing()) {
    // do something while music is playing
}
```

To tell the *MusicHand* object to stop playing a selection, call *stop_music_clip*:

```
musichandptr->stop_music_clip();  // current selection stops
```

The *is_conducting* member reports whether *MusicHand* detected a sound card driver when the program started.

```
if (musichandptr->is_conducting()) {
    // music is supported by this game environment
}
```

The VocalHand Class

VocalHand loads .SFX libraries, which are files of sound effects. .SFX libraries contain multiple sound clips, provided in the .VOC format. A game program can derive from *VocalHand* or instantiate a *VocalHand* object, although many games will use the *Performer* class, which is derived from *VocalHand*.

The *VocalHand* constructor accepts a pointer to the director for which the object is running. If you omit that argument, the constructor builds the object with no associated director, and the class may not have a CUELIST entry or request and stop cues with function calls.

Following is a small class that derives from *VocalHand* to implement sound effects for a game.

```
class SoundTech : public VocalHand  {
    char *sfxfile;
    void initialize()
        { load_sfxlib(sfxfile); }
public:
    SoundTech(char *sfx)
        { sfxfile = sfx; }
};
```

The call to *VocalHand::load_sfxlib* tells the object the name of the .SFX library to load. All the sound clips that can be played by the *VocalHand* object are in that library. A game can instantiate an object of such a class, as the following example shows:

```
static SoundTech *soundtech;

soundtech = new SoundTech("town.sfx");
```

The game that uses such a class can then call *VocalHand* member functions through objects of the derived class, as shown here:

```
soundtech->play_sound_clip(clip);       // play a sound clip
// ...
soundtech->stop_sound_clip();           // stop the sound clip
// ...
if (soundtech->sound_clip_is_playing()) // test if clip is playing
    // sound clip is playing
```

The clip number argument in the *play_sound_clip* function call is an integer that is relative to one. It must be greater than zero and less than or equal to the number of clips in the .SFX library that was loaded for the *VocalHand* object.

Level 3: Performers and VideoDirectors

Abstraction level 3 derives classes from *VocalHand* and *Director*. *Performer* provides basic graphics support, and *VideoDirector* provides video page-flipping support.

The Performer Class

Performer, which supports graphics, is derived from *VocalHand*, which is derived from *Hand*. In addition to being able to request cues, *Performer* loads .GFX libraries, which are files that contain images that you provide in the form of .PCX files. Once *Performer* loads a .GFX library, it can display the images inside the library at any time.

.GFX and .SFX libraries are created using utility programs from the Theatrix toolkit. Chapter 6 explains how these tools work.

The VideoDirector Class

VideoDirector is derived from *Director*. *VideoDirector* supports page-flipping animation, which uses a hidden video page to assemble a scene and then displays it instantly so that the user sees only the finished page.

Level 4: SceneryDirectors

Until now, our discussion has related mostly to the action part of the game. Few games, however, jump immediatly into the action. Most of them have an introductory screen, and many have a trailer screen that comes up after the game is over. Most games have a menu display, too, which allows you to choose from selections such as whether to play another session, get help, change options, exit the game, and so on.

At its fourth level of abstraction, Theatrix implements the *SceneryDirector* class, which implements scenery without animation.

The SceneryDirector Class

Dislaying an information screen seems simple enough. Display a .PCX file and wait for a key. That's about all there is to it, but a few subtleties should be considered. For instance, how should the image be displayed? If displayed on the visual page, the image appears on the screen a line at a time. (It appears quickly, but a line at a time nonetheless. On a slow machine, the user will see this effect.) This might be a desired effect, but it usually makes the game appear to run slowly. An alternative is to load the image into the hidden page and do a page swap so that the image appears all at once. Also, which keys should be used as an acknowledgment? Any key or only certain ones?

The *SceneryDirector* class offers one solution. *SceneryDirector* is designed to be used as a base class:

```
class MyIntroPage : public SceneryDirector
{
public:
    MyIntroPage() : SceneryDirector("myintro.pcx")  { }
}
```

By creating an instance of *MyIntroPage* before any other *Director* objects, you've added an intro page. *SceneryDirector* can be used to display intro screens, help screens, and trailer screens. The demos on the CD-ROM—such as Marble Fighter, Theatris, and Shootout—all use *SceneryDirector*, which displays the image by using a page-swap and then waits for the Enter, space bar, or Esc key to be pressed before it continues.

Level 5: Players and SceneDirectors

Theatrix provides two classes at level 5 that encapsulate the operations of video pages and bitmaps. These classes are *Player* and *SceneDirector*. *Player* is derived from *Performer*, and *SceneDirector* is derived from *SceneryDirector*.

These two classes make it easy to animate multiple sprites simultaneously. At first glance, animating two sprites doesn't seen any more complicated than animating one sprite as in the Planet demo—but it is. With single sprite animation, a scene can be updated simply by erasing the old image (with a portion of the background image) and drawing the new one. This technique doesn't work with two sprites because the sprite that is moving might overlap the sprite that is not moving, so it would erase part or all of the second sprite. In short, to animate two or more sprites, the updating must be coordinated.

Another facet of multiple sprite animation involves Z-order, or the ability of one sprite to consistently appear above or in front of another sprite. This requires the sprites to be updated in a specific order. Both of these issues are addressed and taken care of by the *SceneDirector* and *Player* combination.

Theatrix
User's Guide

"Science is the guide of action."
William Kingdom Clifford

This chapter describes the utility programs that accompany and support the Theatrix C++ class library. You will learn about these subjects:

◇ Graphics file libraries

◇ Sound effects libraries

◇ Palette management utilities

◇ Mouse cursors

◇ Miscellaneous utilities

Managing Graphics File Libraries

GFX libraries are files that contain sprites and other bitmaps. Usually each sprite has its own GFX library, which contains the bitmaps that define all the poses that a sprite can assume. Other bitmaps are props, such as doors that open, numeric displays for showing the game's score, and any other bitmap that the game needs to display over the scenery.

GFXMAKE

Graphics bitmaps are supplied to GFXMAKE in the form of .PCX files. There are two ways to use GFXMAKE: The file names can be included on the command line, or a "list file" can be supplied that contains a list of the .PCX files to be included.

Let's pretend that we are going to write a game in which a character moves around the screen in four directions. We'll need four bitmaps of our character: one with the character moving up, one moving down, one moving left, and one moving right. The construction of the images is up to you. You might want to draw them in a paint program, render them with a 3-D package, or capture them from a picture. Whatever your source is, you need to produce each image in the .PCX format. Almost any format can be converted to the .PCX format using Image Alchemy, which is included on the CD-ROM.[1]

Once you have the four .PCX files of the character moving in four directions, producing a .GFX file is simple. Place the four images in the same directory, and then, in that same directory, execute this command:

```
GFXMAKE test.gfx up.pcx down.pcx left.pcx right.pcx
```

Make sure that GFXMAKE is in the command path. If all goes well (and you've named your .PCX files up.pcx, down.pcx, and so on), the GFXMAKE will create a .GFX file called TEST.GFX, which contains four images. Then, in your game, in a Performer-derived *initialize* member, include this line:

---

[1]The version of Image Alchemy included on the CD-ROM is a demo version, which can convert images of 640 x 480 and smaller resolution. Refer to the Image Alchemy documentation for ordering information.

```
MyPerformer::initialize()
{
    // ...
    load_gfxlib("test.gfx");
    // ...
}
```

Now your Performer will be able to use the *show_image* member:

```
show_image(x,y,1);
```

This line would display the first image (up.pcx) of the TEST.GFX file with its upper left corner located at x/y. Likewise, using 2 as the last parameter would display the second image (down.pcx).

GFXSHOW

GFXSHOW reads .GFX files and displays the images. When you're creating the .GFX file, this utility can be helpful. Had we actually created our TEST.GFX file, we could then type:

```
GFXSHOW test.gfx
```

The contents of our new .GFX library would be displayed. If the images in test.gfx use a palette other than the standard VGA palette, you can supply another parameter after the .GFX libarary:

```
GFXSHOW test.gfx test.pal
```

SHOWPCX

SHOWPCX displays the .PCX file you supply on the command line. Unlike most viewers, SHOWPCX displays images in Mode X.

Managing Sound Effects Libraries

Sound effects libraries contain sound clips built from .VOC files. Usually, each sprite has a library of its own voices and sound effects. A base class often manages the sound effects for its derived sprites.

SFXMAKE

SFXMAKE works like GFXMAKE except that SFXMAKE takes .VOC files as input and creates .SFX files. The .VOC files can be supplied on the command line or in a list file. Let's say that we have a game with two sounds: a gun firing and an explosion. Although the list file syntax is usually used if you have more than two entries, let's use it so that you can see how it works.

First, we prepare the list file:

```
shot.voc
explode.voc
```

Let's call the file sounds.txt. In the directory that contains this file and the two .VOC files, type:

```
SFXMAKE sounds.sfx @sounds.txt
```

Now you can load the file in your game in much the same way you loaded the .GFX library in the preceding example. In a VocalHand-derived class, place this code:

```
void MyVocalHand::initialize()
{
    // ...
    load_sfxlib("sounds.sfx");
    // ...
}
```

In a callback in that same class, you can play the gunfire sound with this command:

```
play_sound_clip(1);
```

Specifying 2 as the parameter would play the explosion.

SFXPLAY

Like GFXMAKE, SFXMAKE has a companion utility that you can use to make sure that your library has been assembled properly.

The command

```
SFXPLAY sounds.sfx
```

allows you to play each sound by entering the number of the sound clip.

Palatte Management Utilities

It's important to understand palettes, because you must deal with them in order to display images that use colors other than the standard VGA colors. We will discuss palettes and everything that you need to know to get around them, but we will not worry about every detail of the VGA hardware.

We have been using 256-color modes. This means that 256 colors can be displayed together at the same time on one screen. The modes in question are capable of displaying virtually any color but can deal with only 256 at a time. When you first put the VGA adapter into Mode X, 256 colors are available. Although these default VGA colors can be used to accomplish quite a bit, they are limited, especially when it comes to displaying rendered pictures or scanned photographs.

You can tell the VGA card to use other colors instead, but managing 256 colors is more than most people want to do. The alternative is to use the palette tools documented here to do the management for you. This technique, if used properly, frees you from having to worry about each color entry but allows you to make full use of the 256 color modes. Follow these steps:

1. Produce a background image .PCX file. This image should fill the whole screen (320 x 240 for Mode X).
2. Produce the individual characters for the scene (also in .PCX format).
3. Extract a palette from the background image using GETPAL (discussed next).
4. Choose one or two sample shots of each character from the game and extract their palettes using GETPAL.
5. Create a master palette with GENPAL (discussed in this chapter), using as input the palettes you extracted from your background and characters.

6. Force all the .PCX files (the background and all images for the character) to use the master palette. This is accomplished with CVTPAL, which will be discussed later in this chapter.

7. Create the desired GFX library using the converted .PCX files. This is done with GFXMAKE.

8. Use the converted background in the game with the *show_pcx* member. The palette in the background .PCX image will be installed into the VGA memory automatically.

Now you can display the background image with the *show_pcx* member of VideoDirector and then display the .GFX images at will.

GETPAL

GETPAL extracts the palette from a .PCX file. Each .PCX file contains its own palette. Utilites such as CVTPAL and GENPAL (which we will discuss next) take palettes as input, so it is necessary to extract the palettes from .PCX files. This is the job of GETPAL. GETPAL is used this way:

```
GETPAL picture1.pcx
```

This command would cause GETPAL to create a palette file called picture1.pal, which would contain an ASCII list of the palette entries. If you don't want the palette output to have the same name as the input .PCX, then include the desired name after the PCX:

```
GETPAL picture1.pcx pal1.pal
```

The resulting palette files can be used as input for CVTPAL, GENPAL or NeoPaint.[2]

CVTPAL

CVTPAL installs a new palette in a .PCX file. Using GENPAL, a palette is generated that contains the colors you want to use. The problem is that now you have a number of .PCX files with random palettes but only a single

---

[2]Use care if you decide to manipulate the palette with NeoPaint. NeoPaint forces color 0 to black and color 255 to white.

palette file. CVTPAL can be used to convert the palette of each .PCX file to the new palette. For example:

```
CVTPAL picture1.pcx pal1.pal
```

This command causes CVTPAL to replace each pixel of picture1.pcx with the closest match it can find based on the new palette found in pal1.pal. In order words, CVTPAL normalizes the image found in picture1.pcx to the palette found in pal1.pal. You should use the palette you create with GENPAL to normalize all the .PCX files in your game. Once these .PCX files have been packaged into .GFX libraries, all the images can be displayed on the same screen at the same time without any palette problems.

GENPAL

GENPAL merges several palettes into one palette, eliminating duplications. The command looks like this:

```
GENPAL 0 first.pal second.pal third.pal
```

This command produces a master palette called new.pal, which is the result of merging the three palettes listed. The zero (the first parameter) is the tolerance level. Zero means that GENPAL will omit only exact color matches. Sending 1 means that GENPAL will omit exact matches and matches that are off by only 1. The higher this number, the more matches GENPAL will find. This lets you tune GENPAL to produce a palette as close to 256 as possible (larger palettes render better graphics). GENPAL reports how many colors are present in the master palette. You can include as many palettes as you like on the command line (until you excede DOS's 128-character limit).

Making Mouse Cursors

Theatrix comes with some mouse cursors already defined. These are fine for general use, but you can define your own mouse cursors with the utility discussed in this section.

GMICE

The GMICE utility program allows you to generate the C++ arrays that
define custom mouse cursor shapes from .PCX files. You begin by defining
your mouse cursors as 16 x 16 bit .PCX files with 256 colors.

Next, you determine the cursor's hot spot, which is the point of focus of
the cursor. The hot spot is the pixel coordinate within the cursor image that
is at the screen coordinate that gets reported to the program for the mouse
coordinates when the cursor is moved or clicked.

GMICE has a table of hot spots already defined:

```
// ------ hotspot table
static struct hs {
    char *fn;
    int x, y;
} HotSpots[] = {
    { "LF",  0,  1 },
    { "RT", 15,  1 },
    { "DN", 14, 15 },
    { "UP", 14,  0 },
    { "UL",  0,  0 },
    { "UR", 15,  0 },
    { "LR", 15, 15 },
    { "LL",  0, 15 },
    { "CN",  7,  0 },
    { "DE",  0,  0 },
    {  0,  0,  0 }
};
```

GMICE relates the two-letter tokens in the table to the first two characters of
the .PCX file's name and uses that vector to select the X and Y values for the
hot spot. To use other file name conventions or different hot spot values, you
must modify this table in GMICE.CPP and recompile the utility program.

To run GMICE, name the output file followed by the .PCX files on the
command line. You can use actual file names or names with wildcards, or
you can specify a list file by using the @ prefix. Here is an example:

```
GMICE mice.cpp *.pcx
```

GMICE produces a file of source code that you compile along with your game program. Here is an example of part of the table that GMICE produces in the source code file:

```
char UPCURSOR[] = { 14, 0, // hotspot x/y
    255,255,255,255,255,255,255,255,255,255,255,255,255,  0,  0,  0,
    255,255,255,255,255,255,255,255,255,255,255,255,255,  0,  0,  0,
    255,255,255,255,255,255,255,255,255,255,255,255,255,  0,  0,  0,
    255,255,255,255,255,255,255,255,255,255,255,  0,  0,  0,  0,  0,
    255,255,255,255,255,255,255,255,255,  0,  0,  0,  0,  0,  0,  0,
    255,255,255,255,255,255,255,  0,  0,  0,  0,  0,  0,  0,  0,  0,
    255,255,255,255,255,255,255,  0,  0,  0,  0,  0,  0,  0,  0,  0,
    255,255,255,255,255,255,255,  0,  0,  0,  0,  0,  0,  0,  0,  0,
    255,255,255,255,255,255,255,  0,  0,  0,  0,  0,  0,  0,  0,  0,
    255,255,255,255,255,255,255,  0,  0,  0,  0,  0,  0,  0,  0,  0,
    255,255,255,255,255,255,255,  0,  0,  0,  0,  0,  0,  0,  0,  0,
    255,255,255,255,255,255,255,  0,  0,  0,  0,  0,  0,  0,  0,  0,
    255,255,255,255,255,255,255,  0,  0,  0,  0,  0,  0,  0,  0,  0,
    255,255,255,255,255,255,255,  0,  0,  0,  0,  0,  0,  0,  0,255,
    255,255,255,255,255,255,255,255,  0,  0,  0,  0,  0,  0,  0,255,
    255,255,255,255,255,255,255,255,  0,  0,  0,  0,  0,  0,  0,255,
      0,  0,  0,  0,  0,  0,  0,  0,  0,  0,  0,  0,  0, 63, 63, 63,
      0,  0,  0,  0,  0,  0,  0,  0,  0,  0,  0,  0,  0, 63, 82, 63,
      0,  0,  0,  0,  0,  0,  0,  0,  0,  0,  0,  0,  0, 63, 82, 63,
      0,  0,  0,  0,  0,  0,  0,  0,  0,  0,  0, 63, 63, 63, 82, 63,
      0,  0,  0,  0,  0,  0,  0,  0,  0, 63, 63, 63, 82, 63, 82, 63,
      0,  0,  0,  0,  0,  0,  0, 63, 63, 63, 82, 63, 82, 63, 82, 63,
      0,  0,  0,  0,  0,  0,  0, 63, 82, 63, 82, 63, 82, 63, 82, 63,
      0,  0,  0,  0,  0,  0,  0, 63, 63, 63, 63, 63, 63, 63, 63, 63,
      0,  0,  0,  0,  0,  0,  0, 63, 82, 82, 82, 82, 82, 82, 82, 63,
      0,  0,  0,  0,  0,  0,  0, 63, 82, 82, 82, 82, 82, 82, 82, 63,
      0,  0,  0,  0,  0,  0,  0, 63, 82, 82, 82, 82, 82, 82, 82, 63,
      0,  0,  0,  0,  0,  0,  0, 63, 82, 82, 82, 82, 82, 82, 82, 63,
      0,  0,  0,  0,  0,  0,  0, 63, 82, 82, 82, 82, 82, 82, 63, 63,
      0,  0,  0,  0,  0,  0,  0, 63, 63, 82, 82, 82, 82, 82, 63,  0,
      0,  0,  0,  0,  0,  0,  0,  0, 63, 82, 82, 82, 82, 82, 63,  0,
      0,  0,  0,  0,  0,  0,  0,  0, 63, 63, 63, 63, 63, 63, 63,  0
    };
```

Use the name of the array in the CURSORLIST declaration when you declare the cursor shape for regions of the screen:

```
CURSORLIST(Town)
    MOUSE_CURSOR(  0,   0, 105, 239, LFCURSOR, look_left)
    MOUSE_CURSOR(106,   0, 211, 199, UPCURSOR, look_forward)
    MOUSE_CURSOR(106, 200, 211, 239, DNCURSOR, look_back)
    MOUSE_CURSOR(212,   0, 319, 239, RTCURSOR, look_right)
ENDCURSORLIST
```

Miscellaneous Utilities

The utilities we have discussed so far have been designed specifically for use with Theatrix. The ywo utilities in this section are general .PCX manipulation tools.

PASTE

PASTE is useful for "pasting" text (or another portion of an image) onto a snapshot, or rendered background. Let's say that you are preparing a help screen. You want a fancy background with text over it (like the help screens in Marble Fighter and Theatris). You could bring the image into a paint program and type text over it, but what if you mess up or decide later that you want to move the text to the left a bit?

PASTE allows you to prepare a separate image, containing only the text, and then paste the text over the original image. If you decide to change the text color or move the text, you make the change in the text image and rerun PASTE. PASTE copies anything that is not color 0 (usually black).

Note that the image to be pasted does not have to contain text at all—you can paste any two images together. They should both be the same size.

REGION

REGION "cuts" a region out of one .PCX file and saves it in another. For example:

```
REGION big.pcx small.pcx 100 100 200 200
```

This command displays big.pcx and then saves the region defined by 100,100 at the upper left corner and 200,200 at the lower right corner. This utility is useful when you want to animate a portion of a background and don't want to save the entire picture.

Theatrix
Reference Manual

"Libraries are not made; they grow."
Augustine Birrell

This chapter is the reference manual to the Theatrix C++ class library that is a part of the included CD-ROM. You use it to look up details about the various components of the library. The chapter includes descriptions of:

◇ The Theatrix class library

◇ Theatrix macros

◇ Global values

◇ Global constants

Class Library Reference

This manual documents those parts of the Theatrix class library that represent its public interface. There are many other classes in the library that this chapter does not discuss because the programmer does not need to access their operations directly. We decided not to address them because you might decide that you need to use them, and that would be a mistake. Later versions of this library could significantly change how certain classes work. For example, the library uses its own linked list and other container classes. Eventually these will be replaced by container classes in the C++ Standard Template Library when that library is formally defined and universally understood.

Director (director.h)

There is usually one *Director* object per screen in a game. The game play is one or more *Director* objects, the menu is another *Director* object, and so on. Any game created with Theatrix must have at least one *Director*.

Constructor

```
Director()    // protected
```

Creates a new *Director* object. Because this constructor is protected, you can create a *Director* only by using derivation. *Director* is a relatively large object, about 3KB, so it should be created with care. Typically, a *Director*-derived class should be created dynamically using the *new* operator.

take_over

```
virtual void take_over()    // protected
```

Runs the *Director*'s cue-dispatching loop. This member function is called automatically by Theatrix. The *take_over* function causes the *Director* to take control of the application. During the execution of *take_over*, all other *Director* objects in the game are idle.

Because *take_over* is called automatically by Theatrix, it is not necessary to call it. It is, however, often useful to override it. For example, overriding *take_over* is a way to ensure that a director runs in a certain keyboard mode (see *Hand::set_hotkeys*). In the overridden constructor, set the new mode, call *Director::take_over*, and then restore the mode.

display

```
virtual void display()    // protected
```

The *display* member function is called automatically by Theatrix when the *Director* is about to take over. By default, this routine does nothing but can be overridden to display backgrounds, initialize variables, and so forth.

hide

```
virtual void hide()    // protected
```

The *hide* member function is called automatically by Theatrix after the *Director* has given up control. By default, *hide* does nothing but can be overridden to clear the screen, display statistics, do a fancy fade-out, and so on.

iterate_director

```
virtual void iterate_director()    // protected
```

iterate_director is called by *Director::take_over* once per cycle of the dispatching loop. You can override this member to perform tasks that must occur more often than a timer can provide. Note, however, that the member will be called at different rates depending on the speed of the processor.

get_next_director

```
virtual const Type_info& get_next_director()    // protected
```

Returns the type identification of the next director that should take control of the game. Theatrix calls this member function automatically after the *Director* has given up control. Unless a previous call to *set_next_director* has been made or the member function has been overridden, the type identification for *StopDirector* is returned, informing Theatrix to terminate the application.

set_next_director

```
void set_next_director(const Type_info *dir)        // protected
```

Informs Theatrix which *Director* should follow the current one.

next_director_set

```
int next_director_set()     // protected
```

Returns 1 if a call to *set_next_director* has been made with other than a null pointer; otherwise, returns 0.

Hand (hand.h)

A *Hand* object is the basic unit in a game. As in a play, a *Hand* (a stagehand) may or may not actually be visible to the audience. A *Hand* has one or several tasks that it knows how to perform, and it relies on its *Director* for its cues, which tell the *Hand* when to perform the task.

Constructor

```
Hand(Director* dir=0)    // protected
```

Creates a *Hand* object. This constructor, like the constructor for *Director*, is protected, which means that in order to use *Hand*, it is necessary to derive from *Hand*. Note that the *Director** parameter is optional. Although it is not mandatory to supply this parameter, a *Director* must be supplied for any of the *Hand* object's cue members to operate. If a *Director* pointer is not supplied during construction, then it should be supplied later with a call to *set_director*. If any of the *Hand* class's member functions is invoked before a *Director* has been set (with either the constructor or the *set_director* member function), a fatal error occurs and the program terminates.

get_mouseposition

```
void get_mouseposition(int *x, int *y, int *b)     // protected
void get_mouseposition(int *x, int *y)             // protected
```

Retrieves information about the mouse pointer. The *x* and *y* parameters are pointers to variables where the data should go. The data values are the location of the mouse cursor in screen coordinates. The *b* parameter retrieves information about the mouse buttons. The *b* parameter has the following bits set if the associated buttons are pressed:

bit 0:   mouse button 1

bit 1:   mouse button 2

bit 2:   middle mouse button

initialize

```
virtual void initialize()    // protected
```

Does nothing. The *initialize* member function is called automatically by Theatrix once and only once per execution of the game. The function is designed to be overridden and is used to perform initialization tasks that need to happen only once, such as requesting cues or loading .GFX and .SFX libraries. (In fact, this is the only member function that should be used to load .GFX and .SFX libararies.) You can also initialize variables at this time.

mouse_cursorshape

```
void mouse_cursorshape(char *bitmap)    // protected
```

Specifies what the mouse cursor should look like. The parameter bitmap is a character array generated by the Theatrix utility program GMICE.

mouse_invisible

```
void mouse_invisible()    // protected
```

Hides the mouse. This should be called after *mouse_visible*.

mouse_visible

```
void mouse_visible()    // protected
```

Makes the mouse visible. This member function usually appears in a *display* member.

my_director

```
Director* my_director()     // protected
```

Returns a pointer to the *Director* on which the *Hand* depends for cues. This is useful if the *Hand* is creating other *Hand*s and needs to supply a *Director* for the constructors.

post_message

```
void post_message(int msg,long data=0)    // protected
```

Posts the message *msg*. Theatrix delivers the message to any *Hand*s that either have requested a cue for the message *msg* or have included it in a shortcut macro. The *data* parameter is optional but can be used to send information, including pointers to more data.

post_netpack

```
void post_netpack(int netpack)    // protected
```

Sends a packet to the serial port. The packet is received by a remote system, generating cues for *Hand*s on that system.

request_hotkey_cue

```
void request_hotkey_cue(int key,callback cb)    // protected
```

Requests a cue when the hotkey *key* is pressed. Calling this routine tells Theatrix that when the user presses the key, execute the callback function. The *key* parameter can be any of the constants that take the form SCAN_XXX. These constants are documented later in this chapter. The callback *cb* should have a return type of *void* and can take a single integer parameter. The parameter sent to the callback is the value *key*.

request_joystickbutton_cue

```
void request_joystickbutton_cue(int b,callback cb)    // protected
```

Requests a cue whenever a joystick button is pressed. Calling this routine is like telling Theatrix, "Whenever the user presses a button, then execute the routine I have written called cb." The callback *cb* should have a return type of *void* and take two integer parameters. The two parameters are the distance from center that the joystick currently is. If the values are zero, then the joystick is centered. The first value is the horizontal position, and the second is the vertical position. The range for these values can be retrieved with *Theatrix::get_joystick_extremes.*

request_joystickmove_cue

```
void request_joystickmove_cue(callback cb)     // protected
```

Requests a cue whenever the joystick is moved. Calling this routine is like telling Theatrix, "Whenever the user moves the joystick, then execute the routine I have written called *cb*." The callback *cb* should have a return type of *void* and take two integer parameters. The two parameters are the distance from center that the joystick currently is. If the values are zero, then the joystick is centered. The first value is the horizontal position, and the second is the vertical position. The range for these values can be retrieved with *Theatrix::get_joystick_extremes.*

request_keystroke_cue

```
void request_keystroke_cue(int key, callback cb)     // protected
```

Requests a cue when the keystroke *key* occurs. Calling this routine tells Theatrix that when the user presses the key, execute the callback function. The *key* parameter can be any of the constants found in **ascii.h** and listed later in this chapter, or it can be a character constant ('a', 'b', and so on). The *cb* parameter is a member function that you write and should have a return type of *void* and take a single integer parameter.

request_message_cue

```
void request_message_cue(int message,callback cb)     // protected
```

Requests a cue whenever the message *message* is posted. Calling this routine tells Theatrix that when the message *message* is posted, to call the callback function. The callback *cb* should have return type of *void* and take two parameters. The first parameter should be an integer, and the second a *long.*

request_mouseclick_cue

```
void request_mouseclick_cue(int b,callback cb)    // protected
```

Requests a cue when a mouse button is pressed. Calling this routine is like telling Theatrix, "Whenever the user presses button *b* on the mouse, then execute the routine I have written called cb." The *b* parameter can be either of the constants LEFTMOUSEBUTTON or RIGHTMOUSEBUTTON. The callback *cb* should have a return type of *void* and take three integer parameters. The first two parameters are the x and y, respectively, of the mouse position, and the last parameter is the button that was pressed.

request_mousemove_cue

```
void request_mousemove_cue(callback cb)    // protected
```

Requests a cue whenever the mouse is moved. Calling this routine is like telling Theatrix, "Whenever the user moves the mouse, then execute the routine I have written called *cb*." The callback *cb* should have a return of type *void* and take three integer parameters. The first two parameters are the x and y, respectively, of the mouse position, and the last parameter is the button that was pressed.

request_netpack_cue

```
void request_netpack_cue(int netpack,callback cb)    // protected
```

Requests a cue whenever a packet is received from a remote computer. Calling this routine is like telling Theatrix, "Whenever a packet is received, then execute the routine I have written called *cb*." The callback *cb* must have a return type of *void* and take a single integer parameter.

request_timer_cue

```
void request_timer_cue(int rate,callback cb)    // protected
```

Requests a cue every *rate* seconds. Calling this routine tells Theatrix that at about *rate* times a second, call the callback function. The *rate* parameter can be an integer from 1 to 18. Using 1 means that the function *cb* is called once a second, and using 18 means that the function is called 18 times a second. The callback *cb* should have a return type of *void* and take no parameters.

set_director

```
void set_director(Director*)
```

This member function is used to tell a *Hand* from which *Director* it should request its cues. If you supply a *Director* pointer as a parameter to the *Hand* constructor, it is not necessary to call this member function.

set_hotkeys

```
void set_hotkeys(int on)    // protected
```

Turns the hotkey mode on and off. By default, the hotkey mode is off. By sending 1 or the constant ON, the hotkey mode is activated. Conversely, sending 0 or OFF turns off the hotkey mode. Remember that keystroke cues are active only if the hotkey mode is off, and hotkey cues are active only if the hotkey mode is on.

set_mouseposition

```
void set_mouseposition(int x, int y)    // protected
```

Forces the mouse pointer to the location specified by *x* and *y*. The move takes effect regardless of the mouse pointer's visibility.

start_director

```
void start_director(const Type_info& next)    // protected
```

Signals Theatrix to put the argument *Director* in control. Before doing so, Theatrix takes control away from the current *Director* in control after calling its *hide* member function.

stop_director

```
void stop_director()                        // protected
```

Signals the *Director* to give up control. When the *stop_director* member function is called, the *Director* currently responsible for supplying cues relinquishes control to the Theatrix scheduling loop, which decides what to do next.

stop_hotkey_cue

```
void stop_hotkey_cue(int key,callback cb)    // protected
```

Prevents future cues from occurring. The logical complement to *request_hotkey_cue*, this member function undoes what *request* did.

stop_joystickbutton_cue

```
void stop_joystickbutton_cue(int b,callback cb)    // protected
```

Prevents future cues from occurring. The logical complement to *request_joystickbutton_cue*, this member function undoes what *request* did.

stop_joystickmove_cue

```
void stop_joystickmove_cue(callback cb)    // protected
```

Prevents future cues from occurring. The logical complement to *request_joystickmove_cue*, this member function undoes what *request* did.

stop_keystroke_cue

```
void stop_keystroke_cue(int key,callback cb)    // protected
```

Prevents future cues from occurring. The logical complement to *request_keystroke_cue*, this member function undoes what *request* did.

stop_message_cue

```
void stop_message_cue(int message,callback cb)    // protected
```

Prevents future cues from occurring. The logical complement to *request_message_cue*, this member function undoes what *request* did.

stop_mouseclick_cue

```
void stop_mouseclick_cue(int b,callback cb)    // protected
```

Prevents future cues from occurring. The logical complement to *request_mouseclick_cue*, this member function undoes what *request* did.

stop_mousemove_cue

```
void stop_mousemove_cue(callback cb)    // protected
```

Prevents future cues from occurring. The logical complement to *request_mousemove_cue*, this member function undoes what *request* did.

stop_netpack_cue

```
void stop_netpack_cue(int netpack,callback cb)    // protected
```

Prevents future cues from occurring. The logical complement to *request_netpack_cue*, this member function undoes what *request* did.

stop_timer_cue

```
void stop_timer_cue(int rate,callback cb)    // protected
```

Prevents future cues from occurring. The logical complement to *request_timer_cue*, this member function undoes what *request* did.

MusicHand (music.h)

MusicHand is not used as a base class for any of the classes in Theatrix. Although it is safe to assume that each graphical character in a game might make sounds, it is not safe to assume that each character might want to play music. *MusicHand* can be used as a base class for your own music-handling class. More often you will instantiate an object of *MusicHand* and use that object in one of your *Director* objects.

Constructor

```
MusicHand(char *sc)
```

Creates a *MusicHand* object. The *sc* parameter is the name of an .XMI file from which the *MusicHand* reads music clips.

initialize

```
virtual void initialize()    // protected
```

Initializes the *MusicHand*. This member function is called automatically by Theatrix.

isconducting

```
int isconducting()
```

Returns 1 if *MusicHand* was able to detect and initialize a sound card. Otherwise, returns 0.

load_score

```
void load_score(char* fname)
```

Loads an .XMI file. This file replaces any file specified at construction.

music_clip_is_playing

```
int music_clip_is_playing()
```

Returns 1 if a clip is currently being played; otherwise, returns a 0.

play_music_clip

```
void play_music_clip(int index)
```

Begins the music clip found at location *index* within the .XMI file supplied to the constructor. The *index* parameter is an integer value that must be greater than zero and less than or equal to the number of music clips in the .XMI file.

stop_music_clip

```
void stop_music_clip()
```

Interrupts a sound clip that is being played. If no clip is being played, the call is ignored.

Performer (perform.h)

Performer provides basic graphics support. Classes derived from *Performer* can load .GFX libraries and display bitmaps on the active video page.

Constructor

```
Performer(Director* dir=0)    // protected
```

Constructs a *Performer* object. If possible, it is recommended that the *Director** parameter be supplied here. If it is not, *set_director* must be called *before* any cues are requested.

get_char_height

```
int get_char_height(char ch)
```

Returns the height (in pixels) of the character *ch*. Note that this value may vary depending on the active .GFX font.

get_char_width

```
int get_char_width(char ch)    // protected
```

Returns the width (in pixels) of the character *ch*. Note that this value may vary depending on the active .GFX font.

get_image_height

```
int get_image_height(int image_number)    // protected
```

Returns the bitmap height (in pixels) of the bitmap located at location *image_number* in the active .GFX library.

get_image_width

```
int get_image_width(int image_number)    // protected
```

Returns the bitmap width (in pixels) of the bitmap located at location *image_number* in the active .GFX library.

get_num_images

```
int get_num_images()    // protected
```

Returns the number of bitmaps contained in the active .GFX library.

load_gfxfont

```
void load_gfxfont(char* fontlibname)    // protected
```

Loads the .GFX font library *fontlibname* and makes it the active font for this *Performer*. A .GFX font is a .GFX library with 36 bitmaps (the alphabet and 10 digits).

load_gfxlib

```
void load_gfxlib(char* libname)    // protected
```

Loads a .GFX file (a .GFX file created with GFXMAKE) into memory and marks it as the active library for this *Performer*. If *libname* has already been loaded by another *Performer*, then it is not loaded again, but it is marked as the active library for this *Performer*. This member function should be called only in an *initialize* routine.

set_gfxfont

```
void set_gfxfont(char* fontlibname)    // protected
```

Marks *fontlibname* as the active font for this *Performer*. Note that it is necessary to call this member function only if the *Performer* needs access to more than one .GFX font library.

set_gfxlib

```
void set_gfxlib(char* libname)    // protected
```

Marks the active library for the *Performer* as *libname*. Note that it is necessary to invoke this member function only if the *Performer* needs to access images in more than one .GFX library.

show_clipped_image

```
void show_clipped_image(int x,int y,int image_number) //protected
```

Displays the bitmap *image_number* of the currently active .GFX library at screen location *x,y*. The bitmaps in the .GFX library are numbered from 1. Unlike *show_image* and *show_frame, show_clipped_image* observes the current clipping boundaries. By default, the clipping boundaries are set to include the whole screen. *show_clipped_image does* support transparency.

show_frame

```
void show_frame(int x,int y,int image_number)    // protected
```

Displays the frame *image_number* of the currently active .GFX library at screen location *x,y*. The bitmaps in the .GFX library are numbered from 1. Unlike *show_image*, *show_frame* does not support transparency. Because it does not, it is faster than *show_image*.

show_image

```
void show_image(int x,int y,int image_number)    // protected
```

Displays the bitmap *image_number* of the currently active .GFX library at screen location *x,y*. The bitmaps in the .GFX library are numbered from 1. The *show_image* function supports transparency (pixels with value zero are not drawn), so this is a typical routine for animation.

show_number

```
void show_number(int x,int y,int number)    // protected
```

Displays the number *number* at *x,y*, using the active .GFX font. *x* and *y* are expressed in screen pixels. *number* should be positive.

show_print

```
void show_print(int x,int y,char* string)    // protected
```

Displays the string at *x,y* using the active .GFX font. *string* should contain only letters, digits, and spaces. *x* and *y* are expressed in screen pixels and refer to the upper left corner of the text.

Player (player.h)

Player is used in conjunction with *SceneDirector*. By using a *SceneDirector* with several *Player* objects, you can animate multiple characters simultaneously.

Constructor

```
Player(char* gl=0,char* sl=0,int intv=1)
```

Creates a *Player* object. *gl* is the .GFX library in which the character's graphics are stored, and *sl* is the .SFX library in which the sound effects for that chracter are stored. *intv* is the update interval for the character. This interval defaults to 1, which means that the *Player* is updated on every tick of the timer. A value of 2 means that the *Player* is updated every two timer ticks. The *intv* argument can be any positive number.

appear

```
void appear()
```

Causes the *Player* to become visible.

clip

```
void clip(int x1,int y1,int x2,int y2)
```

Activates clipping for the *Player*. *x1,y1* indicates the upper left corner of the new clipping region, and *x2,y2* indicates the lower right corner.

disappear

```
void disappear()
```

Causes the *Player* to become hidden.

get_imageno

```
short int get_imageno()
```

Returns the current image number for the *Player*.

getheight

```
short int getheight() const
```

Returns the *Player*'s current height in pixels.

getwidth

```
short int getwidth() const
```

Returns the *Player*'s current width in pixels.

getx

```
short int getx() const
```

Returns the *Player*'s current horizontal position.

gety

```
short int gety() const
```

Returns the *Player*'s current vertical position.

initialize

```
void initialize()    // protected
```

Loads the .GFX file for the player. This member function is called by Theatrix, but it is sometimes useful to override it to include other tasks.

isclipped

```
int isclipped()
```

Returns 1 if a clipping region is active; otherwise, returns 0.

isvisible

```
int isvisible()
```

Returns 1 if the player is visible; otherwise, returns 0.

set_imageno

```
void set_imageno(short int index)
```

Specifies the .GFX bitmap number. The *index* parameter specifies which image to use from the .GFX file. If the *Player* changes from frame to frame, this member function can be used to modify which image is used in the .GFX library to draw the character.

setinterval

```
void setinterval(short int inv)
```

Sets the *Player*'s update interval to *inv*.

setx

```
void setx(short int nx)
```

Sets the *Player*'s current X position to *nx*.

setxy

```
void setxy(short int nx,short int ny)
```

Sets the *Player*'s current X and Y positions to *nx* and *ny*.

sety

```
void sety(short int ny)
```

Sets the *Player*'s current Y position to *ny*.

stillframe

```
void stillframe(short int im,short int wait)
```

Displays image *im* at the current position and delays for *wait* ticks of the timer.

unclip

```
void unclip()
```

Deactivates the current clipping region. If no clipping region has been set, then the call is ignored.

update_position

```
virtual void update_position()
```

Does nothing. The intended purpose for this member function is to be overridden by a derived class. The new member function is then called by *SceneDirector* and should calculate a new position based on the *Player*'s role in your game.

SceneDirector (scenedir.h)

SceneDirector is designed for use with *Player*. Using this combination, it is possible to animate multiple characters simultaneously.

Constructor

```
SceneDirector(char* scfile)
```

Constructs a *SceneDirector* object. *scfile* is a .PCX file that is used as a background for the scene.

display

```
void display()    // protected
```

Clears video, displays the background image, and requests internal cues. This member function is called automatically by Theatrix when the *Director* object first takes control, and it is sometimes useful to override it. When you do, your derived class's member function should call *SceneDirector::display* in addition to whatever the override does.

on_escape

```
void on_escape(int)    // protected
```

Stops the *Director*. If you don't want the *Director* to stop when the Esc key is pressed, then override this function with an empty version.

on_timer

```
void on_timer()    // protected
```

Updates the screen. This is called automatically by Theatrix once each clock tick. You can override the function to add behavior.

SceneryDirector (scenery.h)

SceneryDirector provides a basic, simple interface for displaying background scenery.

Constructor

```
SceneryDirector(char *pcxfile, short int trans = ClearEveryTime)
```

Creates a *SceneryDirector* object. The *pcxfile* parameter is the name of the .PCX file for use as a background. The optional *trans* parameter defines how the *SceneryDirector* displays the background. The default value *ClearEveryTime* means that the whole screen is cleared (to color zero), and then the .PCX file is displayed. Alternatively, using the value *NoTransition* causes *SceneryDirector* to display images without clearing video memory. Also, values greater than or equal to 1 can be sent to the *SceneryDirector* constructor to invoke a fade-in effect.

display_original_scenery

```
virtual void display_original_scenery();
```

Displays the original scenery from the hidden page. Copies the hidden page buffer to the active and visible page buffers.

get_next_director

```
virtual const Type_info& get_next_director()    // protected
```

Returns the ID of the next *Director*. Unless a previous call to *set_next_director* has been made, this member returns *NextDirector*. This member is called by Theatrix and can be overriden to return a specific *Director* identification of your choice.

refresh_display

```
virtual void refresh_display();
```

Sets the active page to be the visible page and what was the visible page to be the active page. Then copies the now-visible page buffer into the active page. This function hides the mouse cursor before doing any page swapping and restores the mouse cursor afterward.

Theatrix (theatrix.h)

Theatrix is the object that encapsulates the whole game. It is designed as a base class for an object that will be instantiated in the *main* function of the program. Any *Director*-derived objects in the game should be created in the constructor of the *Theatrix*-derived class.

Constructor

```
Theatrix(char* str)    // protected
```

Creates a *Theatrix* object. The *str* parameter is a string that appears on the startup screen and is typically the name of the game.

enable_joystick

```
void enable_joystick()
```

Instructs Theatrix that the game uses the joystick. Among other things, this activates the joystick calibration sequence.

enable_netpacks

```
void enable_netpacks()
```

Activates the netpack event system. This is to be used if the game makes use of the serial communications abilities of Theatrix.

go

```
void go(int index=0)
```

This is the member function that makes it all happen. Theatrix initializes itself and puts in charge the *Director* indicated by *index*. The default 0 parameter causes the first *Director* created to be the first to be executed. Sending 1 causes the second *Director* created to be executed first, and so on.

go

```
void go(const Type_info& d)
```

This routine acts just like the previous version except that it starts the game with the *Director* specified as the parameter *d*.

joystick_extremes

```
void joystick_extremes(int *x1, int *y1, int *x2, int *y2)
```

Returns the extreme values that the joystick can return. Because the values returned by a joystick differ from one joystick to another (and from one computer to another), the extreme values that are retrieved during joystick calibration can be retrieved using this member.

set_xms

```
void set_xms(int mode)
```

Activates or deactivates XMS memory usage. Sending 0 or OFF prevents Theatrix from using any XMS memory. Conversely, sending 1 or ON informs Theatrix that if it is available, XMS should be used. By default, XMS memory *is* used. To take effect, this member function must be called before *go* is called.

use_commport

```
void use_commport(int port)
```

Instructs Theatrix to use the serial port *port* for serial communications (netpacks). If *enable_netpacks* is not also called, this call is meaningless (and harmless). By default, Theatrix uses comm 1.

use_video_mode

```
void use_video_mode(int vmode)
```

Instructs Theatrix to use *vmode*, instead of the default video mode defined in **settings.h**. To take effect, this member function must be called before *go* is called.

VideoDirector (viddir.h)

Derived from *Director*, *VideoDirector* provides a set of routines useful in managing graphic pages. Specifically, *VideoDirector* supports page flipping.

Constructor

```
VideoDirector()    // protected
```

Constructs a *VideoDirector* object. Because this is a protected constructor, it is possible to create such an object only by using derivation.

active_page

```
static int active_page()
```

Returns the current active video page. This is always either 0 or 1.

fill_background_buffer

```
void fill_background_buffer(int source_page)    // protected
```

Copies the contents of video page *source_page* to the background buffer page (page 2). Typically, this member function is called after a background has been loaded from disk or constructed on page 0 or page 1. Then portions or all of the background buffer page can be used to restore damaged sections of the active page.

flush_patch

```
static void flush_patch(int x1,int y1,int x2,int y2)
```

Copies a portion of the active page to the visual page. This is the only member function that draws directly to the visual page. This is useful when a change made to the active page must be synchronized and when a complete page flip would be inconvenient.

init_video

```
void init_video()    // protected
```

Clears and resets the page-flipping mechanism. Both pages involved with the page flipping (pages 0 and 1) are cleared to black (color zero), and the page-flipping mechanism is reset.

restore_page

```
void restore_page()    // protected
```

Copies the entire background page (page 2) to the active page. This is useful for erasing all sprites at once.

restore_patch

```
static void restore_patch(int x1,int y1,int x2,int y2)
```

Copies a portion of the background page (page 2) to the active page. This is useful for erasing sprites drawn on the active page. Because a clean copy of the background can be stored in the background page (with a call to *fill_background_buffer*), the restored patch looks like the original.

set_synch_patch

```
static int set_synch_patch(int x1,int y1,int x2,int y2)
```

Marks a patch (or rectangle) of the active page to be copied to the active page later. Several of these patches can be marked in this manner, and then all of them can be synchronized at once with a call to *synch_patches*.

show pcx

```
static int show_pcx(char* pcxfile)
```

Reads *pcxfile* from disk and displays it on the active video page. Also, the palette found in *pcxfile* is installed. If *pcxfile* is missing or corrupted, *show_pcx* returns NOT_OK. If all goes well, it returns OK.

show_video

```
static void show_video(char* fname,int x,int y,int nonstop=0)
```

Plays an .FLC file (video). The FLC file name is specified by the *fname* parameter. *x* and *y* indicate where the video should appear on the screen (upper left corner). The optional *nonstop* parameter can be set to 1 if the video should be played in a continuous loop.

stop_video

```
static void stop_video()
```

Interrupts the .FLC file. If no file is playing, the call is ignored.

swap_video_pages

```
void swap_video_pages()     // protected
```

Displays the active video page and hides the visual page. Typically, *swap_video_pages* is called after a scene has been constructed on the active (hidden) page. The routine then displays the new image, and the new active page (the old visual page) is ready for the construction of the next scene.

synch_patch

```
static void synch_patch(int x1,int y1,int x2,int y2)
```

Copies a portion of the visual page to the active page.

synch_patches

```
static int synch_patches()
```

Copies all the patches marked with *set_synch_patch* from the visual page to the active page. The return value is the number of patches that were marked before the call. Once this member function is called, all the patches are unmarked.

synch_video_pages

```
static void synch_video_pages()
```

Copies the entire visual page to the active page. This is useful for situations in whch it is necessary to synchronize both video pages.

video_playing

```
static int video_playing()
```

Returns 1 if an .FLC file is playing; otherwise, returns 0.

visual_page

```
static int visual_page()
```

Returns the current visual page. This is always either 0 or 1.

VocalHand (vocal.h)

The *VocalHand* class supports sound effects and voices by maintaining libraries of and playing back sound clips in the .VOC format. It is possible to derive directly from *VocalHand* and use the resulting class to do all the sounds for the game, or you can have each *Performer* play its own sounds. The latter is possible because *Performer* is derived from *VocalHand*.

Constructor

```
VocalHand(Director* d=0)
```

Creates a *VocalHand* object. Theatrix automatically detects and initializes the sound card and driver. If no sound card is detected, then calls to *play_sound_clip* are ignored.

get_num_clips

```
int get_num_clips()
```

Returns the number of sound clips in the active .SFX library.

get_sound_clip_length

```
int get_sound_clip_length(int clip_index)
```

Returns the length (in bytes) of the clip at the location *clip_index* in the active .SFX library.

load_sfxlib

```
void load_sfxlib(char* sfxlibname)
```

Loads the sound clip library *sfxlibname* (an .SFX file created with SFXMAKE) into memory. This member function should be called only in an *initialize* routine.

play_sound_clip

```
void play_sound_cilp(int clip_index)
```

Plays the sound clip in the active .SFX library at the location *clip_index*. The clip is played until it is interrupted by another call to *play_sound_clip* or the end of the clip is reached.

set_sfxlib

```
void set_sfxlib(char* sfxlibname)
```

Marks *sfxlibname* as the active sound library for this *VocalHand*. It is necessary to call this member function only if the *VocalHand* must play sound clips from more than one .SFX library.

sound_clip_is_playing

```
int sound_clip_is_playing()
```

Returns TRUE if a sound clip is currently being played, and FALSE if the sound card is idle.

stop_sound_clip

```
void stop_sound_clip()
```

Stops the sound card from playing the rest of a sound clip. If no sound is being played at the time of the call, the call is ignored.

Macros

Theatrix provides a set of macros to connect events to callbacks and to define mouse cursor screen regions. These macros define tables that the system uses to make the associations. Other miscellaneous macros are also discussed here.

The CUELIST (hand.h)

The CUELIST table associates events with callback functions. The program includes the DECLARE_CUELIST statement in a class declaration and puts a CUELIST declaration in the executable code within scope of the class declaration, as shown in this example:

```
class MyHand : public Hand  {
    // ...
    DECLARE_CUELIST
    void on_key_a();
    void on_timer();
};

CUELIST(MyHand)
    KEYSTROKE('a',on_key_a)
    TIMER(1,on_timer)
ENDLIST
```

CUELIST

```
CUELIST(class_name)
```

Begins a CUE table definition. *class_name* is the name of the class that contains the cues.

DECLARE_CUELIST

```
DECLARE_CUELIST
```

Declares that a class will have a CUELIST table. This statement must appear in the class declaration.

ENDCUELIST

```
ENDCUELIST
```

Terminates the CUELIST table.

HOTKEY

```
HOTKEY(key,cue_function)
```

Defines a relationship between the key *key* and the function *cue_function*. This means that whenever the user presses *key*, Theatrix invokes *cue_function* automatically. The *cue_function* function should be provided without class specification and without parentheses.

JOYSTICKBUTTON

```
JOYSTICKBUTTON(b,cue_function)
```

Requests that *cue_function* be called whenever the button *b* is pressed on the joystick. The *b* argument specifies the button and may be BUTTONONE or BUTTONTWO. The *cue_function* callback should be provided without class specification and without parentheses.

JOYSTICKMOVE

```
JOYSTICKMOVE(cue_function)
```

Informs Theatrix that whenever the joystick is moved, *cue_function* should be invoked. The *cue_function* callback should be provided without class specification and without parentheses.

KEYSTROKE

```
KEYSTROKE(key,cue_function)
```

Establishes a connection between *key* and *cue_function*. When the user presses *key*, Theatrix invokes *cue_function*. The *cue_function* function should be provided without class specification and without parentheses.

MESSAGE

```
MESSAGE(msg,cue_function)
```

Instructs Theatrix to invoke the *cue_function* whenever the message *msg* is posted. *cue_function* should be provided without class specification and without parentheses.

MOUSECLICK

```
MOUSECLICK(button,cue_function)
```

Establishes a connection between the mouse button *button* and the *cue_function* callback. The *button* argument may be RIGHTMOUSEBUTTON or LEFTMOUSEBUTTON. When the user presses a mouse button, Theatrix will invoke the *cue_function*. The *cue_function* callback should be provided without class specification and without parentheses.

MOUSEMOVE

```
MOUSEMOVE(cue_function)
```

Informs Theatrix that whenever the mouse moves, *cue_function* should be invoked. *cue_function* should be provided without class specification and without parentheses.

NETPACK

```
NETPACK(packet, cue_function)
```

Requests that if the *packet* is received at the serial port, *cue_function* should be called. *cue_function* should be provided without class specification and without parentheses.

TIMER

```
TIMER(rate,cue_function)
```

Instructs Theatrix to invoke the *cue_function* at *rate* times per second. *cue_function* should be provided without class specification and without parentheses.

The CURSORLIST (scenery.h)

The CURSORLIST table associates events with callback functions. The program includes the DECLARE_MOUSECURSORS statement in a class declaration and puts a CURSORLIST declaration in the executable code within scope of the class declaration, as shown in this example:

```
class MyHand : public Hand  {
    // ...
    DECLARE_MOUSECURSORS
    void click_left();
    void click_up();
    void click_down();
    void click_right();
};

CURSORLIST(MyHand)
    MOUSE_CURSOR(  0,  0,105,239, LEFTARROWCURSOR,  click_left)
    MOUSE_CURSOR(106,  0,211,199, UPARROWCURSOR,    click_up)
    MOUSE_CURSOR(106,200,211,239, DOWNARROWCURSOR,  click_down)
    MOUSE_CURSOR(212,  0,319,239, RIGHTARROWCURSOR, click_right)
ENDCURSORLIST
```

CURSORLIST

```
CURSORLIST(class_name)
```

Begins a CURSOR table definition. *class_name* is the name of the class that contains the cursor list.

DECLARE_MOUSECURSORS

```
DECLARE_MOUSECURSORS
```

Declares that a class will have a CURSORLIST table. This statement must appear in the class declaration.

ENDCURSORLIST

```
ENDCURSORLIST
```

Terminates the CURSORLIST table.

MOUSECURSOR

```
MOUSE_CURSOR(x1,y1,x2,y2,cursorshape,callback)
```

Defines a mouse cursor region and a callback function to be called if the user clicks in that region. The *x1* and *y1* arguments define the upper left screen coordinates. The *x2* and *y2* arguments define the lower right screen coordinates. The *cursorshape* argument is a pointer to a character array that defines the cursor's shape. You can use one of the globally defined constants listed in the next discussion for each cursor shape, or you can design your own and use the GMICE utility program, as described in Chapter 6, to convert your graphical mouse cursor to a character array. The *callback* argument is the address of a function that Theatrix calls when the user clicks the left mouse button within the screen region defined by the coordinate arguments.

Mouse Cursor Shapes (scenery.h)

Following are cursor shape global symbols that you can use for the *cursorshape* argument in the MOUSECURSOR macro. Figure 4.13 (Chapter 4) shows what all the cursors except the default cursor look like. The default cursor is the standard upward-left pointing arrow.

- ◇ UPPERLEFTARROWCURSOR
- ◇ UPARROWCURSOR
- ◇ UPPERRIGHTARROWCURSOR
- ◇ LEFTARROWCURSOR
- ◇ CENTERCURSOR
- ◇ RIGHTARROWCURSOR
- ◇ LOWERLEFTARROWCURSOR
- ◇ DOWNARROWCURSOR
- ◇ LOWERRIGHTARROWCURSOR
- ◇ DEFAULTCURSOR

Assert (debug.h)

Assert

```
Assert(condition);
```

The *Assert* macro works just like the Standard C *assert* macro. Theatrix implements its own version to allow an assertion to find its way to the functions that make an orderly shutdown of the game runtime environment, including the release of interrupt vectors.

Adjusting Theatrix (settings.h)

The following constant values define ranges and operating limits for the library. For most games, the values assigned to these settings suffice, but a large or unusual game may need to change one or more of these values. In this case, modify the value and recompile Theatrix.

DEFAULT_VIDEO_MODE

This is the mode number that Theatrix uses if one is not supplied using *Theatrix::use_video_mode*. This constant is set to 22, which is Mode X, but it can be changed if you want Theatrix to use another mode by default.

MAXDIRECTORS

Theatrix has a limit of 20 *Director*s to a game. If you need to use more, then increment this constant.

MAXFXLIBS

Theatrix allows a game to load as many as 30 .GFX and .SFX libraries. If you require more, increment this constant.

MAXHANDS

Theatrix has a limit of 250 *Hand*s to a game. If you find that this is not enough, then increment this constant.

MAXMESSAGE

Theatrix allows messages ranging in value from 0 to 200. This value can be increased to allow higher values as messages.

MAXNETPACK

Theatrix allows netpacks (packets sent over serial connections) to range in value from 0 to 100. This value can be increased. However, values greater than 255 do not transmit correctly, because the netpack system transfers bytes and a byte cannot contain a number higher than 255.

NUMPATCHES

Theatrix allows as many as 25 synch patches to be set at once (refer to *VideoDirector::set_synch_patch*). If you need more, increment this constant.

Keyboard ASCII Codes (ascii.h)

The global symbols shown in Table 7.1 are ASCII values for the keystrokes that you can use as the *key* argument in a KEYSTROKE statement within a CUELIST table.

Table 7.1 Constants for keystroke cues

Symbol	BIOS Key	Symbol	BIOS Key	Symbol	BIOS Key
END	0x4f00	INS	0x5200	F1	0x3b00
LF	0x4b00	DEL	0x5300	F2	0x3c00
LEFTARROW	0x4b00	ESC	0x001b	F3	0x3d00
HOME	0x4700	ESCAPE	0x001b	F4	0x3e00
UP	0x4800	ENTER	0x000D	F5	0x3f00
UPARROW	0x4800	SPACE	0x0020	F6	0x4000
PGUP	0x4900	SPACEBAR	0x0020	F7	0x4100
RT	0x4d00			F8	0x4200
RIGHTARROW	0x4d00			F9	0x4300
PGDN	0x5100			F10	0x4400
DN	0x5000				
DOWNARROW	0x5000				

Keyboard Scan Codes (scancode.h)

The global symbols shown in Table 7.2 are the scan codes that you can use as the *key* argument in a HOTKEY statement within a CUELIST table.

Table 7.2 Constants for hotkey cues

Symbol	Scan Code	Symbol	Scan Code	Symbol	Scan Code
SCAN_SPACE	0x39	SCAN_F1	0x3b	SCAN_A	0x1e
SCAN_ENTER	0x1c	SCAN_F2	0x3c	SCAN_B	0x30
SCAN_INSERT	0x52	SCAN_F3	0x3d	SCAN_C	0x2e
SCAN_DEL	0x53	SCAN_F4	0x3e	SCAN_E	0x12
SCAN_END	0x4f	SCAN_F5	0x3f	SCAN_F	0x21
SCAN_PGDN	0x51	SCAN_F6	0x40	SCAN_G	0x22
SCAN_PGUP	0x49	SCAN_F7	0x41	SCAN_H	0x23
SCAN_HOME	0x47	SCAN_F8	0x42	SCAN_I	0x17
SCAN_LEFT	0x4b	SCAN_F9	0x43	SCAN_J	0x24
SCAN_UP	0x48	SCAN_F10	0x44	SCAN_K	0x25
SCAN_RIGHT	0x4d			SCAN_L	0x26
SCAN_DOWN	0x50			SCAN_M	0x32
SCAN_BKSPACE	0x0e			SCAN_N	0x31
SCAN_TAB	0x0f			SCAN_O	0x18
SCAN_ESCAPE	0x01			SCAN_P	0x19
SCAN_ESC	0x01			SCAN_Q	0x10
SCAN_CTRL	0x1d			SCAN_R	0x13
SCAN_LSHIFT	0x2a			SCAN_S	0x1f
SCAN_RSHIFT	0x36			SCAN_T	0x14
SCAN_PRINTSCREEN	0x37			SCAN_U	0x16
SCAN_ALT	0x38			SCAN_V	0x2f
SCAN_NUMLOCK	0x45			SCAN_W	0x11
SCAN_SCROLLLOCK	0x46			SCAN_X	0x2d
				SCAN_Y	0x15
				SCAN_Z	0x2c

Controller Button Symbols (standard.h)

The symbols shown in Table 7.3 define button values on the mouse and joystick and are used in statements in the CUELIST table.

Table 7.3 Mouse and joystick button constants

CUELIST Statement	Symbol	Value
MOUSECLICK	LEFTMOUSEBUTTON	1
"	RIGHTMOUSEBUTTON	2
JOYSTICKBUTTON	BUTTONONE	1
"	BUTTONTWO	2

You can also use these symbols as arguments to Theatrix functions that expect button arguments.

Theatrix Technical Specifications

This chapter explains the Theatrix internal class structure and data files. We assume that you understand Theatrix well enough to use it and that now you are interested in knowing more about how it works. This chapter is a technical discussion of the operation of the class library, which will be of interest to programmers who want to enhance or modify the library. It also provides insight into the best ways to take advantage of the software framework when you design your games. You will learn about:

- ◇ How the classes operate
- ◇ How Theatrix uses data files

Classes and Data Structures

The implementation of Theatrix consists of several class hierarchies that combine to support the interface that you learned in Chapters 5 and 7. Those chapters taught you how to use the Theatrix library, so they presented only the public interfaces of the exposed classes and the protected interfaces of the classes from which you derive to build your game. This chapter delves more deeply into how Theatrix works and what the underlying classes are.

Theatrix

You learned to build a game by first deriving a game class from the *Theatrix* class and then having your derived class encapsulate and instantiate the components of the game: scenery, players, directors, sound effects, music, and so on. For this discussion you can refer to **theatrix.h** in Appendix B and, if you want to see more of the details of implementation, to **theatrix.cpp** on the included CD-ROM in \THX\SOURCE\THEATRIX.

A game must instantiate one and only one object derived from the *Theatrix* class before it constructs any of the other components of the game. The *Theatrix* constructor initializes a *current_game* global pointer to type *Theatrix* with its own address after asserting that the pointer is set to zero. That assertion ensures that no other *Theatrix* objects are instantiated. Other parts of the game use the *current_game* pointer to address the game object. Because the pointer is global, your instantiation of the object may be local. The demo games instantiate in their *main* functions an *auto* object of a type derived from *Theatrix*.

List of Directors

The *Theatrix* class maintains an array of pointers to the directors that constitute the game. When an object of type *Director* or one derived from *Director* is constructed, the *Director* constructor adds the object's address to the *Theatrix* class's array of director pointers by calling the

Theatrix::add_director function through the *current_game* pointer. The order of director object pointers in the array represents the logical order of directors in the game. That order figures prominently later.

Message Servers

The *Theatrix* class includes eight event *server* objects. These objects are part of the mechanism that dispatches event messages to components of the game. The complex event sensing and message dispatching procedure spans several classes and uses several data structures. The complexity of this approach provides the most efficient mechanism to achieve the desired result.

Event servers test for hardware events, and, when events occur, the servers cause the dispatching of messages to the callback functions for all game components that have requested cues for the specific events. The servers do not themselves dispatch the messages. That function is done by the *folder* mechanism in the *Director* class, but the event servers launch the folder functions that dispatch the messages.

There are event servers for events related to ASCII keystrokes, hotkey presses, timers, generic messages, mouse clicks, mouse movements, joystick motion and keypresses, and serial port network packets.

Event servers are declared *static* in the *Theatrix* class declaration. They would not need to be *static* to work properly, because there can be only one *Theatrix* object instantiated at any one time. The *static* declaration is used for performance reasons. Event sensing runs constantly, testing every event device for events and launching message dispatching when events occur. By making the server objects *static*, we avoid the overhead added by the compiler to initialize and dereference the *this* pointer for each use of a server object.

Each of the event servers differs according to the device it polls, but they all operate in a similar fashion. You can refer to these header files in Appendix B as you read this discussion:

Server	Header file
Timer	timesrvr.h
Keystroke	keysrvr.h
Hotkey	kdsrvr.h
Message	msgsrvr.h
Mouse click	mcsrvr.h
Mouse movement	mmsrvr.h
Joystick	jssrvr.h
Network packet	netsrvr.h

Each of the header files has an associated .CPP file on the CD-ROM in \THX\SOURCE\THEATRIX.

Messages are dispatched to objects derived from the *Hand* class. The object receiving the dispatch must be associated with an object derived from the *Director* class, either by being derived from *Director* or by receiving cues from the current *Director* object in control of the game. Each *Director* object has tables of event registrations. You will learn more about these tables, which involve objects called *folders* and *handlers*, later in the discussion about the *Director* class.

Event servers poll the devices and report events by calling the *dispatch* function associated with a folder object that contains the registrations of *Hand* functions with events.

The keystroke server is a typical event server. We will discuss its operation, and you can apply that knowledge to your understanding of the other servers.

All server classes are derived from the *Server* abstract base class, which is declared in **server.h**:

```
class Server    {
virtual void startup() { }
virtual void shutdown() { }
public:
virtual void check(Folder&) = 0;
};
```

Some servers override the virtual *startup* and *shutdown* functions if their devices have initialization and shutdown procedures before they can be used. Servers that have no such procedures do not override these functions. The *KeystrokeServer* class, shown next, does not.

```
class KeystrokeServer : public Server  {
public:
void check(Folder&);
};
```

When a *Director* object runs a game, it has a dispatching loop from which it calls the check function for all the device servers. Your program does not concern itself with the dispatching loop. The *Director* class takes care of it. The *Director* class includes folder objects for each of the devices, and *Director* passes to the server's *check* function a reference to the folder object. As you will see later, folder objects are specialized for the devices they support. Here is the *KeystrokeServer::check* function.

```
void KeystrokeServer::check(Folder& fld)
{
  unsigned char ascii,aux;
  fg_intkey(&ascii,&aux);      // test for a keystroke
  if (ascii || aux)
    fld.dispatch(ascii, aux); // pass the keystroke value
}
```

The *KeystrokeServer::check* function tests to see whether the user has pressed a key. If a key has been pressed, the *check* function calls the *dispatch* function associated with the folder object that was passed by reference as an argument. The *check* function passes to the *dispatch* function the two values that represent a keystroke. We used a function call from the *Fastgraph* library to test for the keystroke, but a BIOS call would have done the job just as well. If the user presses an extended key (non-ASCII), the *ascii* variable is set to zero and the *aux* variable is set to the key's keyboard scan code. If the user presses a regular ASCII key, the *ascii* variable is set to the ASCII value of the keystroke ('a', 'A', 'b', 'B', and so on) and the *aux* variable is set to zero.

The server only senses the hardware event. It is the folder's job to determine whether there are game components registered to receive a cue when the particular key is pressed.

Hardware Enable

The *Theatrix* class includes functions that the game application program can call to enable the use of XMS, the joystick, and the serial port for multiplayer games, and to set the video mode. The game program calls these functions after instantiating an object of a class derived from *Theatrix* and before using that object to launch the game, as shown here:

```
class MyGame : public Theatrix  {
  // ...
};

int main()
{
  MyGame mygame;              // instantiate the game object
  mygame.enable_joystick();  // game uses the joystick
  mygame.go();               // launch the game
  return 0;
}
```

System Startup

The game program calls the *Theatrix::go* function to launch the game. The *go* function sets things up so that the first instantiated *Director* object will run the game. To specify starting with a different *Director*, include its class *typeid* or its relative-to-zero position as an argument to the *go* function.

The *go* function calls the *startup* functions for each of the server objects and calls static *startup* functions for the *VocalHand* and *MusicHand* classes, too. These two classes have startup procedures that load and initialize sound effects drivers and MIDI drivers into memory.

The *go* function calls the static *Hand::initialize_hands* member function class to initialize all instantiated *Hand* objects. This is the only time that those objects' initialization function is called, so it is important that the program declare all instances of *Hand* objects for the entire game before calling the *go* function.

The *go* function initializes the video mode and then the mouse. Then the function runs a director-launching loop calling, in succession, *Director::display*, *Director::take_over*, and *Director::hide* for the *Director* object that is being given control. All the game activity for the scene being directed takes place from within these three function calls. When they return, the director-launching loop calls the old director's *get_next_director* function to compute an index to a new director to take over. The index is a subscript into the list of directors that the *Theatrix* class maintains. The director-launching loop continues until its call to *find_director_index* returns –1, which means that the game is over.

System Shutdown

When a game is over, the *Theatrix* object shuts down the event devices and the video mode in the reverse order in which it started them up. Each of the devices has a *shutdown* function that takes care of its own shutdown procedures—releasing interrupt vectors, restoring memory allocations, and so on.

System Abort

The *Theatrix* class includes *fatal* functions that do an orderly close down of the system before aborting. These functions, declared in **theatrix.h** display messages on the screen after restoring all interrupts and the video mode. One of the *fatal* functions accepts a *char** argument that points to the message to be displayed. This function is called from within the library when it finds exceptional conditions that require the program to stop.

The other *fatal* function supports the *Assert* macro, defined in **theatrix.h**. The function accepts two strings and an integer. The first string is the error condition, the second is the name of the source code file where the error was encountered, and the integer is the source code line number. The *Assert* macro replaces the Standard C *assert* macro to allow the game program to make an orderly shutdown of its devices prior to aborting due to a failed assertion.

Hands

The *Hand* base class exists to support the registration of derived class objects for event messages and to support mouse operations. You can refer to **hand.h** in Appendix B during this discussion. Directors and other game components derive from *Hand* so that they can request and receive event messages.

The *Hand* base class has only four data members: a pointer to the *Director* object that is in charge of the *Hand* object (when the *Hand* object is itself a *Director*, this is a pointer to itself); an indicator to tell whether the *Hand* object is using the mouse; a static count of instantiated *Hand* objects; and a static array of pointers to instantiated *Hand* objects.

When a *Hand* object is instantiated, its constructor accepts a pointer to the *Director* that directs the actions of the *Hand*. The object stores that pointer for later use and appends its own address (the *this* pointer) to the array of instantiated *Hand* objects.

Cue Registries

Most of the members of the *Hand* class support the registration of the *Hand* object to receive cues based on events. There are request and stop functions for each of the kinds of cues that a *Hand* can receive.

The **hand.h** file also defines the macros that implement the CUELIST table. When a derived class includes the DECLARE_CUELIST macro, the C++ preprocessor translates that statement into the declaration of a static array of structure objects that represent cues. Each element in the array contains an event code, a data byte, and the address of a callback function. The DECLARE_CUELIST macro also declares an inline function named *GetMessageMap* that returns the address of the array. That function overrides a virtual function in the base *Hand* class that returns a null pointer.

The CUELIST macro expands into the definition of the array that the DECLARE_CUELIST macro declares. There are several other macros (HOTKEY, TIMER, MESSAGE, KEYSTROKE, MOUSECLICK, MOUSEMOVE, JOYSTICKMOVE, JOYSTICKBUTTON, and NETPACK) that declare initializers to the array. The END_CUELIST macro declares the terminal entry and C++ tokens for the array.

The static *Hand::initialize_hands* function iterates through the static array of instantiated *Hand* objects and calls the *GetMessageMap* function of each one. If the function returns a non-null pointer, the program iterates through the array of event structures in the *Hand* object's message map. For each entry, the program requests the appropriate cue for the hand, specifying the callback function in the message map entry.

Directors

Objects of classes derived from *Director* run the game. The *Director* class is derived from the *Hand* class, so *Director* objects may request and receive cues.

One *Director* object at a time is in control of the game. As *Director* objects are constructed, they are added to the list of directors that the *Theatrix* class object maintains. Their order in this list represents their logical order of execution. The first director in the list is the first director given control. When that director relinquishes control, the second director in the list gets control. When the last director in the list relinquishes control, the game is over. Directors relinquish control by calling the *Hand::stop_director* function. If a director wants to pass control to a specific director other than the next one in the list, the controlling director (or one of its other *Hand* objects) calls *Hand::start_director* and passes the *typeid* of the director object that will take control.

Folders

Each instantiated *Director* object has eight objects of classes derived from the *Folder* class, which is declared in **folder.h** (see Appendix B). There is one folder for each of the event devices, and they are all derived from the *Folder* abstract base class. Each *Folder* class has a *dispatch* function that dispatches event cue messages to those *Hand* objects that have registered for the cues. The event servers previously discussed call the *Folder* classes' *dispatch* functions when events are sensed.

We will continue our explanation of events and messages by addressing the keystroke event. Each *Director* contains one *KeystrokeFolder* object, the essence of which is shown here. You can view the entire class in **folder.h** and **keyfold.h** in Appendix B.

```
class KeystrokeFolder : public Folder  {
  EventHandler key[NUMKEYS];
public:
  KeystrokeFolder() : Folder(key, NUMKEYS) { }
  void dispatch(int, int, int);
};
```

The array of *EventHandler* objects in the *KeystrokeFolder* class is the dispatching table. There is one such object for each possible event. In this case, there is one *EventHandler* object for each possible keystroke. The essence of the *EventHandler* class is shown here. You can view the entire class in **handler.h** in Appendix B.

```
class EventHandler  {
  LinkedList<subscription> slist;
public:
  void execute_callbacks(int p1=0, int p2=0, int p3=0);
};
```

Each *EventHandler* object includes a linked list of *subscription* objects. The *subscription* class is declared in **handler.h**:

```
struct subscription  {
  Hand* hand;
  callback cb;
  subscription(Hand*h, callback c) : hand(h), cb(c)
    { }
};
```

The *callback* type is a *typedef* declared in **hand.h** as shown here:

```
typedef void(Hand::*callback)(int,int,int);
```

Each *subscription* object contains the address of the *Hand* object that requested the event cue message and the address of the *Hand* object's callback function. Figure 8.1 illustrates the relationship of directors, folders, event handlers, subscriptions, and callback functions.

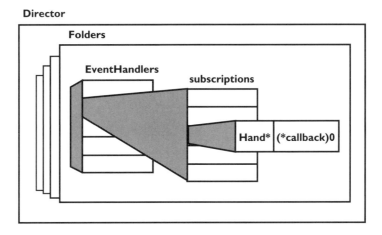

Figure 8.1 Event cue message data structures

A *Folder* object's *dispatch* function uses the data passed to it by the *Server* object's *check* function to determine which event occurred and which callback function to execute, as shown here:

```
void KeystrokeFolder::dispatch(int ascii, int aux, int)
{
  int code=(aux<<8)+ascii;
  if (aux)
    key[aux+AUX_OFFSET].execute_callbacks(code);
  else
    key[ascii].execute_callbacks(code);
}
```

The *KeystrokeFolder::dispatch* function uses the combined argument values of its *ascii* and *aux* parameters to develop a key code and to vector into its array of *EventHandler* objects to select a linked list of subscriptions to service.

Figure 8.2 illustrates the logical relationships between the game components during initialization and game play.

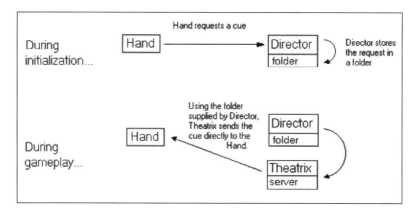

Figure 8.2 Event cue message logical flow

The *EventHandler::execute_callbacks* function iterates through the selected linked list of *subscription* objects and calls the functions that have values in the callback function pointer, as shown here:

```
void EventHandler::execute_callbacks(int p1, int p2, int p3)
{
  Hand* h;
  callback cb;
  subscription *ptr=slist.FirstEntry();
  while (ptr)   {
    h=ptr->hand;
    cb=ptr->cb;
    ptr=slist.NextEntry();
    (h->*cb)(p1, p2, p3);
  }
}
```

VideoDirector

The *VideoDirector* class, declared in **viddir.h** (see Appendix B), is derived from *Director* and handles full screen displays, page buffer management, and playing motion video clips. Some games might derive their director classes directly from *VideoDirector*, but most of them will use *SceneryDirector*, *SceneDirector*, or both. These two classes are discussed in the next section.

The main purpose for the *VideoDirector* class is to encapsulate the full-screen video functions of the graphics library. *VideoDirector* initializes the video system, displays a scene from a .PCX file on the screen, plays .FLC motion video files, and provides functions to manage the three Mode X video page buffers.

The class uses the graphics libraries functions to play .FLC files but does its own timing of the frame rate. An .FLC file includes a field that specifies its frame rate, but if we tell the graphics library to use it and the program displays a mouse cursor, there is an annoying flicker of the mouse. You have to hide the mouse cursor while you display each frame, and the graphics library uses its own built-in delay to implement the frame rate. The mouse cursor is hidden during this delay, resulting in the flicker. Instead of allowing that, we tell the graphics library to ignore the frame rate and to display one frame at a time. The overriding *iterate_director* function gets called once each iteration of the director's loop to check for events, and that function hides the mouse cursor, displays the frame, restores the mouse cursor, and then implements its own delay loop.

VideoDirector supports buffer page management with functions that copy, swap, and synchronize the contents of the three video page buffers. To use these functions, the programmer must understand the relationship between the three buffers and the other functions that write to the buffers. Most of these details are used and hidden by the *SceneryDirector* and *SceneDirector* classes.

VideoDirector supports the display of sprites by providing a low-level patch facility. A *patch* is a rectangular subsection of the screen, usually used to define the space that a sprite occupies. A program can build a table of patch regions by calling the *set_synchpatch* function once for each patch. Later you can use the *synch_patches* function to copy the patch regions from either the visible or the hidden page to the active page. You can also work with individual patches. To use these functions and work with patches, the programmer must understand the relationship between the three buffers and the other functions that write to the buffers. Most of these details are used and hidden by the *SceneDirector* and *Player* classes.

SceneryDirector

The *SceneryDirector* class, declared in **scenery.h** (see Appendix B), supports the display of static scenes where animation is not involved. Game programs use this class to implement information screens, menus, and help screens. *SceneryDirector* is also useful for implementing Myst-like games that involve high-resolution, 3-D modeled, ray-traced scenes where game motion is superimposed over the scenery with .FLC sequences.

SceneryDirector implements most of the mouse operations that games use. The header file defines the DECLARE_MOUSECURSORS, CURSORLIST, MOUSE_CURSOR, and END_CURSORLIST macros. When a derived class includes the DECLARE_CURSORLIST macro, the C++ preprocessor translates that statement into the declaration of a static array of structure objects that represent screen regions. Each element in the array contains rectangle coordinates, a pointer to a bitstream array that defines a cursor shape, and the address of a callback function. The DECLARE_CURSORLIST macro also declares an inline function named *GetMouseCursors* that returns the address of the array. This function overrides a virtual function in the base *SceneryDirector* class that returns a null pointer.

The CURSORLIST macro expands into the definition of the array that the DECLARE_CURSORLIST macro declares. The MOUSE_CURSOR macro declares initializers to the array. The END_CURSORLIST macro declares the terminal entry and C++ tokens for the array.

SceneDirector declares its own CUELIST table to be cued when the user presses the Esc key, space bar, or Enter key. These actions cause the *SceneryDirector* object to call *stop_director* to relinquish control to the next director.

SceneDirector

The *SceneDirector* class is derived from *SceneryDirector*. *SceneDirector* adds support for animated sprite actions and is a companion class to the *Player* class. The *SceneDirector* object in control expects to manage all the currently active *Player* objects. To make that happen, you construct the *SceneDirector* object and then the *Player* objects that it owns. If a game has several animated scenes, you should instantiate the *SceneDirector*s and *Player*s together so that they are properly associated. You can ensure that things work that way by instantiating the *Player* objects from within the constructor of the *SceneDirector* object.

The *SceneDirector* object maintains a list of the *Player* sprites that it controls. The order of that list implements the Z-order of the sprites when they are displayed on the screen, and sprites change their place in the list to change their Z-order as they move among one another. On each tick of the system timer, the *SceneDirector* object iterates through its list of *Player* objects and calls the *displayframe* function of each one so that the *Player*s can update their images and positions and copy the images into the active page. When all the sprites have done that, the *SceneryDirector* object swaps the active page—where the sprites wrote updated images—with the visible page so that the formerly active page is visible and vice versa. Then the *SceneryDirector* object calls *VideoDirector::synch_patches*, which restores the active page to the original background without sprites ready for the next timer tick and frame update cycle.

More Hands

All *Director* classes are derived from *Hand*. Other *Hand* classes implement sprites and play music. This discussion describes them and some of the classes that support them.

Media

Two of the classes derived from *Hand*—*VocalHand* and *Performer*—include objects of classes derived from the *Media* base class. This base class, shown in the file **media.h** in Appendix B, defines the common behavior of sound clips and graphical images.

Theatrix begins a game by loading into memory all the sound clips and graphical sprite images from disk file libraries. A structure named *MediaClip* describes the clips and images with respect to their dimensions, a pointer to their contents, and an offset into XMS where the clip or image can be stored.

There can be many libraries of clips and images. Each sprite usually has its own libraries of sounds and image frames. When the *Hand* object that represents a sprite is initialized, it calls the *Media::load_library* function to load its libraries into memory. The function reads the library and stores the clips or images in XMS if XMS is available, and in conventional memory otherwise.

The *Media* class keeps track of these memory libraries with a static array of objects of the *MediaLib* structure. This structure includes a pointer to an array of *MediaClip* objects, one for each clip or image in the library.

The *GetClip* function provides access to the clips and images. When a *Hand* object wants to make a sound or display its image, it calls *GetClip* with library and clip indexes to specify which clip or image to return.

As far as the *Media* class is concerned, these clips and images are bit streams to be read from a disk file, stored in memory, and returned to callers when callers ask for them. The only difference at this level between graphical images and sound clips is that graphical images have width and height dimensions and sound clips do not. The derived classes *GraphicsMedia* and *SoundMedia* make that distinction and add nothing more to the behavior of the base class.

It is up to the callers to *GetClip* to decide what to do with the bit streams once they have them.

VocalHand

The *VocalHand* class, declared in **vocal.h** (see Appendix B), is derived from the *Hand* class. *VocalHand* objects generate sound effects, and the *VocalHand* class gives the object the behavior needed to do that. The class's public interface includes functions to load sound effects library files, play and stop sound clips from those files, and test to see whether a sound clip is playing.

The *VocalHand* class includes a static object of type *SoundMedia* and an integer that specifies which of several sound libraries the object of the class is using. A Theatrix game maintains one *SoundMedia* object, which contains an array of *MediaLib* objects. At any given time, a *VocalHand* object is using one of those *MediaLib* objects from which to select sound clips to play.

When the *Theatrix* object calls the static *VocalHand::startup* function, the function attempts to load a sound driver program into memory. There are two possible sound driver programs. The first is DIGPAK's driver in a file named **soundrv.com**. Chapter 11 discusses DIGPAK. The other driver is the Sound Blaster's CT-VOICE driver. Both programs are what are known as *loadable* drivers, which means that you load them into memory from within your program and then call functions within them by using offsets from the beginning of the buffer where you loaded the driver. The CT-VOICE driver supports only Sound Blaster sound cards. The DIGPAK driver can be configured to support one of several sound cards.

The *VocalHand::startup* function loads the DIGPAK driver if it exists in the current logged-on subdirectory. Otherwise, it loads the CT-VOICE driver, first testing the SOUND environment variable to see where to find the driver file, which is named **ct-voice.drv**.

The DIGPAK driver has two function entry points in fixed locations from the start of the driver's memory. The first pointer points to the driver's initialization routine. The second pointer points to the driver's de-initialization routine. The program plays and stops sound clips by generating a software interrupt through interrupt vector 0x66 with register values specifying the functions to be performed.

The CT-VOICE driver has one entry point for all operations and uses values in CPU registers to specify the functions to be performed. The entry point is at the beginning of the load module and is a pointer through which you call to use driver functions. The program initializes the CT-VOICE driver by calling functions that set the IRQ, the port, and the address of a status flag that the program uses to test the status of sound clips.

Performer

The *Performer* class, declared in **perform.h** (see Appendix B), is derived from the *VocalHand* class. *Performer* adds the ability to display on the screen graphical images selected from a library of images. A *Performer* object can make sounds and display images of itself.

The *Performer* class includes a static object of type *GraphicsMedia* and an integer that specifies which of several image libraries the object of the class is using. A Theatrix game maintains one *GraphicsMedia* object, which contains an array of *MediaLib* objects. At any given time, a *Performer* object is using one of those *MediaLib* objects from which to select images to display. A *Performer* object uses its *load_gfxlib* function to load its library of images into memory.

When the *Performer* object determines that an image frame is to be displayed, it calls one of the image-displaying functions of its base *Performer* class. That function calls into the *Fastgraph* library to perform the display.

Player

The *Player* class, declared in **player.h** (see Appendix B), is used in combination with the *SceneDirector* class to give sprites the behavior of animation. The *Player* class is derived from the *Performer* class. It maintains information about a sprite's current image number and screen position as well as whether the sprite is currently in view. It also stores information about clipping parameters when a sprite is only partially in view.

A *Player* object assumes that it is being managed by a *SceneDirector* object. The *Player* constructor associates the *Player* object with the currently running *SceneDirector* object. When the *Player* object's *initialize* function is called from the *Hand::initialize_hands* function, the *Player* object loads its graphics and sound effects libraries.

A *Player* object is programmed to refresh its screen image at a regular interval specified as a number of clock ticks. Once every clock tick, the *SceneDirector* calls the *Player::displayframe* function. The *SceneDirector* has prepared the active page to be updated with new sprite images, and *SceneDirector* calls *displayframe* for each sprite in Z-order sequence so that the nearest sprite is called last.

The *SceneDirector* and *Player* classes coordinate the display of the sprites on the background scenery. The game-dependent sprite classes derived from *Player* specify which images from their libraries are to be displayed and where on the screen they are to be displayed.

The *displayframe* function uses a countdown variable to see whether the *Player*'s refresh interval has expired. If it has, *displayframe* calls *update_position*. A class derived from *Player* must provide an *update_position* function that, based on the game's circumstances, establishes the image number and position by calling *Player::setxy* and *Player::set_imageno*. The only valid place to make these changes is from within the *update_position* function. If a sprite class calls those functions from outside the *update_position* function, the *Player* class makes note of that condition, saves the changed values, and applies them just before calling *update_position*.

MusicHand

The *MusicHand* class, declared in **music.h** (see Appendix B), integrates MIDI music files into the game. *MusicHand* is derived from *Hand*, but it has no director. You usually instantiate an object of *MusicHand*, use that object to load an extended MIDI file (.XMI), and play selections from the file.

MIDI songs are supported only through the shareware MIDPAK driver, which is a loadable device driver very much like the DIGPAK driver. The *MusicHand::startup* function loads the driver, initializes it, and establishes communication with it to play songs. You communicate with the driver by using interrupt 0x66, just as you do with the MIDPAK driver.

Unlike .GFX and .SFX files and their drivers, only one .XMI file at a time may be associated with the MIDPAK driver. The *load_score* function allocates memory for the .XMI file, loads it into memory, and calls into the driver to associate the file's memory image with the driver.

Playing, stopping, and testing for music clips are done with calls to interrupt 0x66 with arguments set into the CPU registers.

File Formats

Theatrix uses four types of input files: .PCX files, .GFX files, .SFX files, and .XMI files.

Scenery: PCX

The .PCX format stores background scenery images in 320 x 240, 256-color format. The file consists of header data, a palette record, and an array of color bytes, with one byte per pixel.

Sprites: GFX

.GFX files are generated with the GFXMAKE utility found in the \thx\bin directory of the included CD-ROM. A .GFX file stores a variable number of graphical bitmaps, each of which can be any size under 64KB. Each record is an image stored as a binary stream. Figure 8.3 shows the format of a .GFX file.

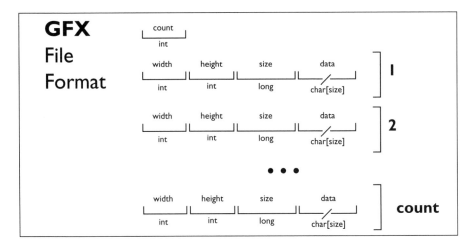

Figure 8.3 The .GFX file format

The data item is an integer that contains a count of the number of image records in the file. This count is followed by the image records themselves. Each record begins with the pixel width and height of the image when it is displayed on the screen. Next is a long integer that contains the size of the image bitmap in bytes. This size field is followed by the image bitmap, consisting of one byte per pixel in the image.

Sound Effects: SFX

.SFX files are generated with the SFXMAKE utility found in the \thx\bin directory of the included CD-ROM. An .SFX file stores a variable number of sound clips, each of which can be any size under 64KB. Figure 8.4 shows the format of an .SFX file.

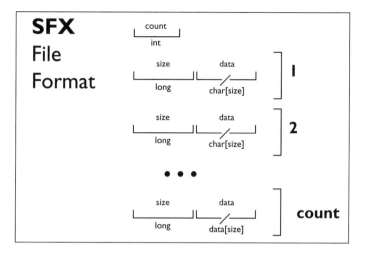

Figure 8.4 The .SFX file format

The .SFX format is similar to the .GFX format except that there are no width and height fields.

Music: XMI

.XMI files are collections of MIDI files. The format is required by the MIDPAK driver. The file is built from standard MIDI files using a utility program named MIDIFORM. The MIDIFORM program is part of the MIDPAK shareware distribution. Chapter 11 discusses MIDPAK.

Shootout (see figure above) is a complex demo game that has the simple, hand-drawn appearance of many arcade-style games. In SkyScrap (see figure below), the player pilots a jet fighter across a scrolling landscape and shoots at other craft that are shooting back. The game uses the joystick or the keyboard to move the jet fighter around and to fire shots. All the games illustrated in this insert are included on the accompanying CD-ROM.

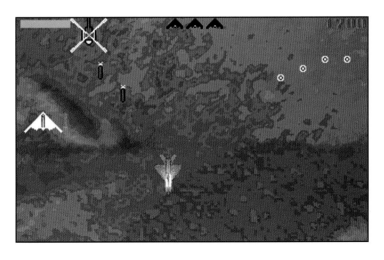

The Marble Fighter demo game pits two players in a kick-boxing match. Both players can be humans, playing at different PCs, or one player can play against the computer. Marble Fighter uses an intro screen, a help screen, and a menu in addition to the action part of the game.

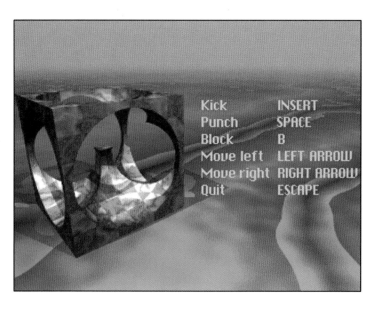

Kick	INSERT
Punch	SPACE
Block	B
Move left	LEFT ARROW
Move right	RIGHT ARROW
Quit	ESCAPE

A tombstone (see figure above) serves as Marble Fighter's menu which is designed so that page flipping can be used to change menu selections. The fighter objects can kick, punch, and block. The fighters use sound effects for hits, groans, and shrieks. The game records the scoring in video slider bars above the fighters (see figure below).

The skaters in these figures were built with NeoPaint. As a skater moves around in a figure eight, the program coordinates where the skater displays. To suggest a third dimension, the game moves the skater up the Y axis when the skater is skating away from the player (see figure above) and down the Y axis when the skater is skating toward the player (see figure below).

The sprites in these figures were built from MORAY 3-D models and rendered with POV-Ray.

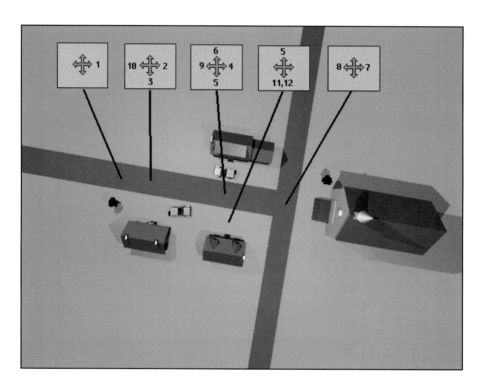

Planning the scenes in a game involves figuring out where the user's viewpoint should be for each scene. The figures show a map of a town by moving the camera high in the sky and pointing it downward. The game's camera locations can be determined for each scene. From these legends it can be determined where to place the camera to render each scene from the 3-D model, and which scene to change to when the user moves away from the current scene in one of the four directions.

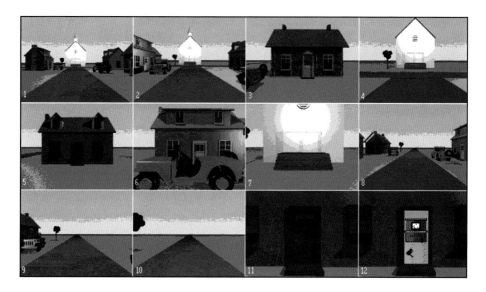

The figure above is a montage of all scenes in the Town demo game. Twelve scenes are not many for a complex game.

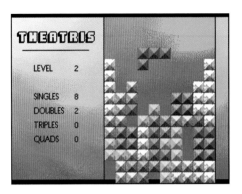

Theatris emulates a type of interactive board game that uses a variable number of games pieces that fall into a pit. This game features a unique menu, the implementation of the pit using grid logic, and data structures that implement the game pieces. The Tic-Tac-Toe demo game (see figure below) is a typical board game. It uses nonanimated sprites and adds sound effects.

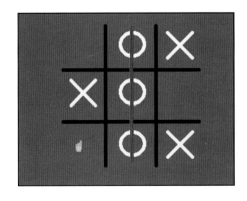

Development Environment

"Winning isn't everything, it's the only thing."
Vince Lombardi (attributed)

We've revealed the innards of a lot of software and data files so far, and we'll expose even more in Chapters 10 and 11. All the different components of a game program can be overwhelming. How does one keep track of all that stuff? How do several programmers on a development team keep in step?

This chapter explains how we organized the development of the demonstration games for this book. There were three programmers writing games and maintaining and modifying the library. Whenever there are multiple programmers, you'll find that concerns of organization, collaboration, and coordination become important. It's easier than you might think to let things get out of control. You can use this example of one project's organization to gather your own resources together and keep them in tow. You will learn how to manage these items:

- ◇ Subdirectories
- ◇ Source code
- ◇ Libraries
- ◇ Utilities and tools
- ◇ Data files
- ◇ Using a network
- ◇ Configuration management

The Game Developer's Subdirectory Structure

Figure 9.1 shows part of the subdirectory structure that you find on the included CD-ROM. This organization reflects the structure that we used to develop the demo games for this book. To keep the figure small, we do not show all the demos—only enough of them to illustrate how we organized our project.

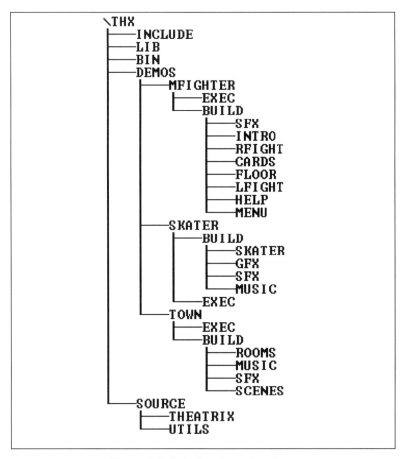

Figure 9.1 Subdirectory structure

Pay close attention to the subdirectories under the DEMOS subdirectories. These are the game projects themselves. Each subdirectory under DEMOS includes all the files needed to build and run one game. Your games might be organized similarly under an appropriately named subdirectory, such as GAMES.

Each game subdirectory has an EXEC subdirectory where the executable game program and its data files are built. The BUILD subdirectory is where we keep all the source code and data to build the game. Below BUILD are more subdirectories for graphical elements, sound effects, video clips, and so on.

Libraries and tools that are not a part of Theatrix (Fastgraph, and so on) are installed in their own subdirectories according to the conventions specified for the programs themselves. We will discuss the organization of these programs later.

Source Code

There are several source code categories that contribute to the game. In addition to your source code, there are the source code to the library, some header files, and the source code to the utility programs.

MAKE.CFG

The subdirectory \THX\SOURCE contains a file named **make.cfg** that you must modify in order to use the makefiles with the demo games. These makefiles include **make.cfg**, which establishes some global macros for making the game. You change those macros to reflect where you have installed the library and tools. Pay careful attention to these macros and double-check to ensure that you set them correctly. They permit the game makefiles to find header files, libraries, and tools.

Listing 9.1 shows **make.cfg** with a typical setup.

Listing 9.1 MAKE.CFG

```
#===============================================================
# MAKE.CFG - common make configuration (!included in makefiles)
#===============================================================
#          --->    User-configurable macros    <---
#---------------------------------------------------------------
# Set DRIVE to where you installed everything
# Example: DRIVE=c:
# (you can override individual DRIVE usages if you install on
# multiple drives>)
#---------------------------------------------------------------
DRIVE=c:
#---------------------------------------------------------------
# Set COMPILER to where you installed Borland C++
# Example: COMPILER=$(DRIVE)\bc45
#---------------------------------------------------------------
COMPILER=$(DRIVE)\bc45
#---------------------------------------------------------------
# Set MODEL to the memory model (t,s,m,c,l,h) of the compile
# Example: MODEL=l (recommended)
#---------------------------------------------------------------
MODEL=l
#---------------------------------------------------------------
# Comment out FGLITE to use Fastgraph commercial edition
#---------------------------------------------------------------
FGLITE=1
#---------------------------------------------------------------
# Set FASTGRAF to where you installed Fastgraph
# Example: FASTGRAF=$(DRIVE)\fg
#---------------------------------------------------------------
FASTGRAF=$(DRIVE)\fg$(FGLITE)
#---------------------------------------------------------------
# Set THEATRIX to where you installed Theatrix
# Example: THEATRIX=$(DRIVE)\thx
#---------------------------------------------------------------
```

```
THEATRIX=$(DRIVE)\thx
#-----------------------------------------------------------------
# Set DTA to where you installed Dave's .TGA Animator
# Example: DTA=$(DRIVE)\dta
#-----------------------------------------------------------------
DTA=$(DRIVE)\dta
#-----------------------------------------------------------------
# Set POVRAY to where you installed POV-Ray
# Example: POVRAY=$(DRIVE)\povray
#-----------------------------------------------------------------
#POVRAY=$(DRIVE)\povray
POVRAY=c:\povray
#-----------------------------------------------------------------
# Borland C++ work space
#-----------------------------------------------------------------
HEADERS=$(DRIVE)\temp\tcdef.sym
#-----------------------------------------------------------------
# Delete the COMPILEDEBUG macro to build without
# debugging information in the .EXE
#-----------------------------------------------------------------
COMPILEDEBUG = -v
#-----------------------------------------------------------------
#      --->     End of user-configurable macros     <---
#=================================================================
#  Set up debugging / nondebugging environment
#-----------------------------------------------------------------
!if $d(COMPILEDEBUG)
LINKDEBUG = /v
!else
COMPILEDEBUG = -DNDEBUG
!endif
#-----------------------------------------------------------------
#  Test for all required user-configurable macros
#-----------------------------------------------------------------
```

```
!if !$d(DRIVE)
!error DRIVE isn't defined
!endif
#--------------------------------------------------------------
!if !$d(COMPILER)
!error COMPILER isn't defined
!endif
#--------------------------------------------------------------
!if !$d(MODEL)
!error MODEL isn't defined
!endif
#--------------------------------------------------------------
!if !$d(FASTGRAF)
!error FASTGRAF isn't defined
!endif
#--------------------------------------------------------------
!if !$d(THEATRIX)
!error THEATRIX isn't defined
!endif
#--------------------------------------------------------------
!if !$d(POVRAY)
!error POVRAY isn't defined
!endif
#--------------------------------------------------------------
!if !$d(DTA)
!error DTA isn't defined
!endif
#--------------------------------------------------------------
THXINC=$(THEATRIX)\include
THXBIN=$(THEATRIX)\bin
THXLIB=$(THEATRIX)\lib\theatrix.lib
FGINC=$(FASTGRAF)\include
FGLIB=$(FASTGRAF)\lib\fg$(FGLITE)$(MODEL).lib
COMPILEPARMS=-d -c -w -m$(MODEL) -H=$(HEADERS) $(COMPILEDEBUG)
INCLUDES=-I$(FGINC) -I$(THXINC)
```

```
COMPILE=bcc $(COMPILEPARMS) $(INCLUDES)
LINK=tlink $(LINKDEBUG) $(COMPILER)\lib\c0$(MODEL)
CLIB=$(COMPILER)\lib\c$(MODEL)
EXEC=..\exec
#-------------------------------------------------------------


.cpp.obj:
    $(COMPILE) {$* }


#-------------------------------------------------------------
POVFILES=$*.def -i$*.pov -o$*.tga
POVSW=+v +x
POVDIRS=-l$(POVRAY)\include -l$(POVRAY)\fonts
#-------------------------------------------------------------


.pov.pcx:
    povray $(POVDIRS) $(POVFILES) $(POVSW)
    alchemy -o -p -8 $*.tga
    del $*.tga
    copy $*.pcx $(EXEC) /Y
    del $*.pcx


#-------------------------------------------------------------
```

Game Source Code

The BUILD subdirectories contain the source code for the game program. We included all of each game's header and .CPP files in this one game-related subdirectory. This subdirectory also contains the game's makefile.

Header Files

In addition to its own header files, a game program must include the header files for the class and function libraries that it uses. To build games, we use the standard C and C++ header files and two other libraries. The header files for the Theatrix class library are stored in \THX\INCLUDE. The header files for the Fastgraph graphics function library are in the \INCLUDE subdirectory under the subdirectory where you install Fastgraph. Make sure that Fastgraph is properly installed and that the THEATRIX and FASTGRAF macros in **make.cfg** are properly set.

Library Source Code

Although you might never need to modify the Theatrix class library, its source code is available to modify or merely for study. The .CPP source code for the library modules is in \THX\SOURCE\THEATRIX. The header files used by the library are the same header files that a game includes, and they are found in \THX\INCLUDE.

Utility Programs Source Code

Theatrix includes several utility programs for building and testing graphical elements and sound effects. The source code for these programs is found in \THX\SOURCE\UTILS.

Game Data Files

In addition to source code files, each game consists of one or more other component files—graphics, sound effects, movies—that contribute to its build. The organization of these elements into subdirectories is usually dependent on how many of them are involved and how the game uses them.

Background Scenery Files

If background scenery files are used just as they come from the paint or ray-tracer tools, you can store their .PCX files directly in the EXEC subdirectory; they need no conversion or other processing to prepare them for the executable game. We usually keep originals in subdirectories under BUILD and allow the makefile to copy them across. This technique permits us to build an entire game starting with an empty EXEC subdirectory.

Often, the scenery palettes must be normalized with one another and with the sprites and cursors in the game. In this case you must put the original copies of the .PCX files in subdirectories and let the makefile build the normalized versions for the EXEC subdirectories. To store these originals, you might use a subdirectory named something like BUILD\SCENES.

Sprite Image Files

A game with a few sprites might store all their images in one .GFX file. More complex games store the images of each sprite in its own .GFX file. Either approach works, but the latter is more manageable. The game build procedure converts collections of sprite frame images into .GFX files, and the makefile contains commands to make these conversions by using the GFXMAKE utility program.

We use a convention where each .GFX file is built from sprite image .PCX files taken from a sprite-dependent subdirectory. For example, the Skater game, which has only three sprites with only one moving sprite, keeps the images for the sprites in BUILD/GFX. The Shootout game—which has seven moving sprites, three doors that open and close, and digits that update a scoreboard—uses subdirectories for each of these sprite components and builds a separate .GFX file for each.

Sound Effects

A game may have one or more .SFX files to contain its sound effects. We usually store the .VOC sound clip files in a subdirectory for each .SFX file to be built. Most of our games use only one .SFX file and have a BUILD\SFX subdirectory to hold the .VOC files that make up the .SFX library file.

MIDI Music Files

A game can have only one .XMI file, no matter how many MIDI clips are used. We use a subdirectory named BUILD\MUSIC to store the .MID files that make up the .XMI library of MIDI songs.

Libraries

The object library for the Theatrix class library is stored in \THX\LIB. The object library for the Fastgraph graphics function library is in the \LIB subdirectory under the subdirectory where you install Fastgraph. Once again, make sure that Fastgraph is properly installed and that the THEATRIX and FASTGRAF macros in **make.cfg** are properly set.

DIGPAK/MIDPAK Drivers

Games that include music need a properly set up MIDPAK driver installed into their EXEC subdirectory. Games with sound effects that are to work with sound cards other than the Sound Blaster need a properly set up DIGPAK driver installed into their EXEC subdirectory.

Setting up these drivers involves the users' participation. They must run the program named SETUP that accompanies the DIGPAK/MIDPAK distribution. You cannot automate this process with a makefile unless you are the only user of your game program. You can, however, include the procedure in your own setup program or batch file that you distribute with your game.

The loadable driver modules do not exist before you run the DIGPAK/MIDPAK SETUP program. The SETUP program generates the files named **soundrv.com**, **midpak.com**, **midpak.ad**, and **midpak.adv**. Those files must be copied into the game's EXEC subdirectory before the game can generate sound and music.

Utilities and Tools

There are some utility programs and graphical and sound-generating tools that you use to build the game's operating environment. The most obvious ones are the compiler and its utilities. The make procedure uses several others discussed here.

Theatrix Utilities

Theatrix includes utility programs that build .SFX sound effect libraries and .GFX graphics libraries and other utilities that normalize palettes among the many graphical elements of a game. The executables of these programs are in \THX\BIN. You must have this subdirectory in your DOS path to run these programs from the makefiles.

POV-Ray

POV-Ray is a ray-tracing program that converts scripted 3-D models into .TGA graphical images. To run the makefile procedure, you must have POV-Ray properly installed and the subdirectory of its executable files in your path. We use POV-Ray to render some of our backgrounds and sprites.

Because of an exclusive publishing agreement between POV-Ray's proprietors and another publisher, POV-Ray is not included on the CD-ROM that accompanies this book. It is, however, freely available, and you may use it without having to pay license or royalty fees. It is available on the CompuServe Information Service in the GRAPHDEV forum.

Image Alchemy

The Image Alchemy utility program converts bitmapped graphics files from one format to another. You must have it installed and its executable subdirectory in your DOS path. We use Image Alchemy to convert from POV-Ray's .TGA output to the .PCX format that Theatrix uses.

DTA

One of the functions of Dave's .TGA Animator (DTA) program is to translate .PCX frame files into .FLC movie files. To use makefiles that build .FLC files, you must have DTA installed and its executable subdirectory in your DOS path.

MIDIFORM

MIDIFORM is a utility program that builds .MID files into the .XMI library format. The program is a part of the DIGPAK/MIDPAK distribution. You must have MIDIFORM installed and its executable subdirectory in your DOS path.

Game MAKEFILE

The makefile in a game pulls together the raw source code, the library files, and the graphical and sound elements to build the executable game, which consists of a DOS executable program, .PCX files of scenery, .SFX files of sound effects, .GFX files of sprite images, and an .XMI file of music. Listing 9.2 is the makefile for the Skater game.

Listing 9.2 *Skater makefile*

```
!include ..\..\..\source\make.cfg

EXEC=..\exec

all : $(EXEC)\skater.gfx  \
      $(EXEC)\skater.sfx  \
      $(EXEC)\skater.xmi  \
      $(EXEC)\pond.pcx    \
      $(EXEC)\skater.exe
   echo done

$(EXEC)\pond.pcx : gfx\pond.pcx
    copy gfx\pond.pcx $(EXEC)\pond.pcx

$(EXEC)\skater.xmi : music\skater.mid
    midiform $(EXEC)\skater.xmi music\skater.mid

$(EXEC)\skater.gfx : skater\skater1.pcx \
                     skater\skater2.pcx \
                     skater\skater3.pcx \
                     skater\skater4.pcx \
                     skater\skater5.pcx \
                     skater\skater6.pcx \
                     skater\skater7.pcx \
                     skater\skater8.pcx \
                     skater\skater9.pcx \
```

```
                    skater\skater10.pcx \
                    skater\skater11.pcx \
                    skater\skater12.pcx \
                    skater\skater13.pcx
  gfxmake $(EXEC)\skater.gfx @skater\skater.bld


$(EXEC)\skater.sfx : sfx\water.voc
  sfxmake $(EXEC)\skater.sfx sfx\water.voc


$(EXEC)\skater.exe : skater.obj $(THXLIB)
    $(LINK) skater,$(EXEC)\skater,, $(FGLIB) $(THXLIB) $(CLIB)
!if $d(FGLITE)
    echo > $(EXEC)\sk.bat $(FASTGRAF)\fgdriver
    echo >> $(EXEC)\sk.bat skater
    echo >> $(EXEC)\sk.bat $(FASTGRAF)\fgdriver /U
!endif
```

Observe the last five lines in the makefile in Listing 9.2. If you build a game program by linking with the Fastgraph Lite object library, running the game requires that you first load the Fastgraph Lite **fgdriver.exe** memory-resident graphics driver program. When the game exits, you should unload the memory-resident driver. The makefile builds a batch file named **sk.bat** that loads the driver, executes the game program, and then unloads the driver when the game program terminates.

Game Executable Files

Following a successful make procedure, all the files needed to run the game should be in the subdirectory named BUILD\EXEC. No other files should be in that subdirectory, so you can copy everything from it to your distribution disk. However, when you use BUILD\EXEC for testing your program, there are residual debugger files with names such as TDCONFIG.TD and TD.TR. You should delete these files before you build a distribution disk.

Remember that there are files associated with our CD-ROM that you may not distribute with your executable programs without first obtaining the necessary licenses. The DIGPAK and MIDPAK drivers have licensing restrictions, which are quite reasonable for commercial distributors and more than friendly to shareware and freeware distributors. You may not under any circumstances distribute the Fastgraph Lite shareware driver. You must obtain a licensed copy of the commercial Fastgraph linkable library and link your executable programs with that library before you distribute anything.

See Chapter 11 for a discussion of all the tools and how to license them.

Network Rendering

Ray-tracing is a time- and processor-intensive procedure. Some of our games have many scenes and sprites that we render with POV-Ray. Each time we change a model, POV-Ray has to render a new image of the scene or sprite frame. POV-Ray is slow.

In managing our project, we found many uses for a network. One of the most productive ones off-loads the rendering task onto a server on the network. We wrote a program named POVNET that runs on a server, waits for .POV model files to render and launches POV-Ray to render, the models into image files.

The POVNET program, described in more detail in Chapter 11, runs in a DOS box in the server (we used a Windows 95 site for the server). Whenever one of us has a new model to render, we copy the .POV model file into a designated subdirectory on the server. POVNET observes the new model and launches POV-Ray. We can monitor its progress from our work stations and retrieve the newly rendered image file to add to our game when POV-Ray has completed rendering it.

Configuration Management

Every software development project has this problem. How do you keep up with all the components of a program or system when more than one programmer are working independently on common or dependent elements of the system? With a one-person project, it is easy to lose control when there are many elements in a complex system. As you add people, the potential for error rises exponentially. A game project might involve many people—

programmers, artists, sound effects specialists, musicians, script designers, and so on. Each of them can be building and adding pieces to the game as development proceeds. Coordination and synchronization of the various pieces and parts can be an arduous task. There are steps you can take to get it under control.

Formal development projects use computer assisted software engineering (CASE) and version-control tools. We think that these tools not only are overkill for a game project, but they also tend to formalize, institutionalize, and bureaucratize an activity that starts out mainly to be fun.

We are going to discuss guidelines that you can use to implement procedures to help you control your project. They work if everyone is easy to get along with and can adjust to inconvenience from time to time. If, however, there are prima donnas on your team who are disagreeable and uncooperative, then these guidelines will not work. Neither will anything else.

The Objective

Your objective in software configuration management is to make sure that everyone works from a common baseline of software components and that when someone changes a part of the system, the following things happen:

◇ The change is tested with the baseline and works as intended.

◇ The change is tested to ensure that it does not interfere with, conflict with, or otherwise compromise the work that others are doing.

◇ When approved, the change is integrated into the baseline and everyone gets the new stuff.

Those objectives seem reasonable and attainable. But anyone who has worked on a software development project of any size knows how elusive these goals can be. Game projects are more fun than other jobs, but they are as susceptible to the vagaries of a disparate staff as any other kind of cooperative enterprise.

The Network

The network is a valuable tool in keeping a grip on the software configuration, especially if the network supports primitive groupware actions such as broadcast messages and protected read or write access at the subdirectory level. Netware, Windows NT, Windows for Workgroups, and Windows 95 all support mail and password-protected read-only access to remote subdirectories.

The Configuration Manager

In a big software development project, configuration management is a full-time job, perhaps even involving a staff of several people who watch over the configuration and keep it under control.

A game project will not usually be that big unless you are building one of those extravaganzas that involve Hollywood actors and who knows what. Nonetheless, on any multiperson software development project, the responsibilities of configuration manager must be assigned. One person should assume those duties, and the other team members must acknowledge and respect that person's authority.

This delegation of authority introduces an anomoly. The boss never wants the mundane duties of configuration manager. Yet the boss is usually writing code. All programmers view configuration management as a pain in the hindquarters—an impediment to getting things done—because it places a wall between them and the current baseline. They have to go through a bothersome procedure to implement a change. The boss, being a programmer, runs into that wall just like everyone else and sometimes uses his or her position to overrule the configuration manager's authority. If you are the boss, don't let that happen.

Nobody likes the configuration manager, so don't take the job if you need to be liked.

The Baseline

The baseline is a read-only repository of source code and raw graphics and sound files. Team members can retrieve files from the baseline, but only the configuration manager can change files in it or add files to it. The baseline represents the currently approved version of the system.

Making Changes

When team members work on parts of the system, they work with local copies of the baseline. The configuration manager maintains a record of which files are likely to change. Therefore, the configuration manager always knows—or should know—which files are being modified by whom, and, in rare cases, which files are concurrently and independently being modified by more than one team member.

When a change is completed, the team member submits it to the configuration manager and the other team members for review. You can use a public subdirectory on the file server for these submissions. The configuration manager then does whatever is necessary to achieve the three objectives listed above, sometimes merging the work of more than one team member to install their respective changes.

If you do all these things, you will maintain control of the configuration of your software. It is, however, a fact of software development that people throw out the time-consuming and bothersome control mechanisms when the deadlines loom near. You will, too. So did we.

Example Game Programs

"Few things are harder to put up with than the annoyance of a good example."
Mark Twain

OK, we understand. Most programmers turn to this chapter first. You want to get to the action straight away. Well, you are right. This is where the real fun starts. We are going to put into practice everything that we discussed in Chapters 1 through 9 (which you may not have read yet) by building some game programs. But if you skipped Chapter 5, you might want to return and read it now. This discussion starts there. Chapter 5 discusses the levels of abstraction at which you can work and explains the Theatrix class library hierarchy. This chapter completes that discussion by describing the demo game programs at each level of abstraction and teaches you how to implement different game features and styles.

Each demo program has lessons to be learned, and our discussions concentrate on what is unique about the lessons and the concepts the lessons introduce. You will learn about:

- ◇ Instantiating and running games
- ◇ Using the joystick and mouse
- ◇ Sound effects
- ◇ Video clips
- ◇ Sprite animation

- ◇ Music
- ◇ Menus and help screens
- ◇ Multiple-player games
- ◇ Games with many sprites
- ◇ Background scrolling

Textmode

The first game is called Textmode because it operates in the PC's text video mode at the lowest level of abstraction in a Theatrix game. Textmode teaches you how to derive a game class from the *Theatrix* class, derive *Director* and *Hand* classes, register for event cues, and use the keyboard and joystick.

The Textmode demo is not a graphics game. The program merely demonstrates abstraction level 1 of Theatrix. By staying in text mode, we can concentrate on program architecture and postpone our discussions of bitmaps and video modes.

The TextModeApp Class

Here is the *TextModeApp* class:

```
class TextModeApp : public Theatrix  {
  TextModeDirector* dir;
public:
  TextModeApp();
  ~TextModeApp()
    { delete dir; }
};


TextModeApp::TextModeApp() : Theatrix("Text Mode Demo")
{
  dir=new TextModeDirector;
  use_video_mode(3);
}
```

When the *TextModeApp* constructor runs, it passes a string to the *Theatrix* constructor. This string appears on the top of the startup display, and you use it in your games as a title. Next, the constructor creates an instance of *TextModeDirector*, to be discussed soon. The call to *use_video_mode* informs Theatrix that the game uses text mode 3 instead of the default video mode.

The *TextModeApp* destructor deletes the *TextModeDirector* object created by the constructor.

The main Function

Here is the Textmode program's *main* function:

```
int main()
{
  TextModeApp app;
  app.enable_joystick();
  app.go();
  return 0;
}
```

The *main* function creates an instance of our *TextModeApp* class. The demo uses the joystick, so Theatrix is notified with a call to *enable_joystick*. Then the program calls the *Theatrix::go* member function through the derived *TextModeApp* object. This function call tells Theatrix to initialize itself and start the game. When that function returns to *main*, the game is over.

The TextModeDirector Class

The following code shows the *TextModeDirector* class:

```
class TextModeDirector : public Director {
  void on_key(int key);
  void on_timer()
    { cout << "timer tick...\n"; }
  void on_joystickbutton1()
    { cout << "joystick button 1\n"; }
  void on_joystickbutton2()
    { cout << "joystick button 2\n"; }
  void on_joystickmove(int x, int y)
    { cout << "joystick moved: " << x << ' ' << y << '\n'; }
  DECLARE_CUELIST
public:
  TextModeDirector() {  }
};
```

The *TextModeDirector* class has five callback functions. The *on_timer* member function displays a message to demonstrate that the function received the cue. The *on_joystickbutton1* and *on_joystickbutton2* functions report that their respective joystick button cues were received. The *on_joystickmove* function reports that the joystick is away from center and what the joystick position coordinates indicate.

The DECLARE_CUELIST statement tells the compiler that a CUELIST table accompanies this class.

The *on_key* function, shown next, contains a switch and tests for two keys: the space bar and the Esc key.

```
void TextModeDirector::on_key(int key)
{
  switch (key) {
    case SPACEBAR:
      cout << "space bar pressed...\n";
      break;
    case ESCAPE:
      stop_director();
      break;
    default:
      break;
  }
}
```

This code demonstrates that a callback function can be used for multiple events. In this case, the *on_key* function is called when either the space bar or the Esc key is pressed.

The CUELIST table, shown next, tells Theatrix to call *on_key* when the space bar or the Esc key is pressed, to call *on_timer* every second, and to call the joystick functions when you wiggle or click the joystick.

```
CUELIST(TextModeDirector)
  KEYSTROKE(SPACEBAR,on_key)
  KEYSTROKE(ESCAPE,on_key)
  TIMER(1,on_timer)
  JOYSTICKBUTTON(BUTTONONE, on_joystickbutton1)
  JOYSTICKBUTTON(BUTTONTWO, on_joystickbutton2)
  JOYSTICKMOVE(on_joystickmove)
ENDCUELIST
```

The Startup Screen

When you run Textmode, it displays the standard Theatrix startup screen shown in Figure 10.1.

Figure 10.1 Theatrix startup screen

```
                        Text Mode Demo


   TIMERSERVER: hooked timer interrupt...
   KEYDOWNSERVER: hooked timer interrupt...
   looking for sound card...
   CT-VOICE driver initialized...
   A220 I10 D1 H5 P330 T6
     using port 220
     using irq 10
   looking for music driver...
   music driver not initialized...


   Move joystick to upper left and press a button
   upper left: 70/70


   Move joystick to lower right and press a button
   lower right: 147/145


   starting...
```

The information displayed on the startup screen depends on what the game includes. The top of the screen is the game's title, which you provide as an argument to the *Theatrix* class constructor. When the *main* function calls *Theatrix::go*, the rest of the screen is displayed.

In this example, the system found the CT-VOICE driver for sound effects, even though Textmode does not use sound effects. The startup screen reports the setting of the BLASTER environment variable and the port and *irq* values that Theatrix has extracted from that variable.

The music driver is not found in this setup, and the startup screen reports that condition.

Because the program has enabled the use of the joystick, Theatrix asks the user to move the joystick and press buttons to calibrate the joystick's extreme values and its center location. Then Theatrix starts the game.

Running the Textmode Demo

The Textmode game's only actions are to write text messages to the screen when its callback functions execute. There are callback functions for the space bar keystroke, the Esc keystroke, timer ticks, joystick buttons, and joystick movements. Figure 10.2 shows a typical Textmode game session.

Figure 10.2 Textmode running

```
joystick moved: -51 0
joystick moved: -51 0
joystick moved: -49 0
timer tick...
timer tick...
timer tick...
timer tick...
joystick button 1
joystick button 1
timer tick...
timer tick...
timer tick...
space bar pressed...
timer tick...
timer tick...
timer tick...
space bar pressed...
timer tick...
```

While the demo runs, you see the "timer tick..." text message displayed once every second. This text is displayed as the result of a timer cue, which was requested to send one cue per second. Now press the space bar. A new text message appears, indicating that the space bar was pressed and the program sent the keypress cue to report that event. Move the joystick around. While the joystick is off center, the system cues the program, and the program displays text messages to report the joystick position. To exit from the program, press Esc at any time.

Timer tick messages are sent once every interval as specified by the CUELIST tables's TIMER statement. Joystick movement messages continue to be sent as long as the user holds the joystick away from the center position. Joystick button messages continue to be sent as long as the user holds the joystick button down. When you press the Esc key, the game stops and exits to DOS.

Mouse

The Mouse program demonstrates the use of the mouse in a game. The program is not so much a game as it is a demonstration. You don't play for points or attempt to vanquish opponents. You just run the program, move the mouse, and observe its effects. Figure 10.3 shows the demo in progress.

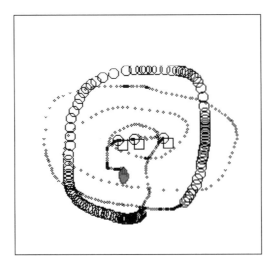

Figure 10.3 Running the Mouse demo

The MouseDemo Class

The *MouseDemo* class is derived from *SceneryDirector* so that it can use the mouse cursor shapes feature of that class:

```
class MouseDemo : public SceneryDirector  {
  void display();
  void hide();
  void on_quit(int,int,int);
  void on_click(int x,int y,int b);
  void on_move(int x,int y,int b);
  void on_centerclick(int, int);
  DECLARE_CUELIST
```

```
   DECLARE_MOUSECURSORS
public:
  MouseDemo()
    { }
};

CUELIST(MouseDemo)
  MOUSECLICK(RIGHTMOUSEBUTTON,on_quit)
  MOUSECLICK(LEFTMOUSEBUTTON,on_click)
  MOUSEMOVE(on_move)
  KEYSTROKE(ESC, on_quit)
ENDCUELIST

CURSORLIST(MouseDemo)
  MOUSE_CURSOR(  0,  0,105, 79,UPPERLEFTARROWCURSOR, 0)
  MOUSE_CURSOR(106,  0,211, 79,UPARROWCURSOR, 0)
  MOUSE_CURSOR(212,  0,319, 79,UPPERRIGHTARROWCURSOR, 0)
  MOUSE_CURSOR(  0, 80,105,159,LEFTARROWCURSOR, 0)
  MOUSE_CURSOR(106, 80,211,159,CENTERCURSOR, on_centerclick)
  MOUSE_CURSOR(212, 80,319,159,RIGHTARROWCURSOR, 0)
  MOUSE_CURSOR(  0,160,105,239,LOWERLEFTARROWCURSOR, 0)
  MOUSE_CURSOR(106,160,211,239,DOWNARROWCURSOR, 0)
  MOUSE_CURSOR(212,160,319,239,LOWERRIGHTARROWCURSOR, 0)
ENDCURSORLIST
```

The cursor shapes called out in the MOUSE_CURSOR statements are taken from the standard shapes that the *SceneryDirector* class provides.

Mouse Events

The program's callback functions draw shapes on the screen by using some of the Fastgraph library's graphical functions. For example, the *on_move* callback function is called whenever the mouse is moved and calls *fg_move* and *fg_circle*:

```
void MouseDemo::on_move(int x,int y,int b)
{
  fg_move(x,y);
  mouse_invisible();
  fg_circle((b & LEFTMOUSEBUTTON) ? 5 : 1);
  mouse_visible();
}
```

Moving the mouse draws a circle. If the left mouse button is not down, the circle is tiny, and the effect is that of scribing a wavy line on the screen. If the left mouse button is down, the program draws a larger circle, which seems to drag the circle around the screen, leaving trails.

Your game programs might or might not use the underlying Fastgraph graphical functions. We use them here only to demonstrate the behavior of the mouse events. Games involving scenery and sprites do not need to address these lower levels of abstraction.

Planet

The Planet demo displays a small moon bouncing around the screen over the top of a large planet. The file named **planet.pcx** contains an image of the background scene, which depicts the planet. The file named **sphere.pcx** contains an image of the sprite.

The game achieves this bouncing effect by doing the following:

1. It draws the background on a hidden video page.
2. It draws the moon on top of the background image.
3. It swaps the video pages so that the newly constructed image becomes visible.
4. It repeats these steps until the Esc key is pressed.

The DemoDirector Class

The *DemoDirector* class displays the background, creates and updates the moon, and ends the demo when the user presses the Esc key:

```
class DemoDirector : public VideoDirector {
  void display();
  void on_timer();
  void on_esc(int);
  Sprite* moon;
  int x,y;
  int xinc,yinc;
public:
    DemoDirector();
};
```

DemoDirector has two callback functions: *on_timer* and *on_esc*. The *display* member is not a callback; it overrides a virtual member function of the base *Director* class. Theatrix calls *display* one time when the *Director* object takes control of the game, so this is where we write our code to display the background.

The *DemoDirector* constructor is shown next:

```
DemoDirector::DemoDirector()
{
  moon=new Sprite("demo.gfx","demo.sfx");
  x=y=20;
  xinc=yinc=INC;
}
```

The first line creates an object of a class called *Sprite*, which we will look at soon. The *Sprite* object is the moon, which moves over the background. Note that the *Sprite* constructor takes two parameters. One is the .GFX library that contains the moon's bitmap image to display on the screen, and the other is the .SFX library, which contains one sound clip. (The moon makes a noise when it changes direction.)

The next two lines in the *DemoDirector* constructor initialize some integer data members. The moon's location starts at screen position 20,20. The *xinc* and *yinc* members are initialized with the constant INC, which the program defines as the value 4. These variables are used to increment the moon's position on each update.

DemoDirector first displays the background on the screen from its overridden *display* member function. *DemoDirector::display* is shown here:

```
void DemoDirector::display()
{
  init_video();
  show_pcx("planet.pcx");
  swap_video_pages();
  synch_video_pages();
  fill_background_buffer(active_page());
}
```

This seems like a lot of code just to display a background, so let's consider what's happened. The functions called by the *display* function are members of the base *VideoDirector* class. The *init_video* member function clears the video pages and initializes the page-flipping mechanism. The *show_pcx* function displays the .PCX file **planet.pcx** on the screen. Three more things need to happen. First, only the hidden page contains the .PCX image at this point. This hidden page is also referred to as the *active* page, because all graphics calls affect the active page instead of the visible page. Recall a previous discussion on page-flipping. While the user is looking at the visible page, we are constructing a new page on the active page. So *swap_video_pages* makes our new image visible, and now we have a new, active page (the page that was previously visible and that, at the moment, contains nothing related to the game).

The second thing that needs to happen is the call to *synch_video_pages*, which synchronizes the two video pages so that they both contain the image that was just constructed and that is now being viewed.

Now one task remains. We need to make a copy of the background that we will never overwrite. This copy is kept in the background page buffer. The call to *fill_background_buffer* makes this copy. The parameter specifies that the active page is the source for our background image. Because both the active page and the visible page contain identical images at this point, it does not matter which page we use.

The *DemoDirector* class needs a CUELIST table:

```
CUELIST(DemoDirector)
   TIMER(18,on_timer)
   KEYSTROKE(ESC,on_esc)
ENDCUELIST
```

The TIMER statement in the CUELIST table tells Theatrix to call our *on_timer* callback 18 times every second and to call our *on_esc* function whenever the user presses the Esc key. Here is the *on_esc* function:

```
void DemoDirector::on_esc(int)
{
   stop_director();
}
```

When the user presses the Esc key, the *DemoDirector* object stops itself.

The *on_timer* function is shown next:

```
void DemoDirector::on_timer()
{
   moon->move_to(x+=xinc,y+=yinc);
   swap_video_pages();
   if (x<5 || x>280)  {
       xinc=-xinc;
       moon->bounce();
   }
   if (y<5 || y>190)   {
       yinc=-yinc;
       moon->bounce();
   }
}
```

This code is more complicated but is not hard to understand. The first line tells the moon to move to a new location. Once the moon has displayed itself, the video pages are swapped so that the new image becomes visible.

The *if* statements after *swap_video_pages* reverse the moon's direction when it gets too close to the edge of the screen. When the moon's direction changes, the *Sprite::bounce* member is called to play a sound effect.

The Sprite Class

The *Sprite* class declaration looks like this:

```
class Sprite : public Performer  {
  char gfxlib[13];
  char sfxlib[13];
  int image;
  int w,h;
  int xq[2];
  int yq[2];
public:
  Sprite(char* gfxlib,char* sfxlib);
  void initialize();
  void move_to(int x,int y);
  void bounce();
};
```

The *Sprite* constructor initializes the object's data members:

```
Sprite::Sprite(char* gfxlibname,char* sfxlibname)
{
  strcpy(gfxlib,gfxlibname);
  strcpy(sfxlib,sfxlibname);
  image=IMAGENO;
}
```

When the game starts, the sprite must load its .GFX and .SFX libraries into memory. Each *Hand* has a virtual member function called *initialize* that is called once per execution of the game when the game begins. This function is where the .GFX and .SFX libraries are loaded. The *Sprite::initialize* member is shown next:

```
void Sprite::initialize()
{
  load_gfxlib(gfxlib);
  load_sfxlib(sfxlib);
  w=get_image_width(image);
  h=get_image_height(image);
  xq[0]=xq[1]=0;
  yq[0]=yq[1]=0;
}
```

The *initialize* function loads its libraries and calls two *VideoDirector* member functions to get the height and width of the image. It sets its initial screen position to 0/0.

The *Sprite::move_to* function changes the moon's position at each tick of the timer. The function is defined this way:

```
void Sprite::move_to(int newx,int newy)
{
  static int qi;
  VideoDirector::restore_patch(xq[qi],yq[qi],
                          xq[qi]+w-1,yq[qi]+h-1);
  show_image(newx,newy,image);
  xq[qi]=newx;
  yq[qi]=newy;
  qi=(qi+1)%2;
}
```

Here we learn more about the page-flipping technique at this level of abstraction. First, *Sprite::move_to* has to erase its old image before drawing the new one, which is not as easy as it sounds. *Sprite* cannot simply remember its location and then erase itself at the same location—it operates on two pages. *Sprite* must maintain a small circular queue in order to track where it was last drawn on each page. The queue can hold only two values: one for each page. Two queues are maintained: one for the X value and a second one for Y.

The *VideoDirector::restore_patch* function copies rectangles from the background buffer to the active page. (Remember that we filled the background buffer with a copy of the background image in *DemoDirector::display*.) The call to *restore_patch* uses the queue to look up where the sprite was drawn on the active page, and *restore_patch* erases the sprite. Then the image is drawn at the new location with a call to *show_image*. Now the queue must be updated with the *newx* and *newy* values. Finally, *qi*, which toggles between 0 and 1 to access the queue, is updated.

The PlanetDemo Class

The *PlanetDemo* class derives from the *Theatrix* class to implement and run the game:

```
class PlanetDemo : public Theatrix  {
public:
  PlanetDemo() : Theatrix("Planet")
    { demo=new DemoDirector; }
  ~PlanetDemo()
    { delete demo; }
private:
  DemoDirector* demo;
};
```

The *PlanetDemo* constructor instantiates a *DemoDirector* object from the free store. The destructor deletes that object.

The main Function

The *main* function instantiates an object of type *PlanetDemo* and calls its *go* function. When the *go* function returns, the game is over:

```
void main()
{
  PlanetDemo demo;
  demo.go();
}
```

Figure 10.4 is a screen shot taken from the Planet demo game.

Figure 10.4 The Planet demo

Tic-Tac-Toe

The Tic-Tac-Toe demo game is a typical board game. It demonstrates the use of the *Performer* class as a base from which to derive nonanimated sprites. The game also adds sound effects. Each move is punctuated by a silly spoken message from the game to the player. Figure 10.5 shows the board with a game under way.

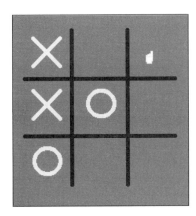

Figure 10.5 The Tic-Tac-Toe board

The game uses a CURSORLIST table to divide the board into its nine segments, as shown here:

```
CURSORLIST(TicTacToe)
    MOUSE_CURSOR( 70,  18, 128,  75, UPCURSOR, position1)
    MOUSE_CURSOR( 136, 18, 200,  75, UPCURSOR, position2)
    MOUSE_CURSOR( 208, 18, 266,  75, UPCURSOR, position3)
    MOUSE_CURSOR( 70,  82, 128, 146, UPCURSOR, position4)
    MOUSE_CURSOR( 136, 82, 200, 146, UPCURSOR, position5)
    MOUSE_CURSOR( 208, 82, 266, 146, UPCURSOR, position6)
    MOUSE_CURSOR( 70, 154, 128, 210, UPCURSOR, position7)
    MOUSE_CURSOR( 136, 154, 200, 210, UPCURSOR, position8)
    MOUSE_CURSOR( 208, 154, 266, 210, UPCURSOR, position9)
ENDCURSORLIST
```

The game player makes the first move by clicking on one of the segments. Each time the player makes a move, the game posts that move and calculates its own next move.

Sound Clips

Before making a move, the game speaks a phrase, the contents of which depend on whether the game is making a winning move, blocking the player's winning move, or simply getting the next available space. Here is how the game identifies the different phrases:

```
enum soundclip {
  iwin = 1,
  youwin,
  tie,
  notthere,
  hmm,
  ohno,
  nowwhat
};
```

A Voice Class

The game uses a *Voice* class to encapsulate the sound effects:

```
class Voice : public VocalHand  {
  void initialize()
    { load_sfxlib("ttt.sfx"); }
public:
  Voice(Director *dir) : VocalHand(dir)
    { }
};
```

Playing Sound Clips

The game instantiates an object of this class and uses the object to speak the phrases in the .SFX library, as shown here:

```
// ---- computer says something
void TicTacToe::say(soundclip clip)
{
  voice->play_sound_clip(clip);
  while (voice->sound_clip_is_playing())
    ;
}
```

Building the .SFX Library

The makefile must cooperate in the building of the .SFX library so that the sound effects are in proper sequence as defined by the *soundclip* declaration. The makefile's entry for building the .SFX file is as follows:

```
$(EXEC)\ttt.sfx : sfx\iwin.voc      \
                  sfx\youwin.voc    \
                  sfx\tie.voc       \
                  sfx\notthere.voc  \
                  sfx\hmm.voc       \
                  sfx\ohno.voc      \
                  sfx\nowwhat.voc
   sfxmake $(EXEC)\ttt.sfx $**
```

Skater

The Skater demo program illustrates sprite animation at the fifth and highest level of abstraction. The Skater demo also uses music and sound effects. You learned from the discussion of Tic-Tac-Toe how to add sound effects to a game. Now we'll discuss how to add music.

The Skater demo is found on the included CD-ROM in the \THX\DEMOS\SKATER directory. The demo involves a skating pond with three skaters. Actually, only one of the skaters is skating; the other two are just standing. The skater is doing a figure eight around both of the standers. The demo illustrates the use of *Player* and *SceneDirector*, and is also an example of how to manage the Z-order of sprites. The skater, in the course of his figure eight, skates at one point behind the far stander, then, at the center of the eight, between the two standers, and, finally, in front of the near stander. This pattern is made possible by changing the skater's Z-order relative to the two standing sprites.

The Pond Class

First, a class named *Pond* is derived from *SceneDirector*:

```
class Pond : public SceneDirector   {
  Stander *stander1;
  Stander *stander2;
  Skater *skater;
  MusicHand *conductor;
  void on_timer();
  void on_enter();
  void display();
  void hide();
public:
  Pond();
  ~Pond();
};
```

Aside from the constructor and destructor, the only member function we'll discuss here is *on_timer*, which is a callback. There are also three pointers that point to the three skaters and a pointer to a *MusicHand* object. (Notice that because two of the sprites don't actually skate in the demo, they are called *Stander*s.) Let's look first at the constructor:

```
Pond::Pond() : SceneDirector("pond.pcx") {
  // --- most distant stationary sprite
  stander1 = new Stander;
  stander1->set_imageno(10);
  stander1->setxy(180,100);
  stander1->appear();
  // --- closest stationary sprite
  stander2 = new Stander;
  stander2->set_imageno(9);
  stander2->setxy(140,130);
  stander2->appear();
  // --- moving sprite
  skater = new Skater;
  conductor = new MusicHand("skater.xmi");
}
```

In addition to creating two *Stander* and one *Skater* objects, the constructor gives instructions to the *Stander* objects. The *set_imageno* member function tells the *Stander* which .GFX library image to use to draw itself. The *setxy* member tells the *Stander* where to stand. Finally, the *appear* member tells the *Stander* that it is visible. *Stander* is derived from *Player*; these member functions are defined in *Player*.

The *Pond* destructor deletes the three objects created in the constructor. The *on_timer* callback function implements most of the *Pond* class's functionality:

```
void Pond::on_timer()
{
  SceneDirector::on_timer();
  if (skater->steps == 0) {
    switch (skater->mode)  {
      case 1:
        // -- front lateral segment
        // -- set moving sprite in front of others
        MoveZToFront(skater);
        break;
      case 3:
      case 7:
        // -- center lateral segment
        // set moving sprite between other two
        // ChangeZOrder(skater,stander2);
        break;
      case 5:
        // -- rear lateral segment
        // set moving sprite behind others
        changeZOrder(skater,stander1);
        break;
      default:
        break;
    }
  }
}
```

Hcrc is how the Z-order is maintained during the figure eight. Each mode of *Skater* represents a segment of the figure eight. Each section in the *switch* statement handles a different segment. For some segments (mode 2, for example), no change in Z-order is needed, but others require that the skater's

Z-order change, and this is done with calls to the *SceneDirector::changeZOrder* member function.

The first thing that the *Pond::on_timer* callback does is to call *SceneDirector::on_timer*. This *Pond::on_timer* member function overrides *SceneDirector::on_timer*, which needs to execute, so the overriding function calls the overridden function. Because *SceneDirector::on_timer* is responsible for updating the *Player* objects, forgetting to call it produces unwanted results.

The Skater Class

Now let's examine the *Skater* class:

```
class Skater : public Player
{
  short int steps;
  short int mode;
  friend class Pond;
  void on_enter();
protected:
  DECLARE_CUELIST
public:
  Skater();
  virtual ~Skater() { }
  void update_position();
};
```

A callback function named *on_enter* is defined, and because the callback is to be connected to the Enter key cue via the CUELIST macros, the DECLARE_CUELIST statement is required. A member function called *update_position* overrides *Player::update_position*, which is called by *SceneDirector* for each frame interval. *Player::update_position* gives the *Player* an opportunity to change its location and image.

The *steps* data member keeps track of how far along the skater is in a segment. It is incremented by *update_position* at each frame interval until it has reached the length of the segment the skater is currently on, whereupon a new segment starts. The *mode* member indicates which segment the skater is on.

The Skater constructor looks like this:

```
Skater::Skater() : Player("skater.gfx","skater.sfx")
{
    setxy(90,145);       // initial position on pond
    set_imageno(1);      // first skater frame
    appear();
    steps = 0;
    mode = 1;
}
```

The *Skater* constructor passes two file names to the *Player* constructor. This is because *Player* loads the .GFX and .SFX files for you.

Player updates the screen automatically. The *Skater* class decides where its sprite should be and what it should look like, and the *Player* class takes care of displaying it.

The *setxy* member function tells *Player* where to draw itself (when the time comes). We saw this member when *Pond* was creating the *Stander* objects. The *set_imageno* function tells *Player* which bitmap image in the .GFX library to use to draw the skater. The *appear* function tells the *Skater* that it is visible. Finally, the *steps* and *mode* data members are initialized.

The *update_position* member function, shown in Listing 10.1, is where all the action occurs. The skater's location is calculated here, depending on the values of *mode* and *steps*.

Listing 10.1 The update_position member function

```
void Skater::update_position()
{
  switch(mode)
  {
    case 1:
    case 3:
    case 5:
    case 7:
      // --- side to side movement
      if (++steps == sidesteps)  {
        steps = 0;
        set_imageno(++mode);
        break;
      }
      if (mode & 2) // modes 3 and 7: to the left
        setx(getx() - sstepincr);
      else
        setx(getx() + sstepincr);
      break;
    case 2:
    case 4:
    case 6:
    case 8:
      // --- front or back movement
      if (++steps == fwdsteps) {
        steps = 0;
        if (mode == 8)
          mode = 0;
        set_imageno(++mode);
        break;
      }
      if (mode < 6)
        sety(gety() - fstepincr);
      else
```

```
        sety(gety() + fstepincr);
      break;
    case 9:
      setinterval(3);    // slow down refresh rate
      set_imageno(13);   // 1st frame of ice-breaking splash
      mode++;
      play_sound_clip(1);
      break;
    case 10:
      set_image(12);     // 2nd frame of ice-breaking splash
      mode++;
      break;
    case 11:
      set_imageno(13);   // 3rd frame of ice-breaking splash
      mode++;
      break;
    case 12:
      set_imageno(11);   // hole in ice
      mode++;
      steps = 0;
      break;
    default:
      if (steps++ == 30)
        stop_director();
      break;
    }
  }
```

The figure eight is broken into eight modes. The odd-numbered modes
represent the left/right segments of the squared figure eight, and the even-
numbered modes represent the far/near segments. When the user presses
Enter (we'll look at that callback next), the mode is set to 9, which initiates a
sequence in which the skater falls through the ice. The cases near the end of
the function handle this sequence.

Now let's look at the *OnEnter* callback function:

```
void Skater::on_enter()
{
  if (mode < 9)  {
    int yp = 35;
    if (mode == 3 || mode == 7)
      yp=25;
    else if (mode > 3 && mode < 7)
      yp=15;
    setxy(getx()-10,gety()+yp);
    mode = 9;
  }
}
```

First, the mode is checked. If it is less than 9, we know that the figure eight is still in progress. If it is, a test determines where the splash sequence should be drawn. Finally, the mode is set to 9, which initiates the splash sequence.

The SkaterDemo Class

The *SkaterDemo* class derives from the base *Theatrix* class and is the vehicle with which the program initializes and runs the game:

```
class SkaterDemo : public Theatrix  {
  Pond* pond;
public:
  SkaterDemo() : Theatrix("Pond")
    { pond=new Pond; }
  ~SkaterDemo()
    { delete pond; }
};
```

The main Function

The *main* function looks like most other *main* functions in a Theatrix game:

```
int main()
{
  SkaterDemo demo;
  demo.go();
  return 0;
}
```

Unlike many of the other demo games, this one's graphical elements—the *Player* objects—deal only with what should be drawn and where. The previous demo (the Planet demo) had to deal with not only what should be drawn and where but also how large the image was and where on the last video page the sprite appeared. Although *Performers* and *VideoDirectors* are powerful, you will probably use *Players* and *SceneDirectors* more often because they encapsulate more of the details of animation than do the classes at the lower levels of abstraction.

The MusicHand Object

The Skater program's *Pond* class has a pointer to a *MusicHand* object. The constructor initializes that pointer:

```
class Pond : public SceneDirector   {
  MusicHand *conductor;
  void display();
  // ...
public:
  Pond();
  ~Pond();
};

Pond::Pond() : SceneDirector("pond.pcx")
{
  // ...
  conductor = new MusicHand("skater.xmi");
}
```

Building the .XMI Library

The file named **skater.xmi** is an Extended MIDI library in the format supported by the MIDPAK driver. The makefile builds the .XMI file from one or more .MID files:

```
$(EXEC)\skater.xmi : music\skater.mid
    midiform $(EXEC)\skater.xmi music\skater.mid
```

In this case, there is only one .MID file, and it is in the BUILD\MUSIC subdirectory for the game program.

Playing a Music Clip

The Skater game plays one music clip from the beginning of the game until the player ends the game or until the music clip completes. The game starts playing the music clip by overloading the *Director::display* function:

```
void Pond::display()
{
  SceneDirector::display();
  conductor->play_music_clip(1);
}
```

The *play_music_clip* function stops any previous music clip that might be playing.

Stopping a Music Clip

If the music is still playing when the player stops the program (by pressing Enter or Esc), the overloaded *hide* function stops the music clip:

```
void Pond::hide()
{
  conductor->stop_music_clip();
  SceneDirector::hide();
}
```

You can stop a music clip at any time in a game by calling the *stop_music_clip* function. If no music clip is playing, there is no effect.

Testing for Music Playing

At every timer interval, the *on_timer* function tests to see whether the skater sprite is still skating and whether the music clip was started and has now completed. If all these conditions are true, the program calls the *on_enter* function to stop the program.

The *on_enter* function is the callback that runs when the user presses the Enter key. This function causes the skater sprite to crash through the ice and then terminates the program. By calling this function when the music stops playing, the program crashes the sprite through the ice at that time:

```
void Pond::on_timer()
{
  if (skater->mode < 9 && conductor->isconducting() &&
      !conductor->music_clip_is_playing())    {
    skater->on_enter();
    return;
  }
  SceneDirector::on_timer();
  // ...
}
```

The *isconducting* function returns true if the game program was able to load and initialize the music driver at the start of the program. The *music_clip_is_playing* function returns true if a music clip is currently being played.

Terminating the Music Driver

When the game is over, the *Pond* destructor deletes the *MusicHand* object, which frees the memory where the object loaded the .XMI library:

```
Pond::~Pond()
{
  delete conductor;
  // ...
}
```

You can instantiate and delete *MusicHand* objects during the course of the game. Only one such object should be instantiated at any one time.

Marble Fighter

The Marble Fighter game pits two players in a kick-boxing match. Both players can be humans, playing at different PCs, or one player can play against the computer. Marble Fighter is the first of our games that uses an intro screen, a help screen, and a menu in addition to the action part of the game.

Intro and Help Screens

An intro screen is a static, full-screen image that the game displays when the program starts. A help screen is a static, full-screen image that the game displays when the player requests help, usually from the menu. Theatrix games implement these screens by assigning them to directors.

Marble Fighter is written at the third level of abstraction, which means that it takes care of its own director navigation. It implements its help and intro screens by using identical constructs. We'll discuss the intro screen here, and you can apply the same understanding to the help screen. This code shows the game's *Intro* class, which implements an intro screen by deriving from *VideoDirector*:

```
class Intro : public VideoDirector  {
public:
  void display();
  void take_over();
  int get_director_id()
    { return INTRO_ID; }
  int get_next_director_id()
    { return MENU_ID; }
};
```

The game instantiates an object of type *Intro* and, by instantiating it as the first director, arranges for that object to be the first director to get control. When a director object gets control, Theatrix first calls the director's *display* function followed by its *take_over* function; derived classes can override these functions and often do. Here are the functions for the *Intro* class:

```
void Intro::display()
{
  init_video();
  show_pcx("intro.pcx");
  swap_video_pages();
}
void Intro::take_over()
{
  while (kbhit()) getch();
  getch();
}
```

The *Intro::display* function calls *VideoDirector* functions to initialize the video system and display the .PCX file that contains the intro page's image. The *Intro::take_over* function does nothing more than wait for a keystroke, at which time it returns to relinquish control. The class's *get_next_director_id* function tells Theatrix which director should be given control next.

The *Intro::take_over* function flushes any pending keystrokes and then waits for a keystroke, after which the function returns control to Theatrix.

Figure 10.6 shows Marble Fighter's intro screen.

Figure 10.6 Marble Fighter's intro screen

Figure 10.7 shows Marble Fighter's help screen.

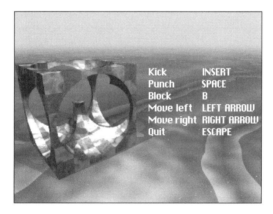

Figure 10.7 Marble Fighter's help screen

Later, at higher levels of abstraction, you will see how the *SceneryDirector* class encapsulates and hides the details of intro and help screens.

Menus

Most games have menus, but seldom does a game have a menu that looks like the menus of other games. This is the way it should be. Marble Fighter uses a tombstone for a menu. Other games, discussed soon, use other kinds of menus. Theatris uses spinning cubes. Shootout uses a bullet as a menu pointer. Skyscrap highlights the current menu selection.

Marble Fighter's menu is derived from *VideoDirector* so that page-flipping can be used to change menu selections. A .PCX file of the tombstone is displayed in the *Menu::display* routine. The menu has callbacks for the Up, Down, and Enter keys. The Up and Down keys change the image being displayed and make a sound. The Enter key stops the director, because when Enter gets pressed a menu selection has been made, and the menu no longer needs to be in control. The *Menu* class is shown here:

```
class Menu : public VideoDirector  {
  int cur;
  MenuItem* item[ITEMS+1];
protected:
  DECLARE_CUELIST
public:
  Menu();
 ~Menu();
  const Type_info& get_next_director();
  void initialize();
  void display();
  void on_up(int);
  void on_down(int);
  void on_enter(int);
  void on_escape(int);
  void on_fight(int);
  void on_help(int);
  void on_quit(int);
};
```

The *Menu* constructor assigns the *item* array with *MenuItem* objects:

```
Menu::Menu() : VideoDirector()
{
  item[1]=new MenuItem(this,PLAY);
  item[2]=new MenuItem(this,HELP);
  item[3]=new MenuItem(this,QUIT);
}
```

Notice that the *item* array is declared with a size of ITEMS+1, because we are not using the element item[0]. The *Menu::display* member function looks like this:

```
void Menu::display()
{
  init_video();
  show_pcx("menu.pcx");
  if (cur!=PLAY)
    item[cur]->display();
  swap_video_pages();
  synch_video_pages();
}
```

In addition to displaying the actual background, the menu displays a specific item if the current item is not equal to the value PLAY, which can happen when selected parts of the game return to the menu process. The .PCX file has been prepared with PLAY selected, so, if *cur* is equal to PLAY, then the menu is correct. Otherwise, the correct menu option is displayed on top of the background scene.

Most of the member functions in the *Menu* class are callbacks. Here is on_up, the callback for the Up arrow keystroke:

```
void Menu::on_up(int)
{
  if (cur>PLAY)
    cur--;
  else
    cur=ITEMS;
  item[cur]->display();
  item[cur]->play_switch_sound();
  swap_video_pages();
}
```

The function decrements the *cur* integer, making sure that if *cur* is as high as it can go, the lowest selection is chosen. The *display* call tells the new current selection to display itself. Then a sound is played. In this menu, each selection makes the same sound, but you could have each selection make a different sound. The call to *swap_video_pages* updates the visible page.

Most of the other callbacks in the *Menu* class look just like the *on_up* callback. Notice that callbacks such as *on_help* are used when the user presses a shortcut key. In the case of *on_help*, if the user presses the H key, the menu jumps directly to the help option. Here is the *on_help* function:

```
void Menu::on_help(int)
{
  if (cur!=HELP)    {
    cur=HELP;
    item[cur]->display();
    item[cur]->play_switch_sound();
    swap_video_pages();
  }
}
```

The callback forces the option to the HELP setting, unless it is already there. Now let's examine how the menu communicates with the rest of the program. First, if the user presses Enter, the current item is selected. The *on_enter* callback function is shown next:

```
void Menu::on_enter(int)
{
  stop_director();
}
```

Pressing the Enter key stops the *Menu* director object. Theatrix determines what to do when it calls the *get_next_director* member function, the return value of which is based on which selection the user made before pressing Enter.

Whenever a director gives up control (when its *stop_director* member is called), Theatrix determines which director to put in charge next. If no director can be found to take over, the application exits. Theatrix determines which director is next by calling the current director's *get_next_director* member. The *Menu* class's *get_next_director* function looks like this:

```
const Type_info& Menu::get_next_director()
{
  if (cur==PLAY)
    return typeid(Match);
  if (cur==HELP)
    return typeid(HelpPage);
  return typeid(StopDirector);
}
```

The *cur* variable was set as the user made selections while viewing the menu screen. If *cur* is equal to PLAY, the *Match* director is next, and its *typeid* is returned. (In Marble Fighter, the game object is of type *Match*.) Likewise, if HELP is the current option, then the *HelpPage* director takes over. If neither is true (if QUIT was selected), then *get_next_director* returns the typeid of the StopDirector class to report to Theatrix that the current director is the last one to run.

Figure 10.8 shows the Marble Fighter menu display.

Figure 10.8 The Marble Fighter menu

The Fight

The action of the Marble Fighter game is controlled by the *Match* class, which is derived from *VideoDirector*. The class instantiates two fighter objects of classes derived from the base *Fighter* class and lets them fight. *Fighter* is derived from *Performer*. In the single-player mode, one of the fighters is the computer itself. The fighter objects can kick, punch, and block. A fighter knows when it has hit its opponent. The fighters use sound effects for hits, groans, and shrieks. Each hit or kick is a score, and the first player to reach the highest possible score is the winner. The game records the scoring in video slider bars above the fighters. Figure 10.9 shows a fight in progress.

Figure 10.9 A Marble fight

When you start the Marble Player game in single-player mode, you can choose to be the left or right player by typing "-left" or "-right" on the command line.

Multiple-Player

Marble Fighter is the only game among the demos that supports multiple players on two PCs. To use this feature, you must connect the two PCs with a modem or a null modem cable and use the command-line options shown in Table 10.1.

Table 10.1 Marble Fighter command-line options

Option	Meaning
-net	specifies multiple players
-com <n>	serial port: <n> = 1 (default) or 2
-left	you will be the left player
-right	you will be the right player

Marble Fighter includes the code for making a direct serial connection. Chapter 11 describes a tool that allows you to use modems at either end of the connection.

To use the serial connection, a game calls the *Theatrix::enable_netpacks* function to cause the serial connection to be acknowledged. Then, if the port is to be other than COM1, the game calls the *Theatrix::use_commport* function, passing the port number as an argument. These calls must be made before calling the *Theatrix::go* function to launch the game. After that, the game can request cues from the remote computer and send cues to the remote computer.

The *Match* class's CUELIST table requests cues for the *Match* class object when certain cues are received from the remote computer:

```
CUELIST(Match)
  // ...
  NETPACK(IM_WAITING,on_waiting)
  NETPACK(I_QUIT,on_quit)
ENDCUELIST
```

You can also use the *Hand::request_netpack_cue* and *Hand::stop _netpack_cue* functions to request and terminate cues. Marble Fighter uses that approach to get remote player cues for the remote fighter object.

Serial cues are eight-bit values. A game sends a cue to the remote computer by calling the *Hand::post_netpack* function.

Town

Town is a Myst-like game. It consists of static full-screen displays, mouse navigation, music clips, sound effects, and one video clip. You can use the *SceneryDirector* class to build games with images that consist primarily of static scenes. The Town demo game uses *SceneryDirector* objects to display its scenery. Town is implemented at the fourth level of abstraction. There is no animation, so there are no *Performer* objects. The Town demo is found on the included CD-ROM in the \THX\DEMOS\TOWN subdirectory.

The Town Class

The Town game consists of 12 scenes, each rendered from a single 3-D model. There is a *Town* class from which 12 subclasses are derived. Each subclass represents one scene in the game. The *Town* class is shown here:

```
class Town : public SceneryDirector {
  static int townct;
  int tune;
  int clip;
  virtual void look_forward() { }
  virtual void look_right()   { }
  virtual void look_left()    { }
  virtual void look_back()    { }
  void on_escape();
  DECLARE_CUELIST
  DECLARE_MOUSECURSORS
protected:
  static MusicHand *conductor;
  static VocalHand *soundtech;
  Town(char *pcx, int tn = 0, int cl = 0);
  ~Town();
  virtual void display();
  virtual void hide();
  void on_timer();
};
```

The *Town* class includes data members that point to objects of *MusicHand* and *VocalHand* classes. These objects play the music and sound effects for the game. The *Town* constructor builds them as shown here:

```
Town::Town(char *pcx, int tn, int cl) :
                SceneryDirector(pcx, NoTransition)
{
  if (townct == 0)    {
     conductor = new MusicHand("town.xmi");
     soundtech = new VocalHand();
     soundtech->load_sfxlib("town.sfx");
  }
  tune = tn;
  clip = cl;
  townct++;
}
```

The *townct* data member is a static reference-counting variable. It ensures that the *MusicHand* and *VocalHand* objects are instantiated and deleted only once. Because *Town* is a base class to 12 subclasses of which there is one object each, this measure is necessary. The *Town* destructor waits until *townct* is zero before deleting the two objects, as shown here:

```
Town::~Town()
{
  if (--townct == 0)  {
     delete soundtech;
     delete conductor;
  }
}
```

CUELIST and CURSORLIST Tables

The *Town* class's CUELIST table captures keystrokes and timer ticks as shown here:

```
CUELIST(Town)
  KEYSTROKE(LF,  look_left)
  KEYSTROKE(UP,  look_forward)
  KEYSTROKE(DN,  look_back)
  KEYSTROKE(RT,  look_right)
  KEYSTROKE(ESC, on_escape)
  TIMER(18, on_timer)
ENDCUELIST
```

The *Town* class has a CURSORLIST table, which controls how the game handles mouse cursors. Here is the CURSORLIST table:

```
CURSORLIST(Town)
  MOUSE_CURSOR(  0,   0, 105, 239, LFCURSOR, look_left)
  MOUSE_CURSOR(106,   0, 211, 199, UPCURSOR, look_forward)
  MOUSE_CURSOR(106, 200, 211, 239, DNCURSOR, look_back)
  MOUSE_CURSOR(212,   0, 319, 239, RTCURSOR, look_right)
ENDCURSORLIST
```

Each MOUSE_CURSOR entry in the CURSORLIST table specifies a region on the screen with the X and Y coordinates of the region's upper left and lower right corners. The MOUSE_CURSOR entries name cursor shapes for the mouse to assume when its pointer is in the entry's region. The entries also specify callback functions to call when the user clicks the mouse in the regions.

The cursor shapes used by the Town game are the standard ones that Theatrix provides. You can build custom cursor shapes. Chapter 4 discusses that procedure.

Callback Functions

The callback functions in the CURSORLIST table are the same as the callback functions associated with arrow keystrokes in the CUELIST table. This approach allows the user to play the game without a mouse by pressing arrow keys.

Playing Music and Sound Effects

The *Town* class overrides its base class's *display* function to turn on the mouse and start any music clip or sound effect associated with the derived *Town* subclass scene. The overridden *hide* function turns off the mouse, music clips, and sound effects.

The *Town::on_timer* callback function keeps a sound effect playing. If the scene has a sound effect and if the sound effect has played to completion, the function starts the sound effect playing again.

The three functions that manage music clips and sound effects are shown here:

```
void Town::display()
{
  SceneryDirector::display();
  mouse_visible();
  if (tune)
      conductor->play_music_clip(tune);
  if (clip)
      soundtech->play_sound_clip(clip);
}
void Town::hide()
{
  if (tune)
      conductor->stop_music_clip();
  if (clip)
      soundtech->stop_sound_clip();
  mouse_invisible();
  SceneryDirector::hide();
}
void Town::on_timer()
{
  if (clip && !soundtech->sound_clip_is_playing())
      soundtech->play_sound_clip(clip);
}
```

Stopping the Game

The *Town::on_escape* callback function executes when the user presses the Esc key:

```
void Town::on_escape()
{
  set_next_director(&typeid(StopDirector));
  stop_director();
}
```

The call to *set_next_director* tells the *SceneryDirector* class to shut down when *stop_director* is called. Ordinarily, a *SceneryDirector* object always switches to the next director in the list of instantiated directors when *stop_director* is called.

The Derived Town Subclasses

There are 12 derived *Town* subclasses, one for each scene in the game. Each scene has a .PCX file associated with it, and some have music and sound clips. Here is a typical *Town* subclass:

```
class Town3 : public Town   {
public:
  Town3() : Town("town03.pcx", 4, 2) { }
  void look_left()  { start_director(typeid(Town2)); }
  void look_right() { start_director(typeid(Town10)); }
};
```

The *Town* constructor accepts as many as three arguments. The first argument is the name of the .PCX file that provides the scene's full-screen image. The second argument is a music clip, if one is to be played when the scene begins. The third argument is a sound clip, if one is to be played when the scene begins. These clip arguments are zero if no clip is to be played. The Town constructor parameters have default arguments of zero, so you can omit the argument values.

Navigating the Town

The *look_left* and *look_right* callback functions override the empty callback functions of the same name in the base *Town* class. There may also be *look_forward* and *look_back* callback functions. These functions specify what to do when the user presses an arrow key or clicks in a mouse region to move forward, backward, right, or left. In most cases, these functions call the *start_director* function, specifying the *typeid* of the *Town* subclass to be started. This action stops the current director and starts the specified director.

Planning the scenes involved figuring out where the user's viewpoint would be for each one. Then, from each such viewpoint, we had to determine which viewpoint would be activated depending on which way the user navigated with the keyboard or the mouse.

To make this analysis easier, we built a map of the town by moving the camera high in the sky and pointing it downward. Then we determined where the game's camera locations would be for each scene. Figure 10.10 is that map with the camera information added.

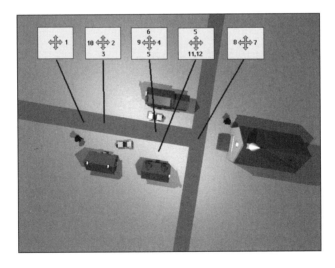

Figure 10.10 A map of the Town

Each of the camera legends in Figure 10.68 indicates the scene number when the camera is pointed in the direction of one of the arrows. From these legends we were able to determine where to place the camera to render each scene from the 3-D model and which scene to change to when the user moves away from the current scene in one of the four directions. Figure 10.11 is a montage of all 12 scenes from the Town game.

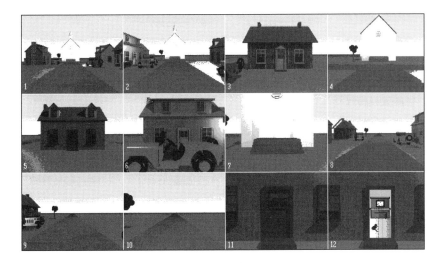

Figure 10.11 The Town scenes

Twelve scenes are not many for a complex game. Myst has more than 2500 scenes. This demo, however, shows you where to start when building games like this.

Playing a Video Clip

The *Town12* subclass does one thing that the others don't do: It plays a moving picture video clip during scene 12. The open door with a cat and a piano in scene 12 of Figure 10.69 is actually one frame of a video clip. The clip wags the cat's tail, rolls the piano roll, and moves the piano keys up and down. Here is the *Town12* class declaration:

```
class Town12 : public Town  {
public:
  Town12() : Town("town11.pcx", 2) { }
  void display()
  {
    Town::display();
    show_video("room.flc", 132, 53, TRUE);
  }
  void hide()
  {
    stop_video();
    Town::hide();
  }
  void look_back()  { start_director(typeid(Town11)); }
  void iterate_director()
  {
    SceneryDirector::iterate_director();
    if (conductor->isconducting() &&
        !conductor->music_clip_is_playing())
      look_back();
  }
};
```

This class uses the same .PCX scenery file that *Town11* uses. By projecting the video clip over the part of the screen that shows the door of the house, the scene seems to open the door and show the motion inside. The call to the base *Town* class's constructor specifies the scene and a music clip to play. The overriding *display* function starts a video clip by calling the *show_video* function. Its parameters are the name of the .FLC file, the X and Y coordinates of the upper left corner where the video clip displays, and a true or false indicator to specify that the clip is to repeat or to play only once.

The overridden *iterate_director* function is called for each loop that the *Director* class processes to run the game. This function permits a game to insert frequent tests and processes that are not related to ticks of the clock. The *Town12* class uses this iteration function to see whether the music clip has finished playing. If it has, the function calls the *Town12::look_back* callback function to move to scene 11.

The TownApp Class

The *TownApp* class derives from *Theatrix* and contains pointers to all the subclasses:

```
class TownApp : public Theatrix {
    Town1 *town1;
    Town2 *town2;
    Town3 *town3;
    Town4 *town4;
    Town5 *town5;
    Town6 *town6;
    Town7 *town7;
    Town8 *town8;
    Town9 *town9;
    Town10 *town10;
    Town11 *town11;
    Town12 *town12;
public:
    TownApp();
    ~TownApp();
};
```

The *TownApp* constructor builds instances of the scene objects using the new operator. The destructor deletes these objects. The program's *main* function looks like the other *main* functions listed in this chapter.

Theatris

Theatris emulates a type of interactive board game that has gained popularity in the past several years. The game uses a variable number of game pieces that fall into a pit. The player fits these pieces together by rotating and moving them with the keyboard. The game employs a grid matrix to implement the tiled pit into which the pieces fall.

We won't go into much detail about the game's implementation. You can read the code and see how most of it works. But several parts of Theatris are worthy of study. The menu is unique, so we describe it here. The implementation of the pit uses grid logic common to many games. The data structures that implement the game pieces are interesting. These details might not be obvious from reading the code, so we explain them here.

The Menu

The Theatris menu is different from other menus in that it indicates the current selection with an animated rotating game piece. Figure 10.12 shows the Theatris menu.

Figure 10.12 The Theatris menu

You can't tell by looking at Figure 10.12, but when you view the menu on the screen, the game piece just to the left of the current selection rotates. As you move the selection up and down with the arrow keys, the new selection's game piece starts rotating and the old one stops. The image frames of each piece on the menu are stored in a .GFX file dedicated to the piece. The

MenuItem class manages the display of each game piece on the menu, and the *Menu* class manages the entire menu.

The *Menu* constructor instantiates three *MenuItem* objects and keeps track of which one is currently selected by receiving keyboard cues for the up and down arrow keys. The *Menu* object also gets a timer cue once every timer tick. The *Menu::on_timer* function manages the rotation, as shown here:

```
void Menu::on_timer()
{
  item[cur]->update();
  swap_video_pages();
}
```

The *MenuItem::update* function, called by *Menu::on_timer*, computes the next frame to be displayed and displays it. When the *update* function returns, *on_timer* calls *VideoDirector::swap_video_pages* because *update* makes its changes to the active page buffer and that buffer needs to become the visible page buffer:

```
void MenuItem::update()
{
  image=(image+1)%numimages;
  show_frame(x,y,image+1);
}
```

Each game piece on the menu is displayed from image frames taken from its own .GFX file. The *numimages* data member is the number of images in that file. The file contains exactly enough images to animate one complete rotation of the piece. Therefore, the expression on the right side of the assignment in the above code always computes the next frame number in the animation sequence.

The game pieces are similar to sprites in that they are animated. However, unlike sprites, the pieces display themselves by using the *VideoDirector:: show_frame* function instead of the *VideoDirector::show_image* function. *VideoDirector::show_frame* uses a graphics feature that superimposes a rectangular graphical image onto the background without considering transparent parts of the rectangle. The game piece images were rendered against the actual background so that their shadows would be projected onto the background. Therefore, the animated images use all the pixels in the frame rectangles.

The Pit

Figure 10.13 shows a Theatris game in progress. The game pieces fall into the pit, and the player fits those pieces together by rotating and moving them with the keyboard.

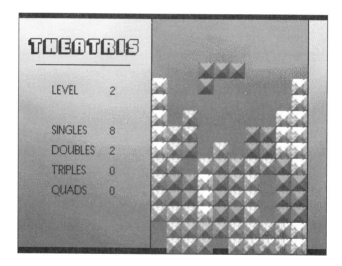

Figure 10.13 A Theatris game

The pit is implemented as a grid, represented by a logical two-dimensional array of tile positions. Each position contains a pointer to an object of type *Block*, a class that implements the game piece. When the pointer is null, the grid position is not filled with a part of a game piece. The outer array is an array of rows. Each row contains an inner array of tile positions and an indicator that says whether the row is fully occupied. Shown next is the organization of these arrays:

```
struct row_array {
  Block* col[PIT_WIDTH];
  int is_full;
};

struct pit_grid {
  row_array row[PIT_DEPTH];
};
```

Game Pieces

Theatris uses seven distinct game pieces. Each piece is made of four square tiles. Figure 10.14 shows the seven pieces.

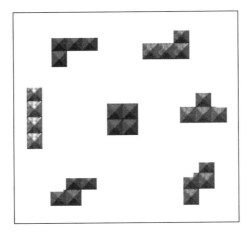

Figure 10.14 The Theatris game pieces

The game pieces are implemented by arrays of coordinates in a five by five grid of tiles. Coordinate 0/0 is the center tile. Tiles to the left of center are addressed as –1 and –2 on the X axis. Tiles to the right of center are addressed as 1 and 2 on the X axis. Tiles above center are addressed as –1 and –2 on the Y axis. Tiles below center are addressed as 1 and 2 on the Y axis.

Each game piece is represented in memory by four arrays of four coordinates. Each array represents the piece at one of its four rotations. Each of the four coordinates in an array specifies a tiled position. These data structures are shown next:

```
struct point  {
  int x,y;
};


struct pointlist  {
  point pair[4];
};


pointlist blueblockinfo[4] = {       //  [0] [1] [2]   [3]
  {{{-1,0}, {0,0}, {1,0},{-1,1},},}, //  XXX XX    X  X
  {{{-1,-1},{0,-1},{0,0},{0,1}, },}, //  X    X  XXX  X
  {{{-1,0}, {0,0}, {1,0},{1,-1},},}, //        X       XX
  {{{0,-1}, {0,0}, {0,1},{1,1}, },},
};
```

Shootout

Shootout is an arcade game that includes many of the features that Theatrix supports. It is the most complex of the demo games, yet it has the simple, hand-drawn appearance of many arcade-style games.

Shootout uses an intro screen to introduce the game and to explain the underlying story. A menu guides users to the help screen, the options screen, and the action. The program is written at the highest level of abstraction, leaving most of the details to the hidden functions of the *SceneryDirector*, *SceneDirector*, and *Player* classes. Figure 10.15 shows the game as it plays out.

Shootout teaches several new lessons. First, the game demonstrates Theatrix's ability to support many sprites. Second, the sheriff's walk is animated using a smooth pace algorithm. Third, the other sprites use clipping to appear in windows, from doorways, and from behind buildings.

Figure 10.15 The Shootout game

Multiple Sprites

In addition to the seven players on the screen, each door on a building is a *Player* object, as is each digit in the scoreboard. To support Shootout, Theatrix must keep pace with 13 sprites all the time, maintaining a refresh rate of 18 frames per second.

Smooth Animation

The sheriff's walking pace in Figure 10.15 must seem natural. When a foot is firmly planted on the street, the rest of the body should move forward without having that foot slide in either direction. The *Sheriff* class implements walking animation with a five-frame sequence that we described in Chapter 4 under "Motion: One Frame at a Time." The *Sheriff::Walk* function implements that sequence:

```
// --- step increments of the sheriff's stroll
short int Sheriff::walkincr[] = { 5,7,6,7 };

void Sheriff::Walk()
{
  setinterval(walkinterval);
  if (++steps == 40)  {
    steps = 0;
    forward ^= 1;
    incr = 1;
    of = 0;
    frame = 0;
    if (forward)    {
      offset = 0;
      setx(FirstX);
    }
    else
      offset = 5;
  }
  else    {
    if (forward)
      setx(getx() + walkincr[of]);
    else
      setx(getx() - walkincr[of]);
    if (++of == 4)
      of = 0;
  }
  frame += incr;
  if (frame == 5)
    incr = -1;
  else if (frame == 1)
    incr = 1;
  set_imageno(frame+offset);
}
```

The *Sheriff::Walk* function is executed once every other clock tick, or approximately nine times per second. The five frame images are numbered 1 through 5 in the .GFX library associated with the *Sheriff* object. The *steps* data member counts the steps. There are 40 steps across the screen, at which time the sheriff changes direction. Each step changes the object's X coordinate and image.

Clipping

When the townspeople and the bad guys come into view, they appear in one of the windows of a building, from out of a door, or from behind a building and down the alley to the street. Their images must be clipped to within the windows and doorframes and the edges of buildings. Except when they appear in windows, the clipping stops after they are in full view.

The *Shootout* class clips the images of the *BitPart* objects when they are about to enter the scene. Clipping is done by calling the *Player::clip* function with four coordinate points to define the rectangular screen region within which the *Player* object can display. The *BitPart* class is derived from the *Player* class, so this action clips the *BitPart* object to display within the window, doorway, or alleyway. Each such entrance is described by a *Portal* object that contains its coordinates.

When a *BitPart* object gets into full view, it unclips itself by calling the *Player::unclip* function. When the object is about to exit the scene, it clips itself to the portal through which it is going to exit.

SkyScrap

In SkyScrap, the player pilots a jet fighter across a scrolling landscape and shoots at other craft that are shooting back. The game uses the joystick or the keyboard to move the jet fighter around and to fire shots.

SkyScrap includes an intro page, a menu, and a help page. Figure 10.16 shows the action page with aircraft flying and rockets being launched.

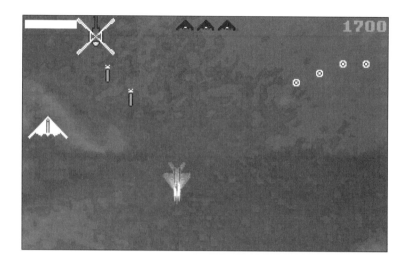

Figure 10.16 The SkyScrap game

The player of SkyScrap is piloting the white stealth aircraft. The ground scrolls from top to bottom, and the other two craft come at the player from the top of the screen. They keep coming. Even when you shoot them down, more of them come at you. The round circles in the upper right corner of Figure 10.16 are shots that the player fired. In this screen shot, the player fired and then moved abruptly to the left side of the screen.

Video Mode

SkyScrap is the only graphical game in our collection of demos that does not use Mode X. Its video mode uses a VGA resolution of 320 x 200.

Joystick

The *Stealth* class is indirectly derived from the *Performer* class, and it gets its cues from its *initialize* function:

```
void Stealth::initialize()
{
  load_gfxlib( "ss.gfx" );
  load_sfxlib( "ss.sfx" );
  request_hotkey_cue(SCAN_LEFT, (callback)&Stealth::OnLeftKey );
  request_hotkey_cue(SCAN_RIGHT,(callback)&Stealth::OnRightKey);
  request_hotkey_cue(SCAN_UP,   (callback)&Stealth::OnUpKey   );
  request_hotkey_cue(SCAN_DOWN, (callback)&Stealth::OnDownKey );
  request_hotkey_cue(SCAN_SPACE,(callback)&Stealth::OnFireKey );
  request_joystickbutton_cue(BUTTONONE,
                                (callback)&Stealth::OnFireKey );
  request_joystickmove_cue(     (callback)&Stealth::OnMove );
}
```

The *OnLeftKey*, *OnRightKey*, *OnUpKey*, and *OnDownKey* callback functions each move the sprite one increment around the screen when the player presses the corresponding key. The *OnFireKey* callback function fires a shot from the player's craft. The increment of movement is controlled by a data member named *MoveLength*, which is initially set to the value 4. This value is the number of pixel positions to move the aircraft for each call of one of the movement callback functions.

We added joystick control to this game by using the joystick's button 1 to fire shots and by writing the *OnMove* callback function to be executed when the player moves the joystick away from the center position. Here is the *OnMove* function:

```
void Stealth::OnMove(int x,int y)
{
    MoveLength = max(abs(x) / 16, 4);
    x > 0 ? OnRightKey() : OnLeftKey();
    MoveLength = max(abs(y) / 16, 4);
    y > 0 ? OnUpKey() : OnDownKey();
    MoveLength = 4;
}
```

Joystick movement events are called when the joystick is moved away from the center position. The X and Y values that are sent as arguments specify the distance in positive (right and up) and negative (left and down) values away from center. The *OnMove* function uses those values to compute the number of pixel positions to move the craft. The further the user moves the joystick from center, the greater the number of pixel positions in the move and, therefore, the faster the craft changes position.

Background Scrolling

As the game progresses, the background scenery, which is a rendered view of the terrain, scrolls vertically beneath the sprites. The program uses a general-purpose background scroller class. The terrain is represented by, in this case, 14 .PCX images, which, if properly placed in a column, would display the complete territory to be covered. Scrolling is achieved first by computing which of these images contribute to the current terrain representation and then by displaying portions of the images in clipped configurations.

The 14 images wrap around so that when the scroller gets to the end of the terrain, it wraps to the beginning.

The scroller class is designed to support scrolling in all directions. To use this feature, you must provide the .PCX files to represent the terrain in a grid. We have not yet used it that way and cannot say for sure that it works except in theory. You can study the SkyScrap game to see how it uses the scroller class and then experiment with it to see how far it takes you.

The Theatrix Toolset

"The game is done! I've won, I've won!"
Samuel Taylor Coleridge

This brief chapter lists the tools and libraries that we collected from shareware and freeware sources. With one exception, they are all included on the CD-ROM that accompanies this book. You will learn what the following tools are and how you can register or license their use.

- ◇ NeoPaint
- ◇ MORAY
- ◇ POV-Ray
- ◇ Alchemy
- ◇ Povnet
- ◇ Blaster Master
- ◇ Dave's .TGA Animator
- ◇ MT—Multi-Track Sequencer/Editor
- ◇ MODEM.BAT
- ◇ Fastgraph 4.0
- ◇ DIGPAK and MIDPAK

About Shareware

Shareware is a technique for marketing software. Several of the tools discussed here and many of the extra games on the included CD-ROM are shareware. We're sure you've heard this before, but please listen up. When a product comes your way through shareware channels, whether on a CD-ROM, from a download, or from a diskette rack, that product is not yours to keep and use forever. You may try it out, but if you plan to use it beyond a trial period, you are required to license or register it and pay whatever fee the author requests. These fees are nominal considering the value received.

Documentation and Support

The tools include documentation in the form of text files that accompany the software. When you license or register the products, you usually get printed documentation, the most current releases of the products, and the right to ask questions of the authors. You can also get help on the various game and graphics forums of the many on-line services that programmers use.

Tools

Following is a short description of each of the tools that you can use to build graphics, sound effects, and video clips. Each listing includes, where appropriate, addresses, phone numbers, and registration costs.

NeoPaint

Neosoft Corp.

354 NE Greenwood Avenue, Suite 108

Bend, OR 97701-4631

503-383-7195 (BBS)

503-389-5489 (VOICE)

503-388-8221 (FAX)

$45

It isn't often that you find a piece of software that looks good, is easy to use, is reliable, and surprises you more each time you use it, but NeoPaint is such a program. NeoPaint supports .BMP, .PCX, and TIFF file formats. This is the best DOS paint program we've seen, and that is saying a lot. The unregistered version is included on the CD-ROM in the \neopaint directory.

MORAY

Lutz Kretzschner

SoftTronics

Munich, Germany

100023,2006 (CompuServe)

$59

MORAY is a 3-D modeler designed for use with POV-Ray (Persistance of Vision ray-tracer). It is a DOS application that employs common 3-D modeler and CAD screen configurations with three side views and an isometric view of the model. You build models by visually and logically combining standard shapes with one another and with textures and surfaces. Those models can be compiled into POV-Ray source code, which can then be rendered by POV-Ray.

The shareware version of MORAY is included on the CD-ROM in the \moray32 directory. The shareware version has all the functionality of the registered version and employs *nag screen* techniques to encourage registration. MORAY is an impressive application and makes using POV-Ray much easier. The version included is the 32-bit version, so memory does not run out quite as quickly as it did in the older 16-bit versions.

POV-Ray

Chris Young

76702,1655 (CompuServe)

POV-Ray (Persistance of Vision ray-tracer) is a great, powerful, and free piece of software. Written by the POV team, which is chaired by Chris Young, POV-Ray is a ray-tracer that uses C-like source language to describe 3-D models, which the program renders into dazzling image files.

We would have included a copy of POV-Ray on the CD-ROM, but an exclusive agreement that the authors have made with another publisher prohibits us from doing so. Fear not, however, because POV-Ray is still free, and it's available from CompuServe's GRAPHDEV forum.

Several of the demo games use images rendered with POV-Ray. We have included the POV-Ray source files that describe these images and the image files themselves. You do not need POV-Ray to build any of our images, but you would need it or another ray-tracer to build your own photo-realistic scenes.

Alchemy

Handmade Software, Inc.

48820 Kato Road, Suite 110

Fremont, CA 94538

800-358-3588 (VOICE)

hsi@netcom.com (Internet)

71330,3136 (CompuServe)

510-252-0909 (FAX)

$79 (MS-DOS version)

Image Alchemy is an impressive and reliable bitmapped graphical file format converter. The demo version converts images that are 640 by 480 pixels and smaller. Image Alchemy supports virtually every graphical file format. Image Alchemy resides on the CD-ROM in the \alchemy directory. The documentation is in a file called **alchemy.doc**.

Povnet

If you have access to two or more computers, Povnet can prove useful. Povnet allows you to use one of the computers as a server to render POV-Ray images. Using a network, POV-Ray source files can be copied to the server where they will be rendered automatically. While the image is rendering at the remote computer, you are free to edit the data file or start on another scene at your local computer. Povnet's executables and source code files reside on the CD-ROM in the \povnet directory.

Povnet was built by the authors of this book, and you may use and distribute it freely. It works better if you make some modifications to POV-Ray. The modified source code files and Povnet are posted on CompuServe under the GRAPHDEV forum. We have not included the modified POV-Ray sources on the accompanying CD-ROM for the same reason that we are not distributing POV-Ray.

Blaster Master

Gary Maddox

210 Camelot Drive

Weatherford, TX 76086

76711,547 (CompuServe)

GO SWREG for registering via CompuServe

$29.95 standard, $49.95 deluxe

Blaster Master is a complete DOS system for recording, editing, and playing sound files on a Creative Labs Sound Blaster. The program is useful for fine-tuning your sound effects and converting between sound file formats, and it has an impressive set of features. It is on the CD-ROM in the \bmaster directory.

Dave's .TGA Animator

David K. Mason

P.O. Box 181015

Boston, MA 02118

76546,1321 (CompuServe)

$35

Dave's .TGA Animator, or DTA, is a utility designed to generate video .FLI or .FLC files from sets of graphical images. This tool allows you to create video files from sets of .PCX or .TGA frame images. The set is processed by DTA into an .FLC file, which can be shown by video player software or used in a game. DTA is on the CD-ROM in the ∫directory.

The DTA program comes with documentation, but the best reference work to it is found in the book *Morphing on Your PC*, written by DTA's author, David Mason. See the Bibliography for details.

MT—Multi-Track Sequencer/Editor

In 1989, M&T books published *MIDI Sequencing in C*, by Jim Conger. The MT software was included with the book. MT is a multitrack sequencer program that runs under DOS and interfaces with MPU-401 MIDI devices. You can use the program along with a compatible MIDI interface card and a MIDI keyboard to record MIDI songs such as the ones that accompany our demo games.

When the book went out of print, Conger released MT as unsupported freeware. The software, including the source code, is the the \MT directory of the CD-ROM.

MODEM.BAT

This batch file allows you to use a modem to connect PCs that are running a game written to use the Theatrix serial port connection for multiplayer sessions. The batch file is located in the \modem directory of the CD-ROM. For instructions on its use, run the batch file with no command-line arguments. This file was prepared by the authors of this book, and you may use it freely.

Libraries

Following is a short description of the two libraries used by Theatrix.

Fastgraph 4.0

Ted Gruber Software

P.O. Box 13408

Las Vegas, NV 89112

702-735-1980 (VOICE)

702-735-4603 (FAX)

702-796-7134 (BBS)

72000,1642 (CompuServe)

Fastgraph Lite is a shareware library of fast graphics functions. Fastgraph is designed specifically as a game libary and was used to write Theatrix. Fastgraph Lite is the shareware version, which supports all the functions of the registered version; it requires a TSR to be resident in memory. You are permitted to use the shareware version of Fastgraph Lite for your own development, but if you want to distribute programs that use the Fastgraph library functions, you must purchase and link with the commercial version of the library. You can get a commercial version of Fastgraph Lite that you can use to distribute programs. As with the shareware version, you must load a TSR before running a program that uses the library. The commercial version of Fastgraph Lite costs $49. For $249, you can also get a full library that you can link with and that needs no TSR to run a program.

The shareware version of Fastgraph Lite version 4.0 is located in the \fgl directory of the CD-ROM.

DIGPAK and MIDPAK

John W. Ratcliff

747 Napa Lane

St. Charles, MO 63304

70253,3237 (CompuServe)

J.RATCLIFF3 (genie)

314-939-0200 (BBS)

$500

DIGPAK and MIDPAK are creations of The Audio Solution, Inc. They provide sound and MIDI support for a large number of sound cards. Both programs can be found in the \DIGMID directory of the CD-ROM. A $500 license fee applies for each driver if you are going to distribute the drivers with your commercial programs. Shareware authors should contact the vendor to discuss terms for distributing shareware copies in advance of receiving any registrations.

The CD-ROM

The software on the CD-ROM that accompanies this book falls into the following categories.

- ◇ Theatrix C++ library
- ◇ Demo game programs
- ◇ Theatrix utilities
- ◇ Additional utilities
- ◇ Games

This appendix describes where the software is located on the CD-ROM and how to install it onto your hard drive.

CD-ROM Organization

Figure A.1 shows the layout of the CD-ROM.

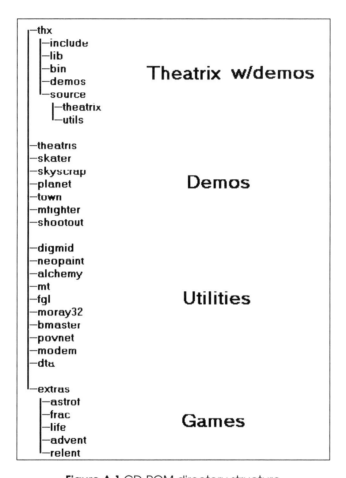

Figure A.1 CD-ROM directory structure

Theatrix Source Code

The Theatrix library source code is kept in two separate directories. The header files are in the **\thx\include** directory, and the source files are in the **\thx\source\theatrix** directory.

Theatrix Examples

The Theatrix examples are contained in directory structures designed to be conducive to a development environment. Table A.1 shows the location of these directories on the CD-ROM.

Table A.1 Demo programs on the CD-ROM

\thx\demos\mfighter	Marble Fighter game
\thx\demos\shootout	Shootout game
\thx\demos\theatris	Theatris game
\thx\demos\skyscrap	SkyScrap game
\thx\demos\town	Town demo
\thx\demos\mouse	Mouse demo
\thx\demos\ttt	Tic-Tac-Toe demo
\thx\demos\planet	Planet demo
\thx\demos\skeleton	Stripped-down demo
\thx\demos\textmode	Text-mode example
\thx\demos\skater	Skater animation demo

As discussed in Chapter 9, each of these directories contains a **build** and an **exec** subdirectory. The **build** subdirectory contains all the source code for the game. The **exec** directory is where the executable and data files are placed by the makefile.

Theatrix Utilities

The source code for the Theatrix utilities is located in the **\thx\source\utils** directory. The executables are in **\thx\bin**.

Installing Theatrix

The easiest way to install the Theatrix software is to copy it onto your hard drive as a complete directory structure. You can do this with the DOS *xcopy* command:

1. Make a directory on your hard drive called **\thx**.

2. Log into that directory.

3. Copy the directory from the CD-ROM with this command:

   xcopy /s d:\thx (if your CD-ROM is the D drive).

Next, install the following software packages from the CD-ROM:

1. Fastgraph

2. DIGPAC and MIDPAC

3. Image Alchemy

4. Dave's .TGA Animation Program

5. POV-Ray[1]

The installation procedures for each of these packages are discussed later in this chapter.

Next, edit the **make.cfg** file in the **\thx\source** directory. The needed changes are discussed in Chapter 9 and in comments in the **make.cfg** file.

The final step is to ensure that the utilities are in the path. The following items must be in the path in order for you to compile the demos from scratch:

1. Your compiler

2. The Theatrix utilities (**\thx\bin**)

3. Image Alchemy

4. Dave's .TGA Animation Program

5. POV-Ray

Once this installation is completed, you are ready to compile. Each demo has a **makefile** in its build directory, and Theatrix itself can be compiled with the **makefile** in **\thx\source\theatrix**.

---

[1] POV-Ray is not included on the CD-ROM. POV-Ray is necessary only for compilation of the demos if the .POV files are replaced or modified. If only C++ source code is modified, then it will not be necessary to invoke POV-Ray.

Other Utilities and Libraries

Blaster Master

Blaster Master is located in the **\bmaster** directory on the CD-ROM. To install the program, copy the contents of the CD-ROM **\bmaster** directory to a directory on your hard drive. The **tutor.doc** file explains the program's interface.

Dave's .TGA Animation Program

Dave's .TGA Animation Program (DTA) version 2.2 is located in the **\DTA** directory. To install the program, copy the contents of the CD-ROM **\DTA** directory into a directory on your hard drive. The file **dta.doc** will get you started, but *Morphing on Your PC*, written by David Mason (author of DTA), is a better source of documentation.

DIGPAC and MIDPAC

Both DIGPAC and MIDPAC are in the **\DIGMID** directory of the CD-ROM. To install, copy the files into a directory on your hard drive. Two **files—digpkapi.doc** and **midpkapi.doc**—supply documentation for using the APIs of the loadable driver modules. Unless you plan to use either package without Theatrix, you won't need to read these files.

Fastgraph

The version of Fastgraph Light supplied on the CD-ROM is 4.0, and it is located in the **\fgl** directory. Fastgraph is installed via the install program supplied by Ted Gruber Software.

1. Change into the **\fgl\fglight** directory of the CD-ROM.
2. Type **install**.
3. Follow the instructions.[2]

---

[2]The Fastgraph install program assumes that you will be installing the Fastgraph include file and the .LIB file into your compiler directory. This is not a good idea, because upgrading or reinstalling your compiler may erase or corrupt these files. We recommend that you install all the Fastgraph files into their own directory.

Once the installation is complete, you will find ample documentation in the .DOC files. If you are installing Fastgraph only for use with Theatrix, you won't need to view these files.

Image Alchemy

Image Alchemy is located in the **\alchemy** directory. To install it, copy the contents of the directory to your hard drive. A sizable documentation file is available by executing the self-extracting archive **manual.exe**. The program also has good command-line help.

Modem

The modem batch file is located in the **\modem** directory. Copy it to your hard drive where it will be in the path. For instructions on its use, run the batch file with no parameters.

MORAY

MORAY resides in the **\moray32** directory. To install, copy the files to your hard drive. There are some example models in the mdl directory, so you many want to use the *xcopy /s* command.

MT

You'll find the Midi Sequencing software (and source code) in the **\MT** directory. Copy the files to your hard drive to install. You will need to run **setup.exe** before using the program.

NeoPaint

NeoPaint version 3.1 is located in the **\neopaint** directory. You can copy the contents of the directory to a directory on your hard drive, or you can use the supplied install program. The latter method configures your printer, so if you intend to print from NeoPaint, you will need to run the install utility. The utility is in **\neopaint\install** and is named **install.exe**.

Povnet

The **\povnet** directory contains the Povnet utility. To install, copy the contents of the directory to a directory on your hard drive. The file **povnet.doc** explains how to set up a dedicated rendering system using Povnet.

Games

The shareware and freeware games on the CD-ROM are all uncompressed. Many can be run directly from the CD-ROM, but it is better to copy them to your hard drive: CD-ROM drives are slow in comparison to hard drives, and some of the games write to configuration files on the disk from which they are run.

Please bear in mind that most of these games are shareware, which means that there is a development group somewhere trying to make a living by letting you try the software before you buy it.

Adventure

The classic Adventure game is on the CD-ROM in the **\extras\advent** subdirectory. Copy the contents of the \extras\advent directory to a subdirectory on your hard drive to install.

Astrofire

Astrofire is a great example of the use of ray-tracing to spruce up a classic game. Modeled after the old Asteroids game, Astrofire offers many levels of flying rocks and aggressive enemies. To install, copy the contents of the **\extras\astrof** directory to an empty directory on your hard drive.

Frac

Frac is hardly new; it has been around for years. This is version 2.0, but only the menus have changed. Frac is a classic 3-D version of Tetris. Copy the files from the **\extras\frac** directory to install.

Life

Conway's classic game of Life is on the CD-ROM in the **\extras\life** subdirectory. To install, copy the contents of the \extras\life directory to a subdirectory on your hard drive.

Relentless

This is a freeware demo version of Relentless. Relentless uses polygon graphics to achieve incredible animated scenes. You must maneuver past guards—either discreetly or forcefully—to escape to freedom. Copy the **\extras\relent** directory, and run **setup.exe** to configure.

Theatrix C++ Header Files

ascii.h

```
// -------- ascii.h
#ifndef ASCII_H
#define ASCII_H

//---------------------- keypad keys
const int            END = 0x4f00;
const int             LF = 0x4b00;
const int       LEFTARROW = 0x4b00;
const int           HOME = 0x4700;
const int             UP = 0x4800;
const int        UPARROW = 0x4800;
const int           PGUP = 0x4900;
const int             RT = 0x4d00;
const int      RIGHTARROW = 0x4d00;
const int           PGDN = 0x5100;
const int             DN = 0x5000;
```

```
const int    DOWNARROW = 0x5000;
const int          INS = 0x5200;
const int          DEL = 0x5300;
const int          ESC = 0x001b;
const int       ESCAPE = 0x001b;
const int        ENTER = 0x000D;
const int        SPACE = 0x0020;
const int     SPACEBAR = 0x0020;
//------------------- function keys
const int           F1 = 0x3b00;
const int           F2 = 0x3c00;
const int           F3 = 0x3d00;
const int           F4 = 0x3e00;
const int           F5 = 0x3f00;
const int           F6 = 0x4000;
const int           F7 = 0x4100;
const int           F8 = 0x4200;
const int           F9 = 0x4300;
const int          F10 = 0x4400;


#endif
```

debug.h

```
// --------- debug.h

#ifndef DEBUG_H
#define DEBUG_H

void fatal(const char *,const char *,int);

#undef Assert
#ifdef NDEBUG
#define Assert(p)    ((void)0)
#else
#define Assert(p) ((p) ? (void)0 : \
          fatal(#p, __FILE__, __LINE__))
#endif

#endif
```

director.h

```
// ----------- director.h

#ifndef DIRECTOR_H
#define DIRECTOR_H

#include <typeinfo.h>
#include "keyfold.h"
#include "kdfold.h"
#include "timefold.h"
#include "msgfold.h"
#include "mcfold.h"
#include "mmfold.h"
#include "jsfold.h"
#include "netfold.h"
#include "hand.h"

// --- director navigation classes (cannot be instantiated)
class NextDirector  { NextDirector()  { } };
class PrevDirector  { PrevDirector()  { } };
class FirstDirector { FirstDirector() { } };
class LastDirector  { LastDirector()  { } };
class StopDirector  { StopDirector()  { } };

class Director : public Hand  {
  void set_keydownmode(int md);
  void add_keystroke_cue(Hand*,callback,int);
  void del_keystroke_cue(Hand*,callback,int);

  void add_keydown_cue(Hand*,callback,int);
  void del_keydown_cue(Hand*,callback,int);

  void add_timer_cue(Hand*,callback,int);
  void del_timer_cue(Hand*,callback,int);
```

```
void add_message_cue(Hand*,callback,int);
void del_message_cue(Hand*,callback,int);
void delete_hand(Hand*);
void submit_message(int,int,int);

void add_mouseclick_cue(Hand*,callback,int);
void del_mouseclick_cue(Hand*,callback,int);

void add_mousemove_cue(Hand*,callback);
void del_mousemove_cue(Hand*,callback);

void add_joystickbutton_cue(Hand*,callback,int);
void del_joystickbutton_cue(Hand*,callback,int);

void add_joystickmove_cue(Hand*,callback);
void del_joystickmove_cue(Hand*,callback);

void add_netpack_cue(Hand*,callback,int);
void del_netpack_cue(Hand*,callback,int);
void post_netpacket(p);

KeystrokeFolder keyinfo;      // director's key subscriptions
HotkeyFolder kdowninfo;       // "hotkey" subscriptions
TimerFolder timeinfo;         // timer subscriptions
MessageFolder msginfo;        // message subscriptions
MouseclickFolder mouseclickinfo;
MousemoveFolder mousemoveinfo;
JoystickFolder joystickinfo;
NetpackFolder netpackinfo;

int downmode;                 // flag for keyboard mode
int done;                     // true while director in control
const Type_info *next_director;
friend class Hand;
```

```
    friend class Theatrix;
protected:
  Director();
  virtual ~Director()             { }
  virtual void take_over();
  virtual void display()          { }
  virtual void hide()             { }
  virtual void iterate_director() { }
  virtual const Type_info& get_next_director()
    {
      if (next_director)
        return *next_director;
      return typeid(StopDirector);
    }
  void set_next_director(const Type_info *dir)
    { next_director = dir; }
  int next_director_set()
    { return next_director != 0; }
  void quit()
    { done=1; }
};

#endif
```

folder.h

```
// ------ folder.h

#ifndef  FOLDER_H
#define  FOLDER_H

#include "handler.h"

class Hand;

class Folder  {
  EventHandler *events;
  int eventct;
  virtual void reset() = 0;
protected:
  Folder(EventHandler* en=0, const int n=0)
    { events = en; eventct = n; }
  virtual ~Folder()
    { }
public:
  virtual void delHand(Hand*);
  virtual void dispatch(int = 0, int = 0, int = 0) = 0;
};

#endif
```

hand.h

```
// -------------- hand.h

#ifndef HAND_H
#define HAND_H

#include <typeinfo.h>
#include <fastgraf.h>
#include "debug.h"
#include "settings.h"

class Hand;

typedef  void(Hand::*callback)(int,int,int);

enum EventCode {
  TERMINAL_EVENT,
  HOTKEY_EVENT,
  TIMER_EVENT,
  MESSAGE_EVENT,
  KEYSTROKE_EVENT,
  MOUSECLICK_EVENT,
  MOUSEMOVE_EVENT,
  JOYSTICKBUTTON_EVENT,
  JOYSTICKMOVE_EVENT,
  NETPACK_EVENT
};

struct Event   {
  EventCode evtype;
  int code;
  callback func;
};
```

```
#define DECLARE_CUELIST                 \
  static Event MessageEntries[];      \
  virtual Event *GetMessageMap()      \
          { return MessageEntries; }

#define CUELIST(hand) \
  Event hand::MessageEntries[] = {

#define HOTKEY(k,fn)            \
    { HOTKEY_EVENT,          k, (callback)fn },
#define TIMER(t,fn)            \
    { TIMER_EVENT,           t, (callback)fn },
#define MESSAGE(m,fn)          \
    { MESSAGE_EVENT,         m, (callback)fn },
#define KEYSTROKE(k,fn)        \
    { KEYSTROKE_EVENT,       k, (callback)fn },
#define MOUSECLICK(b,fn)       \
    { MOUSECLICK_EVENT,      b, (callback)fn },
#define MOUSEMOVE(fn)          \
{ MOUSEMOVE_EVENT,      0, (callback)fn },
#define JOYSTICKMOVE(fn)       \
    { JOYSTICKMOVE_EVENT,   0, (callback)fn },
#define JOYSTICKBUTTON(b,fn) \
    { JOYSTICKBUTTON_EVENT, b, (callback)fn },
#define NETPACK(p,fn)          \
    { NETPACK_EVENT,         p, (callback)fn },

#define ENDCUELIST             \
  { TERMINAL_EVENT, 0, 0 }     \
};

class Director;

class Hand   {
  Director* director;
```

```
      static int numhands;
      static Hand *hand[MAXHANDS];

      static void initialize_hands();
      virtual void request_cues() { }

      void thx_request_keystroke_cue(int key,callback);
      void thx_stop_keystroke_cue(int key,callback);
      void thx_request_hotkey_cue(int scancode,callback);
      void thx_stop_hotkey_cue(int scancode,callback);
      void thx_request_timer_cue(int rate,callback);
      void thx_stop_timer_cue(int rate,callback);
      void thx_request_message_cue(int msg,callback);
      void thx_stop_message_cue(int msg,callback);
      void thx_post_message(int msg,int data1, int data2);
      void thx_request_mouseclick_cue(int msg,callback);
      void thx_stop_mouseclick_cue(int msg,callback);
      void thx_request_joystickbutton_cue(int msg,callback);
      void thx_stop_joystickbutton_cue(int msg,callback);
      void thx_request_mousemove_cue(callback);
      void thx_stop_mousemove_cue(callback);
      void thx_request_joystickmove_cue(callback);
      void thx_stop_joystickmove_cue(callback);
      void thx_request_netpack_cue(int,callback);
      void thx_stop_netpack_cue(int,callback);
      void thx_post_netpack(int);

      virtual Event *GetMessageMap() { return 0; }
      friend class Director;
      friend class Theatrix;
   protected:
      static short int mouseinuse;
      Hand(Director* dir=0);
      virtual ~Hand();
      virtual void initialize()   { }
```

```
virtual void stop_director();
virtual void start_director(const Type_info&);
Director* my_director()  { return director; }
void set_hotkeys(int on);
void request_keystroke_cue(int key,callback);
void stop_keystroke_cue(int key,callback);
void request_hotkey_cue(int scancode,callback);
void stop_hotkey_cue(int scancode,callback);
void request_timer_cue(int rate,callback);
void stop_timer_cue(int rate,callback);
void request_message_cue(int msg,callback);
void stop_message_cue(int msg,callback);
void post_message(int msg,int data1, int data2);
void request_mouseclick_cue(int b,callback);
void stop_mouseclick_cue(int b,callback);
void request_mousemove_cue(callback);
void stop_mousemove_cue(callback);
void request_joystickbutton_cue(int b,callback);
void stop_joystickbutton_cue(int b,callback);
void request_joystickmove_cue(callback);
void stop_joystickmove_cue(callback);
void request_netpack_cue(int,callback);
void stop_netpack_cue(int,callback);
void post_netpack(int);
void init_mouse()
  { fg_mouseini(); }
void mouse_visible()
  { fg_mousevis(1); mouseinuse = 1; }
void mouse_invisible()
  { fg_mousevis(0); mouseinuse = 0; }
void mouse_cursorshape(char *bitmap)
  { fg_mouse256(bitmap+2, *bitmap, *(bitmap+1)); }
void get_mouseposition(int *x, int *y, int *b)
  { fg_mousepos(x, y, b); }
void get_mouseposition(int *x, int *y)
```

```
     { int b; fg_mousepos(x, y, &b); }
   void set_mouseposition(int x, int y)
     { fg_mousemov(x, y); }
public:
   void set_director(Director* d)  { director=d; }
};
// ----------------- Keystroke
inline void Hand::request_keystroke_cue(int key,callback cb)
{
  Assert(director != 0);
  thx_request_keystroke_cue(key,cb);
}
inline void Hand::stop_keystroke_cue(int key,callback cb)
{
  Assert(director != 0);
  thx_stop_keystroke_cue(key,cb);
}
// ----------------- Keydown
inline void Hand::request_hotkey_cue(int key,callback cb)
{
  Assert(director != 0);
  thx_request_hotkey_cue(key, cb);
}
inline void Hand::stop_hotkey_cue(int key,callback cb)
{
  Assert(director != 0);
  thx_stop_hotkey_cue(key, cb);
}
// ----------------- Timer
inline void Hand::request_timer_cue(int r,callback cb)
{
  Assert(director != 0);
  thx_request_timer_cue(r, cb);
}
inline void Hand::stop_timer_cue(int r,callback cb)
```

```
{
  Assert(director != 0);
  thx_stop_timer_cue(r, cb);
}
// ----------------- Message
inline void Hand::request_message_cue(int msg,callback cb)
{
  Assert(director != 0);
  thx_request_message_cue(msg, cb);
}
inline void Hand::stop_message_cue(int msg,callback cb)
{
Assert(director != 0);
  thx_stop_message_cue(msg, cb);
}


inline void Hand::post_message(int msg,int data1=0,int data2=0)
{
  Assert(director != 0);
  thx_post_message(msg, data1, data2);
}
// ----------------- mouseclick
inline void Hand::request_mouseclick_cue(int b,callback cb)
{
  Assert(director != 0);
  thx_request_mouseclick_cue(b,cb);
}
inline void Hand::stop_mouseclick_cue(int b,callback cb)
{
  Assert(director != 0);
  thx_stop_mouseclick_cue(b,cb);
}
// ----------------- mousemove
inline void Hand::request_mousemove_cue(callback cb)
{
```

```
  Assert(director != 0);
  thx_request_mousemove_cue(cb);
}
inline void Hand::stop_mousemove_cue(callback cb)
{
  Assert(director != 0);
  thx_stop_mousemove_cue(cb);
}
// ----------------- joystickbutton
inline void Hand::request_joystickbutton_cue(int b,callback cb)
{
  Assert(director != 0);
  thx_request_joystickbutton_cue(b,cb);
}
inline void Hand::stop_joystickbutton_cue(int b,callback cb)
{
  Assert(director != 0);
  thx_stop_joystickbutton_cue(b,cb);
}
// ----------------- joystickmove
inline void Hand::request_joystickmove_cue(callback cb)
{
  Assert(director != 0);
  thx_request_joystickmove_cue(cb);
}
inline void Hand::stop_joystickmove_cue(callback cb)
{
  Assert(director != 0);
  thx_stop_joystickmove_cue(cb);
}
// ----------------- netpack
inline void Hand::request_netpack_cue(int p,callback cb)
{
  Assert(director != 0);
  thx_request_netpack_cue(p,cb);
```

```
}
inline void Hand::stop_netpack_cue(int p,callback cb)
{
  Assert(director != 0);
  thx_stop_netpack_cue(p,cb);
}
inline void Hand::post_netpack(int p)
{
  Assert(director != 0);
  thx_post_netpack(p);
}

#endif
```

handler.h

```
// ----------- handler.h

#ifndef  HANDLER_H
#define  HANDLER_H

#include <mem.h>
#include "hand.h"
#include "linklist.h"

struct subscription  {
  Hand* hand;
  callback cb;
  subscription(Hand*h, callback c) : hand(h), cb(c)
    { }
};

class EventHandler  {
public:
  ~EventHandler()
    { reset(); }
  void add(Hand*,callback);
  void del(Hand*,callback);
  void delHand(Hand*);
  void execute_callbacks(int p1=0, int p2=0, int p3=0);
  void reset();
  int getnum();
  LinkedList<subscription> slist;
};

#endif
```

jsfold.h

```
// --------------- jsfold.h

#ifndef JSFOLD_H
#define JSFOLD_H

#include "handler.h"
#include "folder.h"

class Hand;

class JoystickFolder : public Folder  {
  void reset_slot(int);
  EventHandler button1list;
  EventHandler button2list;
  EventHandler list;
  friend class JoystickServer;
public:
  void register_joystickbutton(Hand*,int button,callback);
  void unregister_joystickbutton(Hand*,int button,callback);
  void register_joystickmove(Hand*,callback);
  void unregister_joystickmove(Hand*,callback);
  void delHand(Hand*);
  void reset();
  void dispatch(int, int, int);
};

#endif
```

jssrvr.h

```
// ---------- jssrvr.h

#ifndef JSSRVR_H
#define JSSRVR_H

#include "server.h"

class JoystickServer : public Server  {
  friend class Theatrix;
  int dz;
  int xadj, yadj;
  int cx, cy;
  int lx, ty;
  int rx, by;
  int joystick_supported;
  void startup();
  int setting(int *x, int *y);
  void calibrate(char *pos, int *x, int *y);
public:
  JoystickServer();
  void check(Folder&);
};

#endif
```

kdfold.h

```cpp
// ----------- kdfold.h
#ifndef  KDFOLD_H
#define  KDFOLD_H

#include "handler.h"
#include "folder.h"
#include "debug.h"
const int MAXDOWNENTRY = 20;
class Hand;
struct HotkeyEntry  {
  int code;
  EventHandler list;
};
class HotkeyFolder : public Folder  {
  void reset_slot(int);
  void thxregister_key(Hand*,int key,callback);
  int numentries;
  HotkeyEntry entry[MAXDOWNENTRY];
  friend class HotkeyServer;
public:
  HotkeyFolder() { numentries=0; }
  void register_key(Hand*,int key,callback);
  void unregister_key(Hand*,int key,callback);
  void delHand(Hand*);
  void reset();
  void dispatch(int, int, int);
};
inline void HotkeyFolder::register_key(Hand* hand,
                                       int code,callback cb)
{
  thxregister_key(hand,code,cb);
  Assert(numentries <= MAXDOWNENTRY);
}
#endif
```

kdsrvr.h

```
// ------ kdsrvr.h

#ifndef  KDSRVR_H
#define  KDSRVR_H

#include "server.h"

class HotkeyServer : public Server  {
  void startup();
  void shutdown();
friend class Theatrix;
public:
  void check(Folder&);
  static int newtick;
};

#endif
```

keyfold.h

```
// --------- keyfold.h
#ifndef  KEYFOLD_H
#define  KEYFOLD_H
#include "hand.h"
#include "handler.h"
#include "folder.h"
#include "debug.h"
const int NUMKEYS  = 175;
const int AUX_OFFSET = 71;
class KeystrokeFolder : public Folder  {
  int adjust_key(int);
  EventHandler key[NUMKEYS];
  friend class KeystrokeServer;
public:
  KeystrokeFolder() : Folder(key, NUMKEYS) { }
  void register_key(Hand*,int key,callback);
  void unregister_key(Hand*,int key,callback);
  void reset();
  void dispatch(int, int, int);
};
inline int KeystrokeFolder::adjust_key(int k)
{
  if ((k&0xff00) != 0)
    k = ((k>>8)&0xff)+AUX_OFFSET;
  Assert(k >= 0 && k < NUMKEYS);
  return k;
}
inline void KeystrokeFolder::register_key(Hand* hand,
                                    int k,callback cb)
{ key[adjust_key(k)].add(hand,cb); }
inline void KeystrokeFolder::unregister_key(Hand* hand,
                                    int k,callback cb)
{ key[adjust_key(k)].del(hand,cb); }
#endif
```

keysrvr.h

```
// --------- keysrvr.h

#ifndef  KEYSRVR_H
#define  KEYSRVR_H

#include "server.h"

class KeystrokeServer : public Server  {
public:
  void check(Folder&);
};

#endif
```

linklist.h

```
// ----------- linklist.h
// a template for a linked list

#ifndef LINKLIST_H
#define LINKLIST_H

// --- the linked list entry
template <class T>
class ListEntry  {
  friend class LinkedList<T>;
  T *thisentry;
  ListEntry<T> *nextentry;
  ListEntry<T> *preventry;
  ListEntry(T *entry);
};
template <class T>
// ---- the linked list
class LinkedList  {
  // --- the listhead
  ListEntry<T> *firstentry;
  ListEntry<T> *lastentry;
  ListEntry<T> *iterator;
  short int entrycount;
  T *CurrentEntry();
  void RemoveEntry(ListEntry<T> *entry);
  void InsertEntry(T *entry);
  void InsertEntry(T *entry, short int pos);
  void RemoveEntry(short int pos);
public:
  LinkedList();
  virtual ~LinkedList()
    { ClearList(); }
  void AppendEntry(T *entry);
```

```
  void InsertEntry(T *entry, T *curr);
  void RemoveEntry(T *entry = 0);
  T *FindEntry(short int pos);
  short int FindEntry(T *entry);
  T *FirstEntry();
  T *LastEntry();
  T *NextEntry();
  T *PrevEntry();
  T *NextEntry(T *entry);
  T *PrevEntry(T *entry);
  void ClearList();
  short int EntryCount() const
    { return entrycount; }
};
template <class T>
// ---- construct a linked list
LinkedList<T>::LinkedList()
{
  iterator = 0;
  firstentry = 0;
  lastentry = 0;
  entrycount = 0;
}
template <class T>
// ---- remove all entries from a linked list
void LinkedList<T>::ClearList()
{
  ListEntry<T> *lentry = firstentry;
  while (lentry != 0)  {
    ListEntry<T> *nxt = lentry->nextentry;
    delete lentry;
    lentry = nxt;
  }
  iterator = 0;
  firstentry = 0;
```

```
    lastentry = 0;
    entrycount = 0;
}
// ---- construct a linked list entry
template <class T>
ListEntry<T>::ListEntry(T *entry)
{
    thisentry = entry;
    nextentry = 0;
    preventry = 0;
}
template <class T>
// ---- append an entry to the linked list
void LinkedList<T>::AppendEntry(T *entry)
{
    ListEntry<T> *newentry = new ListEntry<T>(entry);
    newentry->preventry = lastentry;
    if (lastentry)
        lastentry->nextentry = newentry;
    if (firstentry == 0)
        firstentry = newentry;
    lastentry = newentry;
    entrycount++;
}
template <class T>
// ---- return the current linked list entry
T *LinkedList<T>::CurrentEntry()
{
    return iterator ? iterator->thisentry : 0;
}
template <class T>
// ---- return the first entry in the linked list
T *LinkedList<T>::FirstEntry()
{
    iterator = firstentry;
```

```
    return CurrentEntry();
  }
  template <class T>
  // ---- return the last entry in the linked list
  T *LinkedList<T>::LastEntry()
  {
    iterator = lastentry;
    return CurrentEntry();
  }
  template <class T>
  // ---- return the next entry following the specified one
  T *LinkedList<T>::NextEntry(T *entry)
  {
    FindEntry(entry);
    return NextEntry();
  }
  template <class T>
  // ---- return the next entry in the linked list
  T *LinkedList<T>::NextEntry()
  {
    if (iterator == 0)
      iterator = firstentry;
    else
      iterator = iterator->nextentry;
    return CurrentEntry();
  }
  template <class T>
  // ---- return the previous entry ahead of the specified one
  T *LinkedList<T>::PrevEntry(T *entry)
  {
    FindEntry(entry);
    return PrevEntry();
```

```
}
template <class T>
// ---- return the previous entry in the linked list
T *LinkedList<T>::PrevEntry()
{
  if (iterator == 0)
    iterator = lastentry;
  else
    iterator = iterator->preventry;
  return CurrentEntry();
}
template <class T>
// ---- remove an entry from the linked list by position
void LinkedList<T>::RemoveEntry(short int pos)
{
  FindEntry(pos);
  if (iterator != 0)
    RemoveEntry(iterator);
}
template <class T>
// ---- remove an entry from the linked list by entry address
void LinkedList<T>::RemoveEntry(ListEntry<T> *lentry)
{
  if (lentry == 0)
    return;
  if (lentry == iterator)
    iterator = lentry->preventry;
  // ---- repair any break made by this removal
  if (lentry->nextentry)
    lentry->nextentry->preventry = lentry->preventry;
  if (lentry->preventry)
    lentry->preventry->nextentry = lentry->nextentry;
  // --- maintain listhead if this is last and/or first
  if (lentry == lastentry)
    lastentry = lentry->preventry;
```

```
  if (lentry == firstentry)
    firstentry = lentry->nextentry;
  delete lentry;
  --entrycount;
}
template <class T>
// ---- remove current or specified entry from linked list
void LinkedList<T>::RemoveEntry(T *entry)
{
  if (entry != 0)
    FindEntry(entry);
  RemoveEntry(iterator);
}
template <class T>
// ---- insert an entry into the linked list ahead of another
void LinkedList<T>::InsertEntry(T *entry, T *curr)
{
  FindEntry(curr);
  InsertEntry(entry);
}
template <class T>
// ---- insert an entry into the linked list by position
void LinkedList<T>::InsertEntry(T *entry, short int pos)
{
  FindEntry(pos);
  InsertEntry(entry);
}
template <class T>
// ---- insert an entry into the linked list ahead of iterator
void LinkedList<T>::InsertEntry(T *entry)
{
  if (iterator == 0)
    AppendEntry(entry);
  else {
    ListEntry<T> *newentry = new ListEntry<T>(entry);
```

```
      newentry->nextentry = iterator;
      if (iterator)  {
        newentry->preventry = iterator->preventry;
        iterator->preventry = newentry;
      }
      if (newentry->preventry)
        newentry->preventry->nextentry = newentry;
      if (iterator == firstentry)
        firstentry = newentry;
      iterator = newentry;
      entrycount++;
    }
}
template <class T>
// ---- return a specific linked list entry
T *LinkedList<T>::FindEntry(short int pos)
{
  iterator = firstentry;
  while (iterator && pos--)
    iterator = iterator->nextentry;
  return CurrentEntry();
}
template <class T>
// ---- return a specific linked list entry number
short int LinkedList<T>::FindEntry(T *entry)
{
  short int pos = 0;
  if (entry == 0)  {
    pos = entrycount;
    iterator = 0;
  }
  else  {
    iterator = firstentry;
    while (iterator)  {
      if (entry == iterator->thisentry)
```

```
            break;
        iterator = iterator->nextentry;
        pos++;
      }
    }
    return pos;
}

#endif
```

mcfold.h

```
// ------ mcfold.h
#ifndef  MCFOLD_H
#define  MCFOLD_H
#include "handler.h"
#include "folder.h"
class Hand;
class MouseclickFolder : public Folder  {
  void reset_slot(int);
  EventHandler leftbuttonlist;
  EventHandler rightbuttonlist;
  friend class MouseclickServer;
public:
  void register_mouseclick(Hand*,int button,callback);
  void unregister_mouseclick(Hand*,int button,callback);
  void delHand(Hand*);
  void reset();
  void dispatch(int, int, int);
};
#endif
```

mcsrvr.h

```
// ---------- mcsrvr.h
#ifndef  MCSRVR_H
#define  MCSRVR_H
#include "server.h"

class MouseclickServer : public Server  {
public:
  void check(Folder&);
};
#endif
```

media.h

```
// --------- media.h

#ifndef MEDIA_H
#define MEDIA_H

#include "xms.h"
#include "settings.h"

// ------- media clip (sound or graphic)
struct MediaClip {
  short int w, h;
  long size;
  char *buf;
  long xoffset;
  MediaClip();
  ~MediaClip()
    { delete buf; }
};

// ---- media library of sound or graphic clips
struct MediaLib {
  char name[13];
  short int clipcount;
  MediaClip* clip;
  short int xms_handle;
  MediaLib();
  ~MediaLib();
};

class Media {
  static short int use_xms;
  short int bufsize;
  char *buffer;
```

```
protected:
  static MediaLib libraries[MAXFXLIBS];
  static short int libcount;
  Media();
  ~Media();
public:
  static void set_xms(int mode)
    { use_xms = mode; }
  void load_library(char *libfile);
  MediaClip& getclip(int lib, int clp);
  static short int library_number(char *fname);
  static short int clipcount(int libno)
    { return libraries[libno].clipcount; }
  virtual int hasdimensions() = 0;
};

class GraphicsMedia : public Media  {
public:
  GraphicsMedia() { }
  virtual int hasdimensions()
    { return 1; }
};

class SoundMedia : public Media {
public:
  SoundMedia() { }
  virtual int hasdimensions()
    { return 0; }
};

#endif
```

mmfold.h

```
// --------- mmfold.h
#ifndef  MMFOLD_H
#define  MMFOLD_H
#include "handler.h"
#include "folder.h"
class Hand;
class MousemoveFolder : public Folder  {
  void reset_slot(int);
  EventHandler list;
  friend class MousemoveServer;
public:
  void register_mousemove(Hand*,callback);
  void unregister_mousemove(Hand*,callback);
  void delHand(Hand*);
  void reset();
  void dispatch(int, int, int);
};
#endif
```

mmsrvr.h

```
// ---------- mmsrvr.h
#ifndef  MMSRVR_H
#define  MMSRVR_H
#include "server.h"
class MousemoveServer : public Server  {
  int ox, oy;
public:
  MousemoveServer()
    { ox = 0; oy = 0; }
  void check(Folder&);
};
#endif
```

msgfold.h

```
// -------- msgfold.h
#ifndef MSGFOLD_H
#define MSGFOLD_H
#include "queue.h"
#include "folder.h"
#include "debug.h"
class Hand;
class MessageFolder : public Folder  {
  EventHandler messagenumber[MAXMESSAGE];
  Queue msgQ;
  friend class MessageServer;
public:
  MessageFolder() : Folder(messagenumber, MAXMESSAGE) { }
  void add_message(Hand*,int rate,callback);
  void del_message(Hand*,int rate,callback);
  void reset();
  void send(int,int,int);
  void dispatch(int, int, int);
};
inline void MessageFolder::add_message(Hand* h,int m,callback c)
{
  Assert(m >= 0 && m < MAXMESSAGE);
  messagenumber[m].add(h,c);
}
inline void MessageFolder::del_message(Hand* h,int m,callback c)
{
  Assert(m >= 0 && m < MAXMESSAGE);
  messagenumber[m].del(h,c);
}
inline void MessageFolder::send(int msg,int data1, int data2)
{
  Assert(msg >= 0 && msg < MAXMESSAGE);
  msgQ.put(msg,data1,data2);
}
#endif
```

msgsrvr.h

```
// ---------- msgsrvr.h

#ifndef  MSGSRVR_H
#define  MSGSRVR_H

#include "server.h"

class MessageServer : public Server  {
public:
  void check(Folder&);
};

#endif
```

music.h

```
// -------- music.h

#ifndef MUSIC_H
#define MUSIC_H

#include "hand.h"

class MusicHand : public Hand  {
  friend class Theatrix;
  char *scorefilename;
  char *score;
  static char *drivers[3];
  static char *driverptr[3];
  static char *realptr[3];
  static void startup();
  static void shutdown();
  static int load_sound_drivers();
  static int init_driver();
  static void terminate_driver();
  static void delete_drivers(int i);
  static int music_supported;
protected:
  virtual void initialize();
public:
  MusicHand(char *sc);
  virtual ~MusicHand();
  void play_music_clip(int index);
  int music_clip_is_playing();
  void stop_music_clip();
  void load_score(char*);
  int isconducting()
    { return music_supported; }
};

#endif
```

netfold.h

```
// -------- netfold.h
#ifndef  NETFOLD_H
#define  NETFOLD_H
#include "queue.h"
#include "folder.h"
#include "debug.h"
class Hand;
class EventHandler;
class NetpackFolder : public Folder  {
  EventHandler packet[MAXNETPACK];
  friend class NetpackServer;
public:
  NetpackFolder() : Folder(packet,MAXNETPACK)  { }
  void add_netpack(Hand*,int p,callback);
  void del_netpack(Hand*,int p,callback);
  void reset();
  void dispatch(int, int, int);
};
inline void NetpackFolder::add_netpack(Hand* h,int p,
                                                callback cb)
{
  Assert(p >= 0 && p < MAXNETPACK);
  packet[p].add(h,cb);
}
inline void NetpackFolder::del_netpack(Hand* h,int p,
                                                callback cb)
{
  Assert(p >= 0 && p < MAXNETPACK);
  packet[p].del(h,cb);
}
#endif
```

netsrvr.h

```
// ------- netsrvr.h

#ifndef  NETSRVR_H
#define  NETSRVR_H

#include "server.h"
class CommPort;

class NetpackServer : public Server  {
    int netpacks_active;
    int port;
    CommPort* commport;
    void startup();
    void shutdown();
    friend class Theatrix;
public:
    void check(Folder&);
    void send(int);
};

#endif
```

perform.h

```
// ------- perform.h
#ifndef PERFORM_H
#define PERFORM_H
#include <fastgraf.h>
#include "vocal.h"
#include "settings.h"
#include "debug.h"
#include "xms.h"
#include "media.h"
class Performer : public VocalHand  {
  static GraphicsMedia gfxlib;
  int curlib;
  int curfont;
  void thx_show_print(int,int,char*);
  void thx_show_number(int,int,int);
protected:
  Performer(Director* d=0);
  virtual ~Performer();
  void load_gfxlib(char*);
  void set_gfxlib(char*);
  void show_image(int x,int y,int imageno);
  void show_frame(int x,int y,int imageno);
  void show_clipped_image(int x,int y,int imageno);
  int get_image_width(int imageno);
  int get_image_height(int imageno);
  int get_num_images();
  void load_gfxfont(char*);
  void set_gfxfont(char*);
  void show_print(int,int,char*);
  void show_number(int,int,int);
  int get_char_width(char);
  int get_char_height(char);
};
```

```
inline void Performer::show_image(int x,int y,int imageno)
{
  Assert(curlib!=-1);
  Assert(imageno>0 && imageno<=Media::clipcount(curlib));
  MediaClip& mc = gfxlib.getclip(curlib,imageno-1);
  fg_move(x,y+mc.h-1);
  fg_drwimage(mc.buf,mc.w,mc.h);
}
inline void Performer::show_frame(int x,int y,int imageno)
{
  Assert(curlib!=-1);
  Assert(imageno>0 && imageno<=Media::clipcount(curlib));
  MediaClip& mc = gfxlib.getclip(curlib,imageno-1);
  fg_move(x,y+mc.h-1);
  fg_putimage(mc.buf,mc.w,mc.h);
}
inline void Performer::show_clipped_image(int x,int y,
                                          int imageno)
{
  Assert(curlib!=-1);
  Assert(imageno>0 && imageno<=Media::clipcount(curlib));
  MediaClip& mc = gfxlib.getclip(curlib,imageno-1);
  fg_move(x,y+mc.h-1);
  fg_clpimage(mc.buf,mc.w,mc.h);
}
inline int Performer::get_image_width(int imageno)
{
  Assert(curlib!=-1);
  MediaClip& mc = gfxlib.getclip(curlib,imageno-1);
  return mc.w;
}
inline int Performer::get_image_height(int imageno)
{
  Assert(curlib!=-1);
  MediaClip& mc = gfxlib.getclip(curlib,imageno-1);
```

```
    return mc.h;
  }
  inline int Performer::get_num_images()
  {
    Assert(curlib!=-1);
    return Media::clipcount(curlib);
  }
  inline int Performer::get_char_width(char ch)
  {
    Assert(curfont!=-1);
    MediaClip& mc = gfxlib.getclip(curfont,ch-48+26);
    return mc.w;
  }
  inline int Performer::get_char_height(char ch)
  {
    Assert(curfont!=-1);
    MediaClip& mc = gfxlib.getclip(curfont,ch-48+26);
    return mc.h;
  }
  inline void Performer::show_print(int x,int y,char* str)
  {
    Assert(curfont!=-1);
    thx_show_print(x,y,str);
  }
  inline void Performer::show_number(int x,int y,int num)
  {
    Assert(curfont!=-1);
    thx_show_number(x,y,num);
  }
  #endif
```

player.h

```
// -------- player.h

#ifndef PLAYER_H
#define PLAYER_H

#include "perform.h"

class SceneDirector;

class Player : public Performer  {
    char *gfxlib;         // name of .gfx file with Player images
    char *sfxlib;         // name of .sfx file with Player sounds
    short int x, y;       // current screen location
    short int px, py;     // previous screen location
    short int h, w;       // current image size
    short int ph, pw;     // previous image size
    short int imageno;    // current image
    short int is_visible; // true if Player is being displayed
    short int ticker;
    short int interval;
    short int clipped;    // true if image is to be clipped
    short int cx1, cy1, cx2, cy2;  // clip coordinates
    short int in_update_position;
    short int posted_x, posted_y;  // posted screen location
    short int posted_imageno;      // posted image
    void displayframe();
    friend class SceneDirector;
protected:
    SceneDirector *director;
    virtual void initialize();
public:
    Player(char *gl = 0, char *sl = 0, int intv = 1);
    virtual ~Player() { }
```

```
        void set_imageno(short int in);
        short int get_imageno()
          { return imageno; }
        short int getx() const
          { return x; }
        short int gety() const
          { return y; }
        void setx(short int nx);
        void sety(short int ny);
        void setxy(short int nx, short int ny);
        short int getheight() const
          { return h; }
        short int getwidth() const
          { return w; }
        void stillframe(short int im, short int wait);
        virtual void appear()
          { is_visible = 1; }
        virtual void disappear();
        int isvisible()
          { return is_visible; }
        virtual void update_position() { }
        void clip(int x1, int y1, int x2, int y2);
        void unclip()
          { clipped = 0; }
        int isclipped()
          { return clipped; }
        void setinterval(short int inv)
          { interval = inv; ticker = 0; }
      };


#endif
```

queue.h

```
// --------- queue.h

#ifndef  QUEUE_H
#define  QUEUE_H

const int QLEN = 50;

struct messageinfo  {
  int msg;
  int data1;
  int data2;
};

class Queue  {
  messageinfo a[QLEN];
  int head,tail;
  int inc(int);
public:
  Queue();
  void put(int,int,int);
  void get(int*,int*,int*);
  int isfull();
  int isempty();
};

#endif
```

scancode.h

```
// ------- scancode.h

#ifndef SCANCODE_H
#define SCANCODE_H

// ------------------------------- MISC
const int          SCAN_SPACE = 0x39;
const int          SCAN_ENTER = 0x1c;
const int         SCAN_INSERT = 0x52;
const int            SCAN_DEL = 0x53;
const int            SCAN_END = 0x4f;
const int           SCAN_PGDN = 0x51;
const int           SCAN_PGUP = 0x49;
const int           SCAN_HOME = 0x47;
const int           SCAN_LEFT = 0x4b;
const int             SCAN_UP = 0x48;
const int          SCAN_RIGHT = 0x4d;
const int           SCAN_DOWN = 0x50;
const int        SCAN_BKSPACE = 0x0e;
const int            SCAN_TAB = 0x0f;
const int         SCAN_ESCAPE = 0x01;
const int            SCAN_ESC = 0x01;
// ------------------------------- rare
const int           SCAN_CTRL = 0x1d;
const int         SCAN_LSHIFT = 0x2a;
const int         SCAN_RSHIFT = 0x36;
const int    SCAN_PRINTSCREEN = 0x37;
const int            SCAN_ALT = 0x38;
const int        SCAN_NUMLOCK = 0x45;
const int     SCAN_SCROLLLOCK = 0x46;
// ------------------------------- F-keys
const int             SCAN_F1 = 0x3b;
const int             SCAN_F2 = 0x3c;
const int             SCAN_F3 = 0x3d;
```

```
const int            SCAN_F4 = 0x3e;
const int            SCAN_F5 = 0x3f;
const int            SCAN_F6 = 0x40;
const int            SCAN_F7 = 0x41;
const int            SCAN_F8 = 0x42;
const int            SCAN_F9 = 0x43;
const int           SCAN_F10 = 0x44;
// ------------------------------- ALPHA
const int             SCAN_A = 0x1e;
const int             SCAN_B = 0x30;
const int             SCAN_C = 0x2e;
const int             SCAN_D = 0x20;
const int             SCAN_E = 0x12;
const int             SCAN_F = 0x21;
const int             SCAN_G = 0x22;
const int             SCAN_H = 0x23;
const int             SCAN_I = 0x17;
const int             SCAN_J = 0x24;
const int             SCAN_K = 0x25;
const int             SCAN_L = 0x26;
const int             SCAN_M = 0x32;
const int             SCAN_N = 0x31;
const int             SCAN_O = 0x18;
const int             SCAN_P = 0x19;
const int             SCAN_Q = 0x10;
const int             SCAN_R = 0x13;
const int             SCAN_S = 0x1f;
const int             SCAN_T = 0x14;
const int             SCAN_U = 0x16;
const int             SCAN_V = 0x2f;
const int             SCAN_W = 0x11;
const int             SCAN_X = 0x2d;
const int             SCAN_Y = 0x15;
const int             SCAN_Z = 0x2c;


#endif
```

scenedir.h

```
// ------- scenedir.h
#ifndef SCENEDIR_H
#define SCENEDIR_H
#include "scenery.h"
#include "viddir.h"
#include "linklist.h"
#include "player.h"
class SceneDirector : public SceneryDirector  {
  static SceneDirector *thisscene;
  static int lastsceneid;
  int snapshot;
  virtual void pre_timer_tick()  { }
  virtual void post_timer_tick() { }
  void scanframes();
  friend class Player;
  void addplayer(Player& pl);
  void on_s(int = 0);
protected:
  LinkedList<Player> plist;
  virtual void display();
  virtual void hide();
  virtual void on_timer();
public:
  SceneDirector(char *scfile, short int trans=ClearEveryTime);
  virtual ~SceneDirector() { }
  void ChangeZOrder(Player *p1, Player *p2)
  { plist.RemoveEntry(p1); plist.InsertEntry(p1, p2); }
  void MoveZToFront(Player *p)
  { plist.RemoveEntry(p);  plist.AppendEntry(p);  }
};
#endif
```

scenery.h

```
// ---------- scenery.h
#ifndef SCENERY_H
#define SCENERY_H
#include "viddir.h"
struct Mice  {
  short int x1, y1, x2, y2; // screen rectangle
  char *cursor;             // cursor hotspot(x,y) mask and map
  callback func;            // function to call if left click
};
#define DECLARE_MOUSECURSORS      \
  static Mice MouseCursorTable[]; \
  virtual Mice *GetMouseCursors() \
    { return MouseCursorTable; }
#define CURSORLIST(scene)       \
  Mice scene::MouseCursorTable[] = {
#define MOUSE_CURSOR(x1,y1,x2,y2,crs,fn) \
    {x1,y1,x2,y2,crs,(callback)fn},
#define ENDCURSORLIST  \
  { -1, -1, -1, -1 }   \
};
extern char UPCURSOR[];
extern char DNCURSOR[];
extern char RTCURSOR[];
extern char LFCURSOR[];
extern char CNCURSOR[];
extern char ULCURSOR[];
extern char URCURSOR[];
extern char LLCURSOR[];
extern char LRCURSOR[];
extern char DEFAULT[];
#define UPPERLEFTARROWCURSOR  ULCURSOR
#define UPARROWCURSOR         UPCURSOR
#define UPPERRIGHTARROWCURSOR URCURSOR
```

```
#define LEFTARROWCURSOR        LFCURSOR
#define CENTERCURSOR           CNCURSOR
#define RIGHTARROWCURSOR       RTCURSOR
#define LOWERLEFTARROWCURSOR   LLCURSOR
#define DOWNARROWCURSOR        DNCURSOR
#define LOWERRIGHTARROWCURSOR  LRCURSOR
#define DEFAULTCURSOR          DEFAULT

const short int ClearEveryTime = -1;
const short int NoTransition = 0;

class SceneryDirector : public VideoDirector  {
  short int transition;
  void show_mousecursor(char *cursor);
  void mousemoved(int x, int y, int);
  void mouseclicked(int x, int y);
protected:
  char *scenery;
  Mice *mousecursors;
  DECLARE_CUELIST
  virtual void display();
  virtual void stop_director()
    { quit(); }
  virtual void on_escape()
    { stop_director(); }
    virtual void on_space()
    { stop_director(); }
    virtual void on_enter()
    { stop_director(); }
  virtual const Type_info& get_next_director();
  virtual void initialize();
  virtual Mice *GetMouseCursors()
    { return 0; }
  virtual void refresh_display();
  virtual void display_original_scenery();
```

```
public:
  SceneryDirector(char *pcxfile = 0,
                    short int trans = ClearEveryTime);
  virtual ~SceneryDirector()
    { }
};

#endif
```

serial.h

```
// ------ serial.h

#ifndef SERIAL_H
#define SERIAL_H

#include <dos.h>
#undef disable

typedef int bool;
const int true = 1;
const int false = 0;

const int systimer = 8;

class Timer {
  int timer;
public:
  Timer()
    { timer = -1; }
  bool timed_out()
    { return timer == 0; }
  void set(int secs)
    { timer=secs*182/10+1; }
  void disable()
    { timer = -1; }
  bool running()
    { return timer > 0; }
  void countdown()
    { --timer; }
  bool disabled()
    { return timer == -1; }
};

const int xon  = 17;
```

```
const int xoff = 19;
const int PICO1 = 0x21; // 8259 Programmable Interrupt Ctrlr
const int PICO0 = 0x20; // "          "              "        "
const int EOI   = 0x20; // End of Interrupt command
// -------------- line status register values
const int XmitDataReady = 0x20;
// ------------ modem control register values
const int DTR = 1;
const int RTS = 2;
const int OUT2 = 8;
// ------------ modem status register values
const int RLSD = 0x80;
const int DSR = 0x20;
const int CTS = 0x10;
// ----------- interrupt enable register signals
const int DataReady = 1;
// ------------- serial input interrupt buffer
const int BufSize = 1024;
const int SafetyLevel = (BufSize/4);
const int Threshold = (SafetyLevel*3);

// ----- com port initialization parameter byte
union portinit   {
    struct {
        unsigned wordlen  : 2;
        unsigned stopbits : 1;
        unsigned parity   : 3;
        unsigned brk      : 1;
        unsigned divlatch : 1;
    } initbits;
    char initchar;
};
struct CommParameters  {
  int port;
  int parity;
  int stopbits;
```

```
    int databits;
    int baud;
};

class CommPort {
  portinit initcom;
  char *mp_recvbuff;
  bool xonxoff_enabled;
  char *mp_nextin, *mp_nextout;
  int buffer_count;
  CommParameters commparms;
  bool waiting_for_xon;
  bool waiting_to_send_xon;
  static CommPort *mp_CommPort;
  int timeout;
  static Timer serialtimer;

  int BasePort()
    { return (0x3f8-((commparms.port-1)<<8)); }
  int TxData()
    { return BasePort(); }
  int RxData()
    { return BasePort(); }
  int DivLSB()
    { return BasePort(); }
  int DivMSB()
    { return BasePort()+1; }
  int IntEnable()
    { return BasePort()+1; }
  int IntIdent()
    { return BasePort()+2; }
  int LineCtl()
    { return BasePort()+3; }
  int ModemCtl()
    { return BasePort()+4; }
```

```
    int LineStatus()
      { return BasePort()+5; }
    int ModemStatus()
      { return BasePort()+6; }
    int irq()
      { return 4-(commparms.port-1); }
    int vector()
      { return 12-(commparms.port-1); }
    int ComIRQ()
      { return ~(1 << irq()); }
    void CommInterrupt();
    friend void interrupt newcomint(...);
    friend void interrupt newtimer(...);
public:
    CommPort(const CommParameters& cp);
    ~CommPort();
    void Initialize();
    int readcomm();
    bool writecomm(int ch);
    void clear_serial_queue();
    bool carrier()
      { return (inp(ModemStatus()) & RLSD) != 0; }
    bool input_char_ready()
      { return mp_nextin != mp_nextout; }
    void SetTimeout(int to)
      { timeout = to; }
    const CommParameters& CommParms()
      { return commparms; }
    void EnableXonXoff()
      { xonxoff_enabled = true; }
    void DisableXonXoff()
      { xonxoff_enabled = false; }
};


#endif
```

server.h

```
// -------- server.h

#ifndef  SERVER_H
#define  SERVER_H

class Folder;

class Server      {
  virtual void startup() { }
  virtual void shutdown() { }
public:
  virtual void check(Folder&) = 0;
};

#endif
```

settings.h

```
// ------- settings.h

#ifndef SETTINGS_H
#define SETTINGS_H

const int DEFAULT_VIDEO_MODE = 22;

const int MAXDIRECTORS = 20; // Directors in one application
const int MAXHANDS = 250;    // limit of Hands in application
const int MAXFXLIBS = 30;    // GFX/SFX libs
const int MAXMESSAGE = 200;  // highest message number available
const int MAXNETPACK = 100;  // highest network packet available

const int NUMPATCHES = 25;   // used only by 'set_synch_patch'
                             // and 'synch_patches'
const int CLOCKTICKS = 18;

#endif
```

standard.h

```
// ---- standard.h

#ifndef STANDARD_H
#define STANDARD_H

enum boolean
{
  False=0, True, FALSE=0, TRUE,
  Failure=0, Success, FAILURE=0, SUCCESS,
  No=0, Yes, NO=0, YES,
  Off=0, On, OFF=0, ON
};

const int ERROR = -1;
const int OK    =  1;
const int NOT_OK = 0;

const int LEFTMOUSEBUTTON = 1;
const int RIGHTMOUSEBUTTON = 2;
const int BUTTONONE = 1;
const int BUTTONTWO = 2;

#endif
```

theatrix.h

```
// -------- theatrix.h

#ifndef  THEATRIX_H
#define  THEATRIX_H

#include <typeinfo.h>

#include "hand.h"
#include "director.h"
#include "scenedir.h"
#include "scenery.h"
#include "ascii.h"
#include "scancode.h"
#include "standard.h"
#include "perform.h"
#include "viddir.h"
#include "music.h"
#include "keysrvr.h"
#include "kdsrvr.h"
#include "timesrvr.h"
#include "msgsrvr.h"
#include "mcsrvr.h"
#include "mmsrvr.h"
#include "jssrvr.h"
#include "netsrvr.h"
#include "keyfold.h"
#include "kdfold.h"
#include "timefold.h"
#include "msgfold.h"
#include "mcfold.h"
#include "mmfold.h"
#include "jsfold.h"
#include "netfold.h"
```

```
class Theatrix  {
  int videomode;
  Director* director[MAXDIRECTORS];
  int dcount;
  static KeystrokeServer kss;
  static HotkeyServer hks;
  static TimerServer ts;
  static MessageServer ms;
  static MouseclickServer mcs;
  static MousemoveServer mms;
  static JoystickServer js;
  static NetpackServer ns;
  int find_director_index(const Type_info& id);
  void add_director(Director* d);
  friend class Director;
protected:
  Theatrix(char* str);
 ~Theatrix();
public:
  void go(int index=0);
  void go(const Type_info&);
  void enable_netpacks();
  void use_commport(int);
  void enable_joystick();
  void joystick_extremes(int *x1, int *y1, int *x2, int *y2);
  void use_video_mode(int vmode);
  void set_xms(int mode);
  static void fatal(const char*,const char*,int);
  static void fatal(const char*);
  static void system_shutdown();
  static Theatrix *current_game;
};
#endif
```

timefold.h

```
// ------ timefold.h
#ifndef  TIMEFOLD_H
#define  TIMEFOLD_H
#include "handler.h"
#include "folder.h"
class Hand;
class TimerFolder : public Folder  {
  EventHandler tick[CLOCKTICKS];
  friend class TimerServer;
public:
  TimerFolder() : Folder(tick, CLOCKTICKS) { }
  void add_timer(Hand*,int rate,callback);
  void del_timer(Hand*,int rate,callback);
  void reset();
  void dispatch(int tickno, int, int)
    { tick[tickno].execute_callbacks(); }
};
#endif
```

timesrvr.h

```
// -------- timesrvr.h
#ifndef TIMESRVR_H
#define TIMESRVR_H
#include "server.h"
class TimerServer : public Server  {
  int tickno;
  void startup();
  void shutdown();
  friend class Theatrix;
public:
  void check(Folder&);
  static int newtick;
};
#endif
```

viddir.h

```
// ---------- viddir.h
#ifndef VIDDIR_H
#define VIDDIR_H
#include "director.h"
#include "settings.h"
const int BUFFERPAGE = 2;
struct FlicHdr {
  long int size;
  char signature[2];
  short int frames;
  short int width;
  short int height;
  short int bitspixel;
  short int reserved;
  long int delay;
  char filler2[108];
};
struct patch_struct  {
  int x1,y1,x2,y2;
};
class VideoDirector : public Director  {
  static int vpage;
  static patch_struct patch[NUMPATCHES];
  static int patchcount;
  static int flicplaying;
  static int flicframes;
  static int flicnonstop;
  static int delay;
  static int first;
  static char flic_context[16];
  static FlicHdr flic_header;
  void on_hs(int);
protected:
```

```
   VideoDirector();
   virtual ~VideoDirector();
   void init_video();
   void fill_background_buffer(int frompage);
   void restore_page();
   virtual void iterate_director();
   virtual void on_s(int = 0);
public:
  static void swap_video_pages();
  static void synch_video_pages();
  static void synch_patch(int,int,int,int);
  static int set_synch_patch(int x1,int y1,int x2,int y2);
  static int synch_patches(int frvpage = 1);
  static void restore_patch(int x1,int y1,int x2,int y2);
  static void flush_patch(int x1,int y1,int x2,int y2);
  static int show_pcx(char* fname);
  static void show_video(char* fname,int x,int y,int nonstop=0);
  static void stop_video();
  static int video_playing() { return flicplaying; }
  static int active_page()   { return 1-vpage; }
  static int visual_page()   { return vpage; }
  static int install_palette(char*);
};


#endif
```

vocal.h

```
// -------- vocal.h

#ifndef VOCAL_HAND_H
#define VOCAL_HAND_H

#include "hand.h"
#include "media.h"
#include "debug.h"

class VocalHand : public Hand  {
  enum Driver {
    nodriver,
    digpakdriver,
    ctvoicedriver
  };
  int curlib;
  static SoundMedia sfxlib;
  static Driver driver;
  static unsigned *isplaying;
  static unsigned port,irq;
  static unsigned playing;
  static void startup();
  static void shutdown();
  void thxplay_sound_clip(int index);
  static void get_soundcard_settings();
  static Driver load_digpak_driver();
  static Driver load_ct_voice_driver();
  static void init_driver();
  static void terminate_driver();
  static void set_port(unsigned port);
  static void set_irq(unsigned irq);
  static void set_status_flag(char* ptr);
  friend class Theatrix;
```

```
public:
  VocalHand(Director* d=0) : Hand(d)
    { }
  virtual ~VocalHand() { }
  void load_sfxlib(char*);
  void set_sfxlib(char*);
  void play_sound_clip(int index);
  int sound_clip_is_playing();
  void stop_sound_clip();
  int get_num_clips();
  int get_sound_clip_length(int index);
};

inline void VocalHand::play_sound_clip(int index)
{
  Assert(curlib!=-1);
  Assert(index>0 && index<=Media::clipcount(curlib));
  thxplay_sound_clip(index);
}

inline int VocalHand::get_sound_clip_length(int index)
{
  Assert(curlib!=-1);
  MediaClip& mc = sfxlib.getclip(curlib,index-1);
  return (int) mc.size;
}

#endif
```

xms.h

```
// ------------ xms.h

#ifndef XMS_H
#define XMS_H

#include <dos.h>

int xms_present();
unsigned xms_available();
int xms_allocate(unsigned);
void xms_free(int);
void copy_xmstoconv(int, char far *, long, long);
void copy_convtoxms(int, char far *, long, long);

#endif
```

Bibliography

Abrash, Michael. *Zen of Code Optimization.* Coriolis Group Books, 1994.

Abrash, Michael. *Zen of Graphics Programming.* Coriolis Group Books, 1995.

Conger, Jim. *C Programming for MIDI.* M&T Books, 1988.

Conger, Jim. *MIDI Sequencing in C.* M&T Books, 1989.

Ferraro, Richard E. *Programmer's Guide to the EGA and VGA Cards,* 2nd Edition. Addison-Wesley, 1990.

Gruber, Diana. *Action Arcade Adventure Set.* Coriolis Group Books, 1994.

LaMothe, André, John Ratcliff, Mark Seminatore, and Denise Tyler. *Tricks of the Game Programming Gurus.* Sams Publishing, 1994.

Lampton, Christopher. *Flights of Fantasy.* Waite Group Press, 1993.

Lampton. Christopher. *Gardens of Imagination.* Waite Group Press, 1994.

Levy, Steven. *Hackers.* Dell, 1984.

Luse, Marv. *Bitmapped Graphics Programming in C++.* Addison-Wesley, 1993.

Mason, David K. *Morphing On Your PC.* Waite Group Press, 1994.

Microsoft Mouse Programmer's Reference. Microsoft Press, 1989.

Roberts, Dave. *PC Game Programming Explorer.* Coriolis Group Books, 1994.

Stolz, Axel. *The Sound Blaster Book.* Abacus, 1992.

Watkins, Christopher, and Stephen Marenka. *Taking Flight.* M&T Books, 1994.

Wilton, Richard. *Programmer's Guide to PC & PS/2 Video Systems.* Microsoft Press, 1987.

Young, Chris, and Drew Wells, *Ray Tracing Creations,* 2nd Edition. Waite Group Press, 1994.

Glossary

3-D model

A computer data structure with data values that represent an image in terms of its component objects positioned and scaled in a three-dimensional coordinate system.

abstraction, level of

The working level of detail and knowledge at which a programmer writes code. At higher levels of abstraction, the underlying system encapsulates and hides more of the lower-level details.

active video page

The video page that the program reads from and writes to. The active video page can be visible or hidden.

analog signal

A waveform represented in its true, continuous form.

animation

The rapid display of a sequence of pictures that, when viewed, depicts a moving object.

ASCII

The American Standard Code for Information Interchange, which associates integer values to numbers, letters, and special characters. Standard ASCII ranges from 0 to 127 and assigns values to digits, upper- and lowercase letters, punctuation marks, form control characters, and special transmission characters. Extended ASCII ranges from 128 to 255 and, on the PC architecture, assigns those values to foreign (non-English) language characters and graphics characters.

background

The image that occupies the full screen in a game and that represents the scenery in a scene.

baud rate

The speed in approximate bits per second that a serial port transmits and receives data.

bitmapped graphics

The format that represents an image as an array of pixel values. There are several such formats for bitmapped graphics data files. The most common ones are .PCX, .BMP, TIFF, and .GIF. Each format is distinguished by the way that it compresses image data and the format of the header data.

.BMP

The bitmapped graphics file format used in Microsoft Windows.

callback function

A user-defined function that the system calls when an event occurs. The game program registers for event notification by requesting that specific callback functions be called for specific events.

controller

A device that the game player uses to control the game. The keyboard, mouse, and joystick are controllers.

conventional memory

The computer memory in the first megabyte of address space.

coordinates

The addressing system that specifies screen pixels in a column/row scheme. The X axis is from zero to the highest horizontal resolution of the screen. The Y axis is from zero to the highest vertical resolution of the screen. Zero/zero addresses the upper left pixel. 320/240 addresses the lower right pixel when the display is operating in Mode X.

CT-VOICE

The loadable driver program that plays sound effects through a Sound Blaster card.

cue

An event that causes a callback function to be called.

digital signal

A waveform represented by digital values sampled at fixed intervals.

event

Something that happens outside of and asynchronous to the game program. Clock ticks, keystrokes, mouse movements, mouse clicks, joystick motion, joystick button presses, and receptions of network packets are events.

.FLC

A video clip file format originated by Autodesk Animator Pro.

flight simulator

A program that simulates aircraft flight. The program's user is the pilot. The program displays an instrument panel and scenery through the windshield of the simulated airplane.

.GIF

Graphics Interchange Format. A proprietary bitmapped graphics file format copyrighted by the CompuServe Information Service.

hidden video page

One of the video pages that contains display data that the user does not see.

interrupt

The interruption of a program's normal procedure of instruction execution, usually caused by a an event—such as a key or button press—associated with a device, such as a controller or system timer.

loadable driver

A program that is read into memory as if it were a data file. The host program executes the driver by calling memory offsets from the beginning of the loaded module or by issuing software interrupts.

message

A function call that the system makes to registered member functions of the game program. Messages report events to the game program.

MIDI

Musical Instrument Digital Interface. A standard for recording and reproducing musical performances as packets of digital information. Each packet represents a note or event. Packets address channels, which are assigned to instrument sounds.

Mode X

The VGA graphics mode with a resolution of 320 by 240 and with 256 distinct colors selected from a palette of 256KB possible colors.

modem

Modulator/demodulator. A device that allows two computers to communicate over voice-quality telephone lines. Each computer connects to its modem through the computer's serial port. Both modems are connected to the telephone lines at their respective sites. One computer originates a call and the other computer answers. After the connection is completed, the two computers communicate as if they were directly connected at their serial ports with a null modem cable.

mouse cursor

The graphical display that represents where the mouse is pointing. A program can specify custom mouse cursor shapes, and it can select from a standard set of mouse cursor shapes.

null modem

A cable that directly connects two computers at their serial ports. The cable connects the transmit line of each computer to the receive line of the other.

paint program

A program that allows you to construct graphical images by using interactive tools to create and manipulate shapes, lines, colors, and textures.

palette

A table of 256 integer values, with each value representing a color. The size of the integers determines the number of colors that the palette can choose from. Each VGA screen display has an associated palette. The data bytes in video memory are vectors into the palette. Each data byte represents a pixel. The pixel's color is determined by its corresponding palette value.

palette normalization

The process whereby several bitmapped images are modified so that they all use a common palette and can be displayed on the screen at the same time.

patch

The sound assigned to a MIDI instrument.

.PCX

A bitmapped graphics file format associated with ZSoft's PC Paintbrush program and supported by the Windows Paintbrush program in Windows versions prior to Windows 95.

perspective

The visual property of sprite image components wherein more distant images are rendered smaller and higher on the screen's Y coordinate than closer ones.

photo-realism

The quality of a computer-generated image that makes it almost seem to be a photograph. Often associated with ray-traced images.

pixel

Picture element. One dot on a video screen.

quantize

To smooth the pattern of notes played by a MIDI sequencer to a lowest common resolution, such as the eighth note.

ray casting

Building an image of a scene by casting rays from the viewing position until they intersect objects, at which time the pixel values of vertical strips are computed. Ray casting depends on computer models of symmetrical and perpendicular geometric shapes such as walls and corridors.

ray tracing

Building an image from a 3-D model that includes light sources and a viewing position. The model specifies shapes, textures, and surfaces. The shapes can have logical and hierarchical relations with one another. The ray-tracing program computes the color value of each screen pixel by tracing from the light sources through transparent objects to the first opaque object that the ray intersects and then back to the viewing position.

render

To produce a displayable image from a 3-D computer model.

resolution

In video displays, the number of horizontal and vertical pixels that a video mode can display. In digital waveform recording, the minimum and maximum values that a sample can represent expressed as the number of bits in a sample.

sample

In digital signal processing, the single value of a point on a waveform. In music reproduction, a note played by an instrument and recorded to be combined with other recorded samples in the electronic reproduction of a musical selection.

sampling rate

The rate, expressed in samples per second, at which samples are made during the recording of a digital waveform.

scan code

The eight-bit value that the keyboard transmits to the computer when the user presses a key.

scanner

A device that scans a drawing, photograph, or other image into a bitmapped graphics format in the PC.

scenery

See "background."

sequencer

A device that reads files of MIDI data and transmits the packets to synthesizers. A sequencer can also record MIDI files by reading the notes played on a synthesizer.

serial port

The communications port that connects one PC with another either directly or indirectly through a modem. Programs in two computers can communicate through their serial ports.

simulation

A computer model of a real-world object, event, place, or combination of the three.

sound clip

A binary stream that represents the recording of a voice or sound effect. The stream includes a header block that defines the sampling rate and resolution of the sound clip.

sprite

An animated character in a game.

super VGA

A video controller card, compatible with VGA, that is capable of more colors and higher resolution than VGA.

synthesizer

A device that produces musical sounds electronically.

system clock

The hardware interrupt that occurs at appoximately 18.2 times per second.

texture mapping

Creating the image of an object's surface by covering the surface of the object with repetitions of a single tile that contains an image of the texture.

.TGA

Targa. A bitmapped graphics file format developed by AT&T.

TIFF

Tagged Image File Format. A bitmapped graphics file format developed by Aldus.

timer

A software counter that counts down from a programmed value to zero or from zero to the value of the timer. Timers can increment or decrement at each click of the system clock or as a function of the processor speed.

transpose

Change the key signature of a musical composition, adjusting all the notes appropriately.

VGA

Virtual Graphics Array. The video controller card used in most PCs.

video buffer

A contiguous area of memory that holds video display information.

video clip

A sequence of still frame images that can be displayed as a motion picture. The program does not alter the sequence or position of any of the frames while the video clip plays.

video mode

The way that the video controller displays data. The mode specifies pixel resolution and number of colors. Modes are associated with the video controllers. The VGA can use all the modes of earlier PC video controllers and adds several modes of its own. Some modes are graphics modes. Others are text modes. In graphics modes, the value of a byte of video memory specifies the color at a pixel location. In text modes, the value of a word of video memory specifies an ASCII value to be displayed and its color attributes.

video page

One of several video buffers that the program can address. Only one video page at a time is visible to the user. The others are hidden.

visible video page

The video page that contains the display data that the user sees.

VOC

A sound clip file format originated by Creative Labs' Sound Blaster.

wire frame model

A computer model built of vectors that connect to represent the edges of shapes.

Z-order

The order of a sprite relative to the other sprites in the Z coordinate, which defines which sprites would display on top of—and, therefore, in front of—which other sprites when sprite images intersect.

INDEX

G

About the CD-ROM

The contents of the CD-ROM are briefly outlined here.
See Appendix A for descriptions and installation details.

The Theatrix library and demos is in the **\thx** directory.

Blaster Master is located in the **\bmaster** directory.

Dave's Targa Animator (DTA) is located in the **\DTA** directory.

Both DIGpack and MIDpack are in the **\DIGMID** directory.

The version of Fastgraph Light is located in the **\fgl** directory.

Image Alchemy is located in the **\alchemy** directory.

The modem batch file is located in the **\modem** directory.

Moray resides in the **\moray32** directoryYou'll find the Midi Sequencing software (and source code) in the **\MT** directory.

Neopaint version 3.1 is located in the **\neopaint** directory.

The **\povnet** directory contains the Povnet utility.

The Adventure game is on the CD-ROM in the **\extras\advent** subdirectory.

Astrofire is located in the **\extras\astrof** directory.

Copy the files from the **\extras\frac** directory to install.

Conway's game of Life is on the CD-ROM in the **\extras\life** subdirectory.

Copy the **\extras\relent** directory.